Given to us by Scott & Carol Thomas 2021 December for Christmas

The ANOINTING

RODNEY HOWARD-BROWNE

The ANOINTING

Unless otherwise noted, all scriptures are from the King James Version (KJV): King James Version, public domain.

Scripture quotations marked (NLT) are taken from the Holy Bible, New Living Translation, copyright ©1996, 2004, 2015 by Tyndale House Foundation. Used by permission of Tyndale House Publishers, Inc., Carol Stream, Illinois 60188. All rights reserved.

"Scripture quotations taken from the Amplified® Bible (AMPC), Copyright © 1954, 1958, 1962, 1964, 1965, 1987 by The Lockman Foundation. Used by permission. www.Lockman.org"

Scripture quotations marked MSG are taken from THE MESSAGE, copyright © 1993, 1994, 1995, 1996, 2000, 2001, 2002 by Eugene H. Peterson. Used by permission of NavPress. All rights reserved. Represented by Tyndale House Publishers, Inc.

Scripture quotations marked TPT are from The Passion Translation®. Copyright © 2017, 2018 by Passion & Fire Ministries, Inc. Used by permission. All rights reserved. ThePassionTranslation.com.

The Anointing

ISBN 978-1-64440-344-0

Copyright © 2018 by Rodney Howard-Browne

Published by River Publishing

P.O. Box 292888, Tampa, FL 33687 USA

Printed in the United States of America. All rights reserved under International Copyright Law. Content and/or cover may not be reproduced in whole or in part, in any form, without the express written consent of the Publisher.

Contents

1. Understanding the Anointing
   Laying the Foundation 1
2. Increasing the Anointing
   Through Relationship with God 19
3. Increasing the Anointing
   Through Prayer and Worship 35
4. Increasing the Anointing
   Through the Word and Hearing His Voice 45
5. Increasing the Anointing
   Through Building Your Character 60
6. Increasing the Anointing
   Through Yielding to Him 76
7. Release and Transfer the Anointing
   Letting It Flow Through You 90
8. The Glory of God
   The Goodness of God Revealed 116
9. Impartation of the Anointing
   Pouring Out the Anointing on Others 136
10. The Ministry of Laying On of Hands
    Imparting Blessings and Life to Others 155
11. The Price of the Anointing
    It May Cost You Everything 171
12. Special Anointings
    Not Your Ordinary Assignment 186

13	Do You Have Fresh Oil Or Stale Oil?	
	Fill Up with the Oil of Joy	196
14	The Powers of the World to Come	
	Tasting of the Heavenly Gift	213
15	The Fire of God	
	Don't Leave Home Without It	228
16	To You, In You, and Through You	
	Understanding Your Eternal Purpose	245
17	The Double Portion Anointing	
	Dying to Self…Paying a Double Price	257
18	Walking in Your Calling	
	Called, Anointed, Appointed	269
19	Don't Take the Anointing for Granted	
	Guard the Anointing	282
20	What Will You Do With the Anointing?	
	Don't Let the Devil Steal Your Seed	294
	About the Author	309
	Connect	312
	Other Books and Resources by Rodney Howard-Browne	313
	The River at Tampa Bay Church	318
	River University	320
	The Great Commission	322

1
UNDERSTANDING THE ANOINTING
Laying the Foundation

*I*n July 1991, I was preaching a meeting in San Diego, California. One night during the message I began to prophesy. This is what the Lord said: "The great men and women of God that I am using in the earth today are not being used because they are something special. I am using them for one reason, and one reason alone. It's because **they've touched Me and I have touched them**." Every man and woman of God, who has been mightily used by God, is a person who has humbled themselves before Him, pressed into His presence, and allowed Him to do a work in their heart.

Many times, when you look at the men and women of God that He is using, you think He must have His favorites—one blue-eyed boy that He favors over another—but that's not the case. Yes, some people are especially gifted and called by God for a specific purpose, but anyone who desires to be used can press in and touch the hem of His garment.

This anointing is available to everyone who hungers. This is why we should never allow spiritual jealousy to enter in to our lives just because He doesn't use us in the same way He uses others. Remember, that a Pharisee named Gamaliel recognized this when he said: *"And now I say unto you, Refrain from these men, and let them alone: for if this counsel or this work be of men, it will come to nought: But if it be of God, ye cannot overthrow it; lest haply ye be found even to fight against God"* (Acts 5:38–39). I pray that we would have as much sense as this Pharisee and stop trying to be the watchdogs over the Church. The time is short—Jesus is coming soon, and we must learn to flow together and stop fighting one another. Criticism is of the flesh and it must pull others down in order to look good. Humility is of the Spirit and will lay down its life to lift up others. It is impossible to receive from an anointing you criticize.

The Lord wants everyone to be touched by His power and anointed by His Holy Spirit. When we are born-again, the Holy Spirit comes into our heart to live. The Apostle Paul wrote in Romans 8:9: *"But ye are not in the flesh, but in the Spirit, if so be that the Spirit of God dwell in you. Now if any man have not the Spirit of Christ, he is none of his."* Then, when we are baptized in the Holy Ghost, we receive His power (Acts 1:8). John the Baptist said that Jesus would fill us with the Holy Ghost and fire (Matthew 3:11; Luke 3:16). The reason for this fire-power is to turn each of us into a bold witness for Christ.

Jesus told His disciples in Mark 16:15: *"Go ye into all the world, and preach the Gospel to every creature."* He said signs would follow them that believe. *"In my name shall they cast out devils; they shall speak with new tongues; they shall lay hands on the sick, and they shall recover"* (v.17–18). *"And they went forth, and preached everywhere,* **the Lord working with them, and confirming the word with signs following***"* (v. 20, emphasis added). God was working with them, confirming His Word. He wants to work with us, but we first have to learn how to work with Him, so that He, in turn, can work with us. The best place to start is with Jesus, who spoke of His own anointing in Luke 4:14–19:

> And Jesus returned in the power of the Spirit into Galilee: and there went out a fame of him through all the region round about. And he taught in their synagogues, being glorified of all. And he came to Nazareth, where he had been brought up: and, as his custom was, he went into the synagogue on the Sabbath day, and stood up for to read. And there was delivered unto him the book of the prophet Esaias. And when he had opened the book, he found the place where it was written, The Spirit of the Lord is upon me, **because he hath anointed me to preach the Gospel** to the poor; he hath sent me to heal the brokenhearted, to preach deliverance to the captives, and recovering of sight to the blind, to set at liberty them that are bruised, To preach the acceptable year of the Lord. (Emphasis added.)

People want to be where the anointing is—where the presence of God is being manifested. Luke 5:15–17 tells us that as Jesus began to preach, and people were being healed by Him, great multitudes came to hear and see Him. Verse 17 reveals what was drawing them: the power of God—the manifested presence of God—was in their midst.

> But so much the more went there a fame abroad of him: and great multitudes came together to hear, and to be healed by him of their infirmities. And he withdrew himself into the wilderness, and prayed. And it came to pass on a certain day, as he was teaching, that there were Pharisees and doctors of the law sitting by, which were come out of every town of Galilee, and Judaea, and Jerusalem: **and the power of the Lord was present to heal them** (Emphasis added).

WHAT IS THE ANOINTING?

It is the manifest presence of the Lord, or you can say it is the presence and the power of God manifested.

We know that God is omnipresent, which means He *is* everywhere, but it is evident that He is not *manifested* everywhere. He manifests Himself on specific occasions to specific people as He sees fit. He also shows up where there are people looking for Him, seeking after Him—where there are hungry and thirsty people—where He is respected, honored, and made welcome.

Why is the anointing so important? Well, first of all, Jesus was anointed by God before He began His earthly ministry. *"And John bare record, saying, I saw the Spirit descending from Heaven like a dove, and it abode upon him"* (John 1:32). *"How God anointed Jesus of Nazareth with the Holy Ghost and with power: who went about doing good, and healing all that were oppressed of the devil; for God was with him"* (Acts 10:38) If He was anointed, we need to be anointed. Read again the words in Luke 4:18–19:

> **The Spirit of the Lord is upon me, because he hath anointed me to preach the Gospel** to the poor; he hath sent me to heal the brokenhearted, to preach deliverance to the captives, and recovering of sight to the blind, to set at liberty them that are bruised, To preach the acceptable year of the Lord. (Emphasis added.)

The anointing is the signature of God. It is the fingerprint of God on a person whom God uses to bring glory to His Kingdom. I don't know about you, but I want to say: "Lord, mark me with Your finger—may I be marked for all eternity." Many people do not understand or recognize the anointing, because of misconceptions and/or religious traditions. They have never met, seen, or experienced God's presence, so they don't know what to expect, or they just don't expect anything at all. It is important to know what the anointing is, to know when it is being manifested, and to discern when the manifestation is real and when it is not. Why is this so important? Because, you do not want to follow a ministry or a leader if his or her "anointing" is not from God.

You must recognize that there are different kinds of anointings, which we will look at later and that what is manifested this week may be different from last week, because there are different flows to the

Spirit of God. You have to get the mind of the Lord for the moment. That means you must be a yielded vessel, someone who will totally abandon yourself to flowing with the Spirit of God. Jesus said in John 5:19: *"The Son can do nothing of himself, but what he seeth the Father do: for what things soever he doeth, these also doeth the Son likewise."* John 3:34 (AMPC) says: *"For since He Whom God has sent speaks the words of God [proclaims God's own message], God does not give Him His Spirit sparingly or by measure, but boundless is the gift God makes of His Spirit!"*

This indicates that Jesus had the Spirit without measure; He was not lacking in any power or gift. Another version puts it this way: *"For he is sent by God. He speaks God's words, for God gives him the Spirit **without limit**"* (John 3:34, NLT). In other words, there was no limit to the Holy Spirit's power in and through Jesus. Yet, when He went to Nazareth where He had grown up, He could do no mighty work because of their unbelief. What does that tell you? Circumstances and situations (and attitudes) have to be favorable for the anointing to begin to flow.

> And he went out from thence, and came into his own country; and his disciples follow him. And when the sabbath day was come, he began to teach in the synagogue: and many hearing him were astonished, saying, From whence hath this man these things? and what wisdom is this which is given unto him, that even such mighty works are wrought by his hands? Is not this the carpenter, the son of Mary, the brother of James, and Joses, and of Juda, and Simon? and are not his sisters here with us? And they were offended at him. But Jesus, said unto them, A prophet is not without honour, but in his own country, and among his own kin, and in his own house. And he could there do no mighty work, save that he laid his hands upon a few sick folk, and healed them. And he marvelled because of their unbelief. And he went round about the villages, teaching.
>
> MARK 6:1-6

You could say that the anointing is God's electricity. If you understand how electricity flows, you know there is a good conductor, there is a bad conductor, and there is a short circuit. There are places we go where there are good conductors and the anointing flows, because there are hungry people who place a demand on the anointing, just as you would flip a switch to turn on a light. Then there are other places you may preach where the anointing goes out, but it comes right back and smacks you in the forehead. It feels like playing a game of racquetball, because there is no demand on the anointing—no hunger; no thirst; no receptivity; no demand.

So, we know that God is omnipresent—He is present everywhere at the same time—but we also know (and it is obvious) that He is not manifested everywhere. There are many churches around the world today where the Lord is not manifested, and unfortunately, in America, some people have it down to such a fine art they can have church without God. They can preach without the anointing. They can conduct their services without the manifesting of God's presence. But look at their results concerning people being saved, healed and set free. Or should I say, non-results?

I am going to use electricity here again, because it is the closest thing I can find, in the natural, to compare to, or explain, the anointing. Did you know that Benjamin Franklin did not invent electricity? It has been around from Creation. It just took Benjamin Franklin researching his theory about electricity to find out how to grab hold of it. The same is true of Thomas Edison and many other men we credit with great inventions. They didn't create those things. They just found out how certain things—if put together in the right combination—would work.

If today's knowledge had been in place, a Boeing 747 could have flown hundreds of years ago. The Wright brothers didn't invent flight. Birds were flying long before the Wright brothers climbed into their plane. In fact, even Leonardo da Vinci had an interest in building a "flying machine" from the time he was a child. He drew sketches of his ideas, and built at least one resembling a helicopter, but never flew it because he didn't have access to the materials and technology we have today. He had knowledge of things far beyond the common knowledge of the day.

Many times, people who know and understand more than those around them are misunderstood and persecuted. During the Middle Ages, people were burned at the stake because they said the world was round when everyone was sure it was flat, and if you sailed beyond a certain point you would go over the edge. Those who tried to prove it was round were called witches. The religious church was responsible for most of the witch-hunts, in part because of their fear of the unknown or the supernatural. Ignorance, you say? Well, it is no different today. Many people are so afraid of the Holy Ghost anointing that instead of being open to learning more about it, they attribute His work to the devil. The Pharisees did the same thing to Jesus.

The moment you start demonstrating the anointing and the power of God, some people become terrified. If a preacher or evangelist prays for someone and they fall under the power of the anointing, they say, "It must be the devil. How did he do that? How did he lay his hands on somebody and they fell to the floor? That has to be the devil." They think that everything supernatural is of the devil. Well, let me tell you, God is more "super" natural than the devil. God's power is greater than the power of the enemy.

The Pharisees and Sadducees accused Jesus of operating under demon powers. But they were wrong. Jesus did only good works. It is God who anointed Jesus of Nazareth with the Holy Ghost and with power. *"He went about doing good, and healing all that were oppressed of the devil; for God was with Him"* (Acts 10:38). The source of the power is manifested in and through the fruit of the ministry. Good power—good fruit.

God created everything—the universe, people, and angels. The devil is a created being and was perfect in every way until iniquity was found in him. God's power is greater than the power of the enemy, yet if you travel in some religious circles, you find the devil is the one getting the glory. He is all they talk about. In many churches, they spend an inordinate amount of time talking about, and binding, devils.

Yes, we have authority over demons. We don't have to beg; we do need to command, and they have no choice but to obey. We need to rather spend our time praising God and lifting Him up. When we do that, the demons will **run** out of the place.

Now, the devil is not my subject here—Jesus Christ is; He said: *"And I, if I be lifted up from the earth, will draw all men unto me"* (John 12:32). However, if you take the devil out of some preachers' vocabularies, they have nothing to preach about, because the devil is more real to them than Jesus is. I can only say, "To Hell with the devil," because that's his final destination. I mention him only to tell you that he is defeated. Ephesians 4:27 says: *"Neither give place to the devil."* You should memorize that verse…keep it in your heart and mind so you don't exalt him above measure.

In Luke 10:1–16, Jesus sent seventy more disciples out into the harvest, instructing them how to make disciples and heal the sick. They came back rejoicing over their victories, but Jesus did not respond as they expected. Look at verses 17–20:

> And the seventy returned again with joy, saying, Lord, even the devils are subject unto us through thy name. And he said unto them, I beheld Satan as lightning fall from Heaven. Behold, I give unto you power to tread on serpents and scorpions, and over all the power of the enemy: and nothing shall by any means hurt you. Notwithstanding in this rejoice not, that the spirits are subject unto you; but rather rejoice, because your names are written in Heaven (vv. 17–20).

Jesus basically said, "So what?" They should not have come back rejoicing that they had power over the spirits, but rather that their names were written in the Lamb's Book of Life. He had seen Satan fall from Heaven, so He knew when He sent the disciples out that the demon spirits would be subject to them.

People try to explain away the supernatural with their traditions. If they could have talked to Jesus after He visited His hometown, they would have told Him the reason He didn't do any miracles was because He didn't pray enough or fast enough. They didn't understand He had the Spirit without measure, and it didn't matter what He did or did not do. It had to do with where the people's hearts were. It had to do with what their attitude was. If your heart is wrong and your attitude is wrong, then you will not place a demand upon the anointing, just like the example of using the light switch to turn on the electricity. The electricity (the anointing) is there, but if you do not flip the switch (place a demand), you will not receive the benefits of the electricity.

Many other people touched Jesus the day the woman with the issue of blood touched Him, but she got her miracle because her touch was different. Their touch was an inquisitive one, just to say, "I touched Him." But her touch was a faith touch—expecting a miracle—knowing that if she could just make contact, His anointing power would heal her. She had faith in Jesus to heal her—through the hem of His garment—even if He was unaware. Of course, when her faith touched His clothes, the power flowed through Him into her, and He felt it. Instead of being angry, He pronounced her healed and whole through her faith (*See* Mark 5:25–34.)

We see a lot of hype in the church world today, people following so-called celebrities, resembling something we see in Hollywood. It's almost like a World Wrestling Federation spirit has crept into the church. People think that if the B3 organ is cranking at just the right pace, the louder the better, then God will move. Many believe that if enough people are jumping up and down in the aisles and waving flags, you will see the moving of the Spirit of God. It's fine to get excited about Jesus, but it is not the outward things we do that will move God. It's the attitude of our hearts.

The Quakers were first called Quakers because that's what they did. When the anointing came on them, they began to quake, but after a while some just quaked because they were Quakers, even without the anointing. Some people today sing certain songs to get the people worked up until they start to shake and weep, but without the anointing from God they will not produce lasting fruit. Some people sing and shout but are no more anointed than a duck is a Delta Air Lines pilot. There is a difference between getting stirred up in the Spirit and being stirred up in the emotions of the flesh.

When people don't understand what the anointing is and how it operates, they work too hard trying to get it. I have had to get up in meetings and stop everybody and tell them: "It's just not that hard." My heart breaks and I want to weep, because they are trying so hard to grab hold of God. They are striving so hard to get something from God, but they are not open to receive. It is not hard—it is easy. They are trying to get an anointing with rituals and all sorts of rigmarole, and it doesn't work. Isaiah 55:1 (AMPC) says: *"Wait and listen, everyone who is thirsty! Come to the waters; and he who has no money, come, buy and eat! Yes, come, buy [priceless, spiritual] wine and milk without money and without price [simply for the self-surrender that accepts the blessing]."*

You can't work for anything God has to offer. You receive it by faith and by self-surrender. It is the self-surrender that receives—activates—the blessing in your life.

I once asked the Lord why some people never seem to sense His presence. He told me that it's because they are so caught up in their daily lives and the cares of this world, deceitfulness of riches, and lust of other things, that their minds and their thoughts are far from Him. Most of their waking moments are spent in the natural realm, not in the spiritual realm. It's like trying to listen to your favorite radio program when you have it tuned to the wrong station. You won't hear what you are looking for. But when you make an adjustment, deep down in your spirit, you find that the signal comes through loud and clear. It's that easy. God does not speak to your head. He speaks to your heart. We have to quiet our heads and listen to our hearts. Together with spending time in the Word of God, praying in the spirit—in tongues—helps you to quiet your thoughts and become more sensitive to the voice of the Spirit.

It is so easy. Some of the greatest anointings ever to come on me have happened outside of the meetings. I have been at home, sitting in my study, and had to get up out of my chair. The power of God hit me so hard I was woozy. The power of God was all over me. Once when I was driving down the road, praying for someone on the phone, it was all I could do to concentrate and focus on keeping the car headed down the highway.

It's important to know that music, worship and all the other things we have around us enhance the anointing, but if your anointing can't work "in the raw," without any outside help, it isn't worth much. I like to take people out of their environment and drop them in the middle of nowhere, and then watch to see how the anointing works. I have proven what the Lord has given us, with no music, no choir…nothing. Just the preaching of the Gospel.

I walked into a high school one day, with six hundred young people looking at me, and said: "Hi! My name's Rodney Howard-Browne." They didn't know who I was, or what was about to happen. They had no expectations, but I began to preach the Word, and forty-five minutes later, the power of God hit that place like a tornado. There was no music and no band—just the power of God. Now, I'm not against these things, I'm just saying that the church places too much emphasis on all these peripheral things and not on what really gets the job done. They think you have to be inside a church building to see God move. They think you have to sing a special song.

No! When you preach the Word, the anointing shows up. It is the anointing, the presence of God manifested, that draws men and women to Jesus, so you must look for His manifested presence. I constantly look for His presence on me and in me, because He lives in me. You have that privilege also, if you are saved and have the Holy Spirit living in you. People don't even need to know your name if the anointing is on you, they will be ministered to. The only name they really need to know is the Name of Jesus!

THE ANOINTING IS THE SUPERNATURAL EQUIPMENT TO GET THE JOB DONE

In other words, when God anoints you to do something, He empowers you, He graces you, He enables you, and infuses you. He endows you with a supernatural ability to accomplish the task. God would never call you to do something without anointing you to do it. When He calls you, He anoints you and He equips you, so that you have enough to get the job done without any outside help or support. The anointing is all you need. I'd rather have the anointing than any other help I could get. I like what I once heard that Smith Wigglesworth said: "I'd rather have the anointing on me for five minutes than to own the world with a gold fence around it and my name engraved on every brick."

One of the reasons people have a problem in understanding the anointing is that it is like the wind. You can't really see the wind, but you can feel the wind, and you can see the results of where it has been. The wind can change. You may ask which way the wind is blowing, but you can't always tell, because it's swirling first one way and then another. The anointing is like the wind. Jesus said: *"The wind bloweth where it listeth, and thou hearest the sound thereof, but canst not tell whence it cometh, and whither it goeth: so is every one that is born of the Spirit"* (John 3:8).

A Spirit-filled Christian full of the Holy Ghost is like the wind—hard to pin down. When you are under the anointing, you are frustrating to someone who is living in the natural. The only way you can fellowship is for them to get under the same anointing, so the Spirit of God is blowing you in the same direction. A person totally moved by the anointing of God is an enigma to others, like reading a mystery novel with no ending—a real who-done-it. Was it the butler in the kitchen with the candlestick, or Mrs. Green in the conservatory with the knife? The religious mind will look at the anointed person, trying to understand, but will always fall short because they are trying to reason with the natural mind.

Things done under the anointing are spiritual and are only understood spiritually by those who possess the Holy Ghost. 1 Corinthians 2:14-16 says:

UNDERSTANDING THE ANOINTING

But the natural man receiveth not the things of the Spirit of God: for they are foolishness unto him: neither can he know them, because they are spiritually discerned. But he that is spiritual judgeth all things, yet he himself is judged of no man. For who hath known the mind of the Lord, that he may instruct him? But we have the mind of Christ.

Those whom God appoints, He anoints. Without the anointing, it is hard to do. It's like bathing with your socks on. It's uncomfortable. It's like driving with the brakes on. It's like chewing food with no teeth. When you are under the anointing it's easy to chew—you have teeth. That explains why the devil has no power over you: he has no teeth—Jesus knocked his teeth out. The worst he can do is "gum" you. He got "defanged" at Calvary. How can you do God's work without His equipping? We need His anointing to do what He's called us to do.

We need to follow and obey the anointing. The wind may be blowing in a different direction today than it was yesterday. We must follow the Holy Ghost and hear what the Lord is saying, not be blown about in every direction by the winds of man's doctrine. If you notice a yachtsman or a kitesurfer—they have learned to work with the wind to get where they are going. If they ignore the wind or go against it, it will not be well with them. You can go with or against the wind, but the wind will win every time.

The number one way to learn about the anointing is to follow the ministry of Jesus as recorded by His disciples: Matthew, Mark, Luke and John. Several people have told me that they wish they could have lived in Jesus's day, so they could attend His meetings, but I already had the privilege of doing that, in the pages of His Book. You can "go" to every one of Jesus's crusade meetings. Sit and watch Him preach and teach, watch how He functions, and observe how He relates to the people. Sit at the pool of Bethesda with its five porches, where the multitude of blind, halt, maimed and withered people lay, and look at the angel coming down, stirring the water. Then, see the humble Galilean walk right up to a man who had been there for thirty-eight years.

When Jesus saw him lie, and knew that he had been now a long time in that case, he saith unto him, Wilt thou be made whole? The impotent man answered him, Sir, I have no man, when the water is troubled, to put me into the pool: but while I am coming, another steppeth down before me. Jesus saith unto him, Rise, take up thy bed, and walk. And immediately the man was made whole, and took up his bed, and walked.

JOHN 5:6–9

We read in Acts 4:13: *"Now when they saw the boldness of Peter and John, and perceived that they were unlearned and ignorant men, they marveled; and they took knowledge of them, that they had been with Jesus."* Something happens to you when you've been with Him…you are marked. There's a fragrance of the Rose of Sharon and the Lily of the Valley on your garments. Wherever you go, you carry that with you; you are so full of the anointing of God that when you walk into a room, the very atmosphere of the room will change. It doesn't matter what has been going on before you got there; when you are full of the anointing—the Spirit of God—the tone of the place will change when you walk in the door.

When you play your instrument, full of the Holy Ghost, the anointing will flow through your hands onto that instrument and fill the room. Many people play, but there is not that "special something" that you remember long after you leave them, because they don't have the anointing. There are many virtuosos I would not even cross the street to listen to, because they may be talented, but they are not anointed. It's the anointing that changes people. Don't ever forget that. The anointing makes you unique, different from everyone else. The anointing does not merely touch lives, it changes them forever!

People often ask me how I judge the things that are happening in the Body of Christ. I judge things by the anointing. Everything has an anointing rating for me. Anointed—not anointed—anointed "wannabe"—or pretending, which is strange fire (Hophni and Phinehas and Nadab and Abihu). I am serious; it doesn't take me long to click through the channels on the television to judge what is on. Fred Flintstone has more anointing than some of the ministries on television, because at least he speaks in "tongues." "Yabba dabba doo. Yabba dabba doo." I'm not criticizing ministry; I'm talking about anointing or no anointing. If you don't know the difference, you could run around here, there and everywhere, like a chicken with its head chopped off—not sure if you're coming or going. It is necessary to understand the anointing if you want to be a believer God will use.

I don't have to listen to a whole message to know if the anointing is there or it's not. If you have truly experienced and been touched by the anointing, you can recognize if God is present or not. I just look at the speaker, and I can tell you if the anointing is on that person. People come in to our meetings—total strangers—and I see the anointing on them. I don't need a background check, because even if we have never met, I can see the anointing. God's presence has a way of revealing the hearts. When people are under the microscope of the anointing, it will tell the story.

Every believer—yes, **every** believer—is anointed. Take your finger, point it right between your eyes and say: "I am anointed." You were anointed when you got saved and filled with the Holy Spirit. Jesus told the woman at the well: *"But **whosoever** drinketh of the water that I shall give him shall never thirst; but the water that I shall give him shall be in him a well of water springing up into everlasting life"* (John 4:14, emphasis added).

YOU ARE A WELL

Are you a "**whosoever**"? Did you drink at His well? There's a well on the inside of you when you are born-again, but you have to draw the water out. That's why Isaiah 12:3 declares: *"Therefore with joy shall ye draw water out of the wells of salvation."* In all my studies on the subject of the anointing, I have never seen God use the anointing of a depressed minister, because the anointing does not follow depression—it only follows joy. Why? Because joy is the bucket that brings the water up from the well. You will always see more anointing in a happy ministry than in a sad ministry. The anointing follows the joy—a joyful spirit and a joyful heart.

So, where is the well? It's in your spirit, deep down on the inside of you. You have to bring it up from your innermost being, because you are a living water dispenser. The water has to come forth from the wells of salvation, but some people have a pulley problem. In our meetings we see people, bless their hearts, who have been saved for many years, but they have lost their bucket; their rope broke, and their pulley froze. We are just trying to get their pulley operating again, get them a new rope and a new bucket, so that they can learn how to get water out of their well.

That's what I am presenting to you. You are a walking well. Are you letting the fresh water of the Spirit flow freely from your well? If not, why not? What's blocking the flow? You have to learn how to tap into the Greater One who lives on the inside of you.

What awesome things could be accomplished if men and women of God would grab on to this truth. All God needs from you is a yielded vessel. That means you are yielded to Him, regardless of how you are feeling, or what the circumstances are.

YOU ARE A RIVER
John 7:37–39 gives us Jesus's words about the living water:

> In the last day, that great day of the feast, Jesus stood and cried, saying, If any man thirst, let him come unto me, and drink. He that believeth on me, as the scripture hath said, out of his belly shall flow rivers of living water. (But this spake he of the Spirit, which they that believe on him should receive: for the Holy Ghost was not yet given; because that Jesus was not yet glorified.)

Jesus said…out of your belly will come the water. We know a river doesn't begin at the ocean or on the delta. It begins high up in the mountains as just a little trickle. It is a tiny stream that ends up being a powerful river, like the mighty Mississippi. The flow of the living water is just the same. It doesn't matter how small the trickle is initially, but it matters what it's going to become as you let it flow. Out of your belly will flow a river of living water. Point to your belly and say, "Out of my belly shall flow rivers of living water."

Everyone who is born-again is a well. You can live your whole life with just the well, but Jesus said that "out of your belly" God has destined you to be a river. Is your well flowing out of you like a river? Do you know why a river stops flowing downstream? It is because someone or something has built a dam. If you have been dammed up, it is time for the dam to break. That is why the Lord told me to get people under the anointing, so there will be a crack in the wall, and the river will begin to flow again. Lives will be touched and changed; captives will be set free.

One of the most drastic changes in someone's life was seen in the life of the Apostle Paul. (*See* Acts 9:1–9.) Here's a man in total opposition to the Kingdom of God, a man on a mission to destroy the church. He was a man who was very well educated, so he knew what he was doing, but something happened to change everything. It was not that he was persuaded intellectually. He had a head-on collision with Jesus and was engulfed by the presence of the Holy Spirit—and his whole life changed. Notice verse 5. He asked a question and answered it in the same sentence: "Who art Thou, Lord?" He met Jesus for the first time and knew He was Lord. When the anointing comes on you, it's going to touch you and it's going to change you.

I would say that everyone needs to see the light, because when the light of Heaven shines in your heart, all the darkness will flee. When the light of Heaven shines in your heart, it will brand you with the imprint of Heaven. Just as a rancher brands his cattle to show ownership, so you are branded with the insignia of Heaven. Everywhere you go people will look at you and know you belong to Heaven.

That's what happened to Saul of Tarsus on the Road to Damascus. He was struck blind, but Jesus opened his eyes to the Truth. At some point, he was caught up into Heaven and received divine revelation concerning what Christ did for us through His death and resurrection, even things he was forbidden to speak about (2 Corinthians 12:1-4). The Lord then used him to write two-thirds of the New Testament.

That's what God wants to happen to every single one of us. He wants to take Heaven's brand and burn it into our hearts. No amount of scrubbing can get it off.

You can even try to run from God. I heard the testimony of the preacher who was discouraged and thought he would go back to his old life. He drove to a town two hours away—went into a bar and while he was drinking, an old drunk on the other side saw him and said: "Hey, you! Why are you running from God?" He left his drink and ran out and got in the car and drove home.

You can't hide it. When you're marked with Heaven, you may want to run away, but there is not a car that can take you fast enough to get away from Heaven's mark. When God puts His finger on you, your life will never be the same again. I am convinced that if you will yield to His calling, God will touch you in a supernatural way, and mark you with His finger so that only time and eternity will reveal what Heaven will do in and through your life.

THE LORD CAN DESTROY ANY YOKE

Finally, one last verse for our foundation on the study of the anointing is found in Isaiah 10:27: *"And it shall come to pass in that day, that his burden shall be taken away from off thy shoulder, and his yoke from off thy neck, and the yoke shall be destroyed because of the anointing."* The Lord can destroy any yoke. The yoke that man puts on you and the yoke the devil puts on you. The devil burdens people with his heavy yoke of bondage, but the anointing destroys that yoke. It has not merely been broken, as some say, it has been destroyed! We are free, because of the Cross of Calvary, to walk in the anointing He has provided for us.

Let's look now at some of the ways the devil will try to put the yoke back on believers, and God's solution for those who want to walk in the anointing and be used in His service. *"But ye have an unction from the Holy One, and ye know all things"* (1 John 2:20). *"But the anointing which ye have received of him abideth in you, and ye need not that any man teach you: but as the same anointing teacheth you of all things, and is truth, and is no lie, and even as it hath taught you, ye shall abide in him"* (1 John 2:27).

2

INCREASING THE ANOINTING

Through Relationship with God

Before we look at the ways you can increase the anointing in your life, let's briefly look again at what the anointing is…and then what it is not. As I said in Chapter 1, the anointing is the manifest presence of God. We read the words of Jesus in John 4:14: *"But whosoever drinketh of the water that I shall give him shall never thirst; but the water that I shall give him shall be in him a well of water springing up into everlasting life."* Every born-again believer is anointed of God when the Holy Spirit comes to live in us, but our anointing is not always manifested.

In Matthew 3:16–17, we see the account of Jesus's baptism by John the Baptist and His anointing by the Spirit of God: *"And Jesus, when he was baptized, went up straightway out of the water: and, lo, the heavens were opened unto him, and he saw the Spirit of God descending like a dove, and lighting upon him: And lo a voice from Heaven, saying, This is my beloved Son, in whom I am well pleased."*

From the moment that Jesus was baptized, He was anointed for ministry. His life had a specific purpose, and God anointed and empowered Him to fulfill it. Jesus testified of His own anointing when He stood in the synagogue and read from Isaiah 61:1–2, which prophesied of the coming Messiah. Then He confirmed that the scripture was fulfilled that day, because He was that "sent one." Read His words in Luke 4:18–19, 21:

> The Spirit of the Lord is upon me, because he hath anointed me to preach the Gospel to the poor; he hath sent me to heal the brokenhearted, to preach deliverance to the captives, and recovering of sight to the blind, to set at liberty them that are bruised. To preach the acceptable year of the Lord. And he began to say unto them: This day is this scripture fulfilled in your ears. . .

Even though the people in the synagogue of Nazareth that day did not receive Him, the fact is that He was the Anointed One and nothing could change that. God's plans and purposes **will** be fulfilled if we will obey. We don't choose—God does. But when He does, we must believe and obey. Jesus did not do any miracles prior to His anointing. Once He was anointed, He operated in that powerful level of anointing during the three-and-a-half years of His ministry—from the time He was baptized by John until His death. We read the disciple John's words (John 21:25) concerning the miracles of Jesus: *"And there are also many other things which Jesus did, the which, if they should be written everyone, I suppose that even the world itself could not contain the books that should be written."*

As I stated earlier, it is evident, if we study closely the life and ministry of Jesus, that God gave Him the Spirit without measure. Look at the words of John the Baptist in John 3:34–35: *"For he whom God hath sent speaketh the words of God: for God giveth not the Spirit by measure unto him. The Father loveth the Son, and hath given all things into his hand."* Another version says, *"God gives him the Spirit without limit"* (v. 34, NLT).

Jesus was full of the manifest presence and power of God. God had given Jesus the special grace to do the job He had sent Him to do. Let me emphasize what I said in Chapter 1: When God calls you; He graces you; He empowers you; He enables you; He anoints you; and He equips you to do the job He has called you to do. The anointing is tangible, and it is transferable. This is essential for you to know when God calls you to do something. He will never call you to do something He has not empowered you to do. If He calls you to a foreign country, He will give you the anointing to function in that foreign country. If He calls you to be a pastor, teacher, or evangelist, He will give you the anointing necessary for you to fulfill that calling.

If God calls you to sing, He will anoint you to sing. You will be a blessing. You won't empty the building. Anytime God calls you to do something, your anointing will bring Jesus into the room every single time and it will run the devil out. That's our job; run the devil out and bring Jesus in.

THE ANOINTING IS NOT A FORMULA—IT IS A RELATIONSHIP

I have had the privilege of teaching on the subject of the anointing for over twenty-nine years in the morning meetings of our campmeetings and ministers' meetings, as well as thousands of revival services conducted in sixty nations of the world. And what a joy it has been! I have hardly touched the surface of the depths of the subject of God's anointing, but I can tell you one thing for sure. When it comes to increasing the anointing in your life, you must understand that the anointing is not a formula—it is a relationship. Some people seem to think if they can watch the right person and copy what he does, then their success will be the same as the person they are copying. Not so; it doesn't work that way.

David found that out when they put Saul's armor on him, he was totally incapacitated. (*See* 1 Samuel 17:1-58.) He couldn't move because Saul's armor was too heavy for him. He had to shed the armor and stay with the slingshot—the weapon God had allowed him to perfect out in the fields. He knew it was the slingshot that had brought him to that place, and it was the slingshot that would keep him there. David went with what worked for him. He could not wear Saul's armor. But he was confident in his ability to use a sling.

In the natural, a sling was no match for Goliath's weapons, but David was **anointed** to use a sling. David acknowledged that it was God who helped him. David recognized that if he was able to take out the lion and the bear, he could take out the giant Goliath the same way—with what was familiar to him. So, he stayed with the anointing God had given him. If he had worn Saul's armor, the story of David would have ended differently. He would have been slaughtered. You cannot wear another person's mantle, just as you cannot wear another person's anointing. (We will look at that more in a later chapter.) You must discover your own, which comes from building your own relationship with the Lord.

Wives, you cannot have a relationship with the Lord based on your husband's relationship with Him. The same applies to husbands, children, or parents. You can't use someone else's—you must develop a relationship of your own. Many people want to have a line of communication with the Lord just like their pastor has, but they never take the time to get acquainted with God. Knowing *about* God is not the same as *knowing Him personally*, and that does not come through a formula, but by building a relationship with Him.

In the early days of my ministry, in 1980, I loved to read books on the great men of God and their ministries. I remember reading a book about Smith Wigglesworth, the British evangelist, which inspired me to want to have a ministry just like his. What a great man of God he was. I read how he would set his alarm for 4:00 in the morning, get out of bed, have communion, and then dance around the bed and pray in tongues for hours. I said to myself, *"Oh! That's it—that is it!"*

So, I got one of those big alarm clocks that you wind up and when the thing rings the whole house comes awake. I would set the alarm for 4:00 in the morning, and have my juice and cracker ready, right there on my bedside table. I'd wake up and have communion, get up out of the bed and dance, and then pray in tongues for three hours—and fall asleep again. I would wake up about 11:00 feeling so condemned because I couldn't stay awake to pray. But you can't do all that when you go to bed at midnight. You cannot keep that kind of a schedule on four hours of sleep. I tried for several weeks to do it, and then beat myself up over not being able to do it.

I felt I had to do it if I was going to increase the anointing on my life. Finally, the Lord asked me, "What are you doing?" I answered, "Lord, you know—Wigglesworth." The Lord replied; "But you are not Wigglesworth. That was *his* relationship with me. You can't do something because someone else is doing it. You must do what I tell *you* to do." What a lesson!

But it didn't stop me. I went out and found some other formulas. I tell you, I tried everything. I read about one preacher who would go to his room at 2:00 in the afternoon, lock his door and not speak to anyone. He would preach his sermon to himself—five times. I said, "That's it! That's the key to increasing the anointing on your life and your ministry." So, at 2:00, I locked my door and told everyone not to speak to me. "I am getting anointed." I prayed and studied and prayed and studied. By 7:00, when I got to the service, I was so worn out I was yawning between sentences.

Everybody wants to increase their anointing, but they don't realize that the Holy Spirit is not a formula; He's a person. You have to learn to flow with Him. "Hang out" with Him. Relax with Him. He's not uptight, and He is not "religious," either. The things that offend you don't necessarily offend Him. Some of the fleshly things you tolerate are what offends Him.

That is why it is so vitally important for everyone who is going to be used of God to have an encounter with Him. If Saul of Tarsus needed an encounter, then you need one. If the apostles in the early church needed one, then you need one. **Everything must come out of your encounter with God.**

Preachers are the worst when it comes to formulas. They know all of them. They have learned all the "do-it-yourself methods." They wrote the books on "Flowing in the Spirit for Dummies," and "The Idiot's Guide to the Anointing." They seem to think if they can find the best way and patent it, they will be successful. There is only one problem with that: after you patent yourself, all you are is just another copy.

The Lord has an original plan for you, and He has an anointing that He wants to pour out on you. There are anointings just waiting to be released upon the earth for the end-time harvest. Are you hearing me? If you use a formula, trying to get an anointing, you will never achieve the heights and depths of the anointing God has made available to you. You'll never know who you could have been had you only allowed the third person of the Godhead to rise up big on the inside of you.

People try so hard to get some kind of anointing, because they don't want to be left out. No one wants to feel like an oddball; everyone wants to be accepted, doing what everyone else is doing. When I first came to America, the Lord told me: **"Find out whatever everybody else is doing, do the opposite, and it will be Me."** People would ask me, "What are you saying?" because it was different from what they were used to hearing.

Preachers often go to conferences, then preach other's sermons and prophesy other's prophecies. My messages on the anointing have not come from watching other preachers on television. They are fresh words that come as a result of my relationship with God. I'm talking about a message that's going to get the job done. There are too many redundant messages being preached that would be better off not being spoken. I want something that is going to move mountains… something that will shake nations. When we started our ministry, we wondered, "What does this, or that, person think?" However, I realized that, ultimately, it didn't matter what they thought or said. It only matters what Heaven says and what Heaven thinks.

THERE IS A PRICE TO PAY

There is a price to pay to have the anointing. You have to die to the opinions of man. Remember this: any dead fish can float downstream, but it takes a real live fish to go upstream. Everybody wants to follow the crowd, but the way of the anointing is often a lonely path. Sometimes even those who come with you will fall asleep, and you'll end up at your Gethsemane alone.

As we travel around the world, we meet people all the time whose lives are cluttered up with formulas. This one is doing his little thing, that one is doing their little thing. It's very disappointing when you find people who just got saved and are on fire for God, but they are just being fed formulas instead of the reality of the Word. The purest form of a believer is one who is newly saved, because new creatures in Christ are on fire for God. They may have just come out of a life of drugs and alcohol and all kinds of disasters, but Jesus has saved them, and they are so excited they are radical. I mean **radical**. They witness everywhere. They go through the drive-thru at Burger King and say: "I'll take a double whopper; God loves you; bow your head right now."

All they care about is Jesus. They are radically on fire. If you can keep them just like that, they'll do more good for the Kingdom of God and more damage against the kingdom of Hell than you can ever believe. But God forbid they get in the path of Brother and Sister Bucket-mouth, the spiritual ones who've been "in the way" for forty years, who will say: "Don't worry. That's just the zealousness of youth. Why, we've been 'in the way' for many years. Just give them a few more years, and they will find out what it's really like to serve God. They are rejoicing now but wait until the day the devil gets a hold of them." I heard one preacher tell people coming to the altar call, "Now the battle has begun." I wanted to ask him what he meant and then he said, "Now, the devil is going come after you."

Hold it! They just got saved. The devil had them before, but now they have been born-again. It's not "the battle has just begun," but "the victory has just been won!"

New Christians have simple, childlike faith. That's what it takes to get the job done. It's not complicated. A new believer can do more damage to the enemy than anyone because of their simple faith and the fire of God they possess. They need to be encouraged, not discouraged, to trust in the greatness of God, share the Gospel, and to see the miracles that follow the preaching of the Word.

Jesus's messages were simple, but powerful. Some preachers try to make things so difficult, I have to say: "Sorry, Buddy, you lost me there. That is just too complicated." Those who are new in the faith are always in danger of "religious" people trying to put them back into captivity…back into the chains Jesus has just broken off their lives. Just like certain Jews kept trying to pressurize the early Church converts to be circumcised. Religion is a man-made structure. It does not allow freedom; it is built on a set of rules and practices. Religion places burdens on people and does not help them to bear them (Matthew 23:4). Jesus did not give us rules to follow; He gave us commandments to live by: Love God with all your heart, mind and strength, and love others as you love yourself.

The Apostle John wrote to the church at Ephesus in Revelation 2:4: *"Nevertheless I have somewhat against thee, because thou hast left thy first love."* Can you remember how excited you were when you first were saved? You were so on fire for the Lord you couldn't do enough for Him. But, over time, you lost your first love and let your relationship with Him slip. You began to adopt a formula for living the Christian life. Certain things became such habits they began to resemble rules and regulations that were no different from many other religions or cults.

There are many things required of a person when they are in a cult, such as bowing down so many times a day, always facing a certain direction. They must chant a mantra and do various rituals at set times to comply with all the rules necessary to attain a new level. They place the word of man above the Word of God. As I have traveled around the world, I have visited Pentecostal and Charismatic groups that were more like cults than churches—full of religious tradition.

INCREASING THE ANOINTING

The worst thing that can happen to an on-fire, new believer is to get caught up in religion, because they are just coming out of one type of bondage and now they are going into another. They used to snort cocaine and now they have a new addiction, "snorting" religion. When they were serving the devil, they drank alcohol to get drunk. Now they sit in a dead church where there is nothing to drink, because there are no wells with rivers of living water flowing out from them. All that is left is just the vinegar of religion and tradition.

"And it shall come to pass in that day, that his burden shall be taken away from off thy shoulder, and his yoke from off thy neck, and the yoke shall be destroyed because of the anointing" (Isaiah 10:27). The anointing destroys yokes and bondages, and it destroys sin. But it cannot do anything with religion—your own set of beliefs—whatsoever is not of faith is sin and any belief that is not of Him is *unbelief.* *"And he that doubteth is damned if he eat, because he eateth not of faith: for whatsoever is not of faith is sin"* (Romans 14:23). Remember, Jesus could do no mighty work in His hometown because of unbelief. Whole denominations are caught in the grip of unbelief, and you will find no anointing where you find unbelief.

Let's take a look at George, a new believer, full of the Holy Ghost, who is praying for the sick and seeing them healed. When his car breaks down, he lays hands on it and it starts working again. He is so excited he even prays for his dog. He is full of the joy of the Holy Ghost, thanking God all the time for his new life. "I was full of the devil, but now I am serving Jesus. Thank You, Lord." Miracles are happening all around him, because God is using him. Then he visits a new church, and they tell him about a special seminar he should attend. It's about the armor of God. And, being a new Christian, George doesn't know about the armor, so they begin to tell him all about it, piece by piece. "Boy, you are going to be in trouble if you don't know about that. The devil's going to get you."

He is so excited to go, because if *they* tell him he needs the armor, then he must need to learn about it. So, he goes to the seminar and gets all the books and all the tapes. He sits through the whole series and listens as they tell him: "Don't even get out of bed without the armor. Don't leave home without it." They give him a sheet of paper with all the different things he needs to do. It takes ten minutes to put on each part of the armor, so he needs to get up at 6:00 in the morning, giving him enough time to do it all. In fact, on the bedside table is a little man in armor with an alarm clock in his belly that George bought with the tape series.

So, he sets his alarm for 6:00 the next morning and spends the next hour putting on the armor. Now it is 7:00, and George realizes he hasn't showered, shaved, or brushed his teeth. But, he has bigger problems. He is late as he hurries off to go to another seminar, where he listens and buys all the tapes and books about praying in the Spirit. He must have those, because the only way to increase the anointing is to pray in the Spirit for an hour a day.

The next morning when the little armored man rings, he puts on the armor until 7:00, prays in the Spirit until 8:00 and realizes he has not shaved, he has not showered or brushed his teeth. But that's the least of his worries, because he can't be late for today's seminar. In this seminar, he is taught that in order to be anointed you must read forty chapters in the Bible each day. Now he wonders when he will find time to do that. But he finds a new "quick scan" Bible that gives him the main points so he can get through in no time.

The little armored man rings the next morning and George goes through the same routine until now it is 9:00 and he still hasn't showered, shaved or brushed his teeth. But, that is the least of his problems. He has to go to another seminar. At this one, he is taught about the demon spirits over territories and told if he is to be effective for God he must go to the library and pick up books on the area where he lives. He is instructed to especially study how it was founded, and if pirates were involved in settling there. If so, a pirate spirit inhabits the region and now it is George's job to do warfare against the pirate spirits in his area. He is now a Holy Ghost Ghostbuster.

The following morning, George wakes up to the tune of "Ghostbusters" and realizes that he is feeling oppressed. He used to be on fire for God, and loved winning souls to Jesus, but now his day is taken up with rules, regulations, and learning about the mark of the beast and generational curses. And he still hasn't showered, shaved or brushed his teeth. But, that is the least of his worries. Now he has lost his first love.

The devil knows that if Jesus is still your first love, you will be on fire for God; you will have a love relationship with Jesus, and the joy of your salvation will fill your heart. He knows he can't stop you then. That's why he comes to try to bind you with rituals and "dos and don'ts," and formulas that mean absolutely nothing.

Now you may be thinking: "But, I thought the armor was important." Yes, it is, but it doesn't take an hour to put it on. I put mine on and wear it all the time. I even sleep in it. Who told you to take it off?

You ask: "What about praying in the Holy Spirit?" You can do that any time you want to, but you don't have to set a time to do it. There is still the trash to take out, the kids to take to school and meals to prepare. Who made it so hard?

Jesus said, *"My yoke is easy, and my burden is light"* (Matthew 11:30).

No matter what formula you adopt, if you miss doing it for one day, condemnation will set in. Your relationship with the Lord is not because of your great works—it's all because of His grace. People are so worried about how they pray. They think, "Did God accept my prayer?" What is God looking for in us? David found the answer. *"He that hath clean hands, and a pure heart..."* (Psalm 24:4). God is looking for a pure heart.

The anointing is not a formula—it is a love relationship with Jesus Christ of Nazareth, the Son of the living God. Here is the key: do only what He tells you to do. There are those who are building another ark of the covenant and parading it around as though it is some holy thing. They don't realize the Holy Ghost came out of that holy Tabernacle made with the hands of man, never to dwell there again, but to come live in your heart and my heart.

Oh, how easily man goes back into bondage! The things they do, and the things they buy to get closer to God, end up taking them further away from Him.

That's why over the years I have told churches and congregations everywhere we go that we did not come to burden them. We do not leave them in shackles and chains, but we promise to set them free by the power of the Word of the Almighty God. The most devastating thing to us, when we return later, is to see that some those dear ones, who had been set free, are now back in handcuffs again. It is pathetic.

Look at what Job said (Job 42:5): *"I have heard of thee by the hearing of the ear: but now mine eye seeth thee."* You may have heard of Him, but when you see Him in all His glory and splendor, you will never be the same. The fire of God will grab hold of you and consume you. You will say like the prophet of old: *"But his word was in mine heart as a burning fire shut up in my bones..."* (Jeremiah 20:9). Glory to God!

Look around you. Where are the John G. Lakes? Where are the Smith Wigglesworths and the Charles Finneys of today? They were not copies taken from a religious copy machine but were born out of a relationship between themselves and Almighty God. Pray that God will raise up more people with godly hearts like theirs...men with the fire of God in their bones.

Then when you go out to preach, it will not be the words that you have read in this book. It will be Almighty God's words that come from your mouth. If He is real to you, His words will come from a heart that is in relationship with Him. There are millions of people still in captivity, bound by sin. Oh, that you may grab on to these truths and tell them all that was purchased for them at Calvary. Let the fire of Heaven burn bright in your life so that everything done for Him would be done out of your relationship with Him. Don't let your life slip back into rituals and tradition. Don't settle for religion. Who wants the imitation when they can have that which is real? I want what is real!

I am not some maverick; I have tested these truths on the field. I am not alone; I have sat and spoken with great men and women of God, many of them in their nineties. There is an army of men and women who have gone on before me who would back me in my passion for these truths. Heaven backs me up when I tell you that you can only break the captives free from religion and tradition by the anointing and the outpouring of the Living Water, Jesus Christ. Set them free to serve God the way He meant for them to serve, and revival will break out.

It is all based on your freedom, because if you go forth in bondage, they'll come under the same bondage you have. You can't set people free when you're bound. Go out in your anointing and your freedom, and you will see nations shaken.

The number one reason for the lack of the move of God is not sin. Everywhere we go in the world, we see results. Sinners are being saved, running to get in the Kingdom. The number one reason for the lack of the move of God is religion. People tell me, "Don't rock the boat." Well, I didn't come to rock the boat. I came to turn it over!

If the Lord has shown you there is some generational thing you need to break off your life, don't make a doctrine of it. If He has told you to pray in tongues for an hour, then do it. But don't go running around, telling everybody: "I pray in tongues for an hour." If He told you to read forty chapters in your Bible every day, do it. Do whatever He tells you to do. But don't try to force it on other people. I know what I am telling you from my own experience.

When I first started in ministry, I was mean. I would walk into the room when Adonica was trying to feed Kirsten, our oldest child, and begin to admonish her: "You should be praying. I am the only one carrying this whole ministry. It's a heavy load for one person to carry."

What an idiot! It was the truth, but not a kind thing to say to my wife. People wonder why marriages break up. Some people get so super-spiritual they spend all of their time praying instead of taking care of their jobs, their homes, and their families. Praying is good, but it is *not* your number one priority; praying must come, not out of religious duty, but out of your relationship with God. There is a time to pray, and a time to get up and do what you need to do and what God has told you to do. Love God and love people—anything else is extra.

It would have been wrong for David to tell the entire army to go get a slingshot. It was wrong for them to tell him to use Saul's armor. Just use what works. If it doesn't bring results, then don't do it. It's a form of insanity to do the same thing over and over, expecting a different result. It is completely unproductive for you to keep doing something over and over that doesn't bring results. If it doesn't work, forget about it. We don't have time to mess with something that doesn't work.

DEVELOP YOUR RELATIONSHIP WITH THE LORD

We must recognize that everything we do *for* God is done *with* Him, through the love relationship we have with Him. Our relationship with Him is more important than anything we can do for Him. Anyone in the business world knows that it is easier to work with someone you are in association with than to just "do a deal." An association is much longer lasting and more effective than working with strangers.

Some people only call on God when they need Him, without first establishing a connection. They treat God like He is a "one-night-stand," just calling on Him in a time of need. They want His help, but they turn away from Him once the deal is done. It is important to know that relationships bring strength for the future. God is looking for people who not only need His help but want to build a relationship with Him.

I tell ministers and evangelists all the time that their ministry will go much smoother if they establish a rapport with pastors and churches. I have always done that, even to my detriment at times. But don't be afraid to establish relationships. Some people are afraid they will be hurt, so they don't even try. I can assure you that you are not running a risk when you develop a relationship with the Lord. The only one who will get hurt is the devil.

I have talked with many in the Pentecostal flow, or experience, whose whole relationship with the Lord is based around a manifestation. Whether it is tongues, or some manifestation that happens when the anointing is flowing in the service. I can tell you they are not developing a relationship with the Lord. I can invite you to a party where we have balloons and streamers, and we can enjoy cake and ice cream, but that doesn't mean we are developing a relationship. You can hang around the

Lord and He may shower you with gifts, but as for me…I am not there just for the party. I want a relationship with the Lord.

I would be hurt if my children only showed up when I threw them a party. I taught my children—and they learned very quickly—they could go with me when I left the house, or they could stay home. They always asked where I was going, and I told them, "Come with me and you'll see." Sometimes when I wouldn't tell them, they would stay at home. Then when I returned I told them where I had gone, and they were sorry they hadn't come along.

"Daddy, why didn't you tell us where you were going?" they asked. I explained that the decision should be based on wanting to be with their daddy, not just where he was going. It took several times of missing major events before they decided they had better hang around Daddy, because that's where "it happens."

Your decision to spend time with your Father and build a relationship with Him is the same principle. Do you want a love relationship or just what He can give you? Job had learned that lesson when he said (Job 42:5): *"I have heard of thee by the hearing of the ear: but now mine eye seeth thee."* It is one thing to hear about someone, but when you really get to meet that person it is different.

I have been in situations where someone would talk about another preacher in a critical manner. I would ask, "Oh, do you know them?"

They usually answer, "No, but I have heard about them."

I answer, "Well, I happen to know them and you are talking totally untrue rubbish."

Many people have only heard about God, but I actually know Him, so when someone says untrue things about Him I know they are not true; they are just rubbish.

Now, I'm pointing you to a relationship with Him. "Tell me what to do, Brother Rodney." No, let Him tell you what to do. If He is sleeping in the back of the boat, sometimes you just need to go snuggle up. Don't do all the talking. Let Him tell you what to do when He is ready. Bless God, if I was in the boat with Him, I would tie a rope to

His foot and tie the other end of it to my foot and go to sleep. Where Jesus is, that's where I am, because we are in a relationship.

Some of the things I am going to share with you may not fit into your present relationship with the Lord. You may have to build them into your relationship with Him. Don't just treat them as a formula and think they are necessarily going to work for you. Let me tell you, you can achieve a certain success in your ministry without the anointing. You can build a half-decent ministry by just getting all of your ducks in a row, doing everything you are supposed to do, and even getting the funding for it. But whether God breathes on it—and whether there is any eternal fruit—is another story. When we do it in God's plan and will, it produces gold, jewels, and precious stones. When we do it in our flesh, it's wood, hay, and stubble.

Now let's look at some other ways you can increase the anointing in your life.

3

INCREASING THE ANOINTING

Through Prayer and Worship

We have established what the anointing is and how to recognize the difference between having a relationship with God and following religion's formulas. Now is a good time to start asking God how He plans to use the anointing in your life and decide how willing you are to increase your anointing in order to do what He has planned for you. There are several things that will guarantee you a closer relationship with the Lord which, in turn, will increase your anointing.

A LIFESTYLE OF PRAYER

The first thing you should place on your list of things to increase your anointing is what I call "A Lifestyle of Prayer." Many people have a ritualized prayer life, but that's not what Jesus taught. Prayer is communicating with God, but it is not one-sided, because God also wants to communicate with you. You talk to Him—He talks to you. In 1 Thessalonians 5:17, the Apostle Paul tells us to *"pray without ceasing."* Some ask how you can pray without ceasing, but it is not praying on your knees all day and night; it is living in a spirit of prayer. You can be crying out to God wherever you are and whatever you are doing. Your thought life can be with God all the time.

We read in Jude 20: *"But ye, beloved, building up yourselves on your most holy faith, praying in the Holy Ghost."* We used to hear people talking about being "prayed up," but you can stay "prayed up" when you pray in the Holy Ghost. You will grow spiritually as you stay in touch with God. As a believer, who wants to be used of God, there are two kinds of prayers you should be praying on a regular basis.

- **A Prayer of Consecration.** As a Spirit-filled child of God, we should want His will to be done in our lives above our own. Jesus prayed this prayer in the Garden of Gethsemane: *"Father, if thou be willing, remove this cup from me: nevertheless not my will, but thine, be done"* (Luke 22:42). He knew what He was anointed to do and wanted only to do His Father's will.

- **A Prayer of Repentance.** 1 John 1:8–9 says: *"If we say that we have no sin, we deceive ourselves, and the truth is not in us. If we confess our sins, he is faithful and just to forgive us our sins, and to cleanse us from all unrighteousness."* Sin separates us from God. We need to get rid of it quickly, through acknowledgement of the sin, repentance toward God, and receiving His forgiveness. We must keep our hearts right with God, not only to avoid sin's penalty, but because of our relationship with Him, and our love for Him. We live right, because we love Him. We never want to hurt Him or our relationship with Him.

Many Christians have a daily quiet time—a very quiet time. No communication takes place. But that is not what God intends for prayer to be. Many people never learn that God not only hears us, but He also wants to talk to us. Actually, we need to develop an even greater ability to *listen* than we have in talking. Some people are very skilled at talking but have never learned to listen. We all know someone we dread having to call on the phone, because we know it will be a one-sided conversation. Yabba, yabba, yabba, hardly stopping to breathe. You may have something important to tell them, but you can't get a word in edgeways.

The same thing happens when we meet with the Lord. He's trying to talk to us, but He can't get a word in, because we do all the talking. He may want to give us some valuable information, but we are just there to deliver what we want to tell Him. We are so anxious to talk we are not listening to what He wants to tell us. So, we must develop a two-way communication with the Lord. It's not good to go to Him and unload our prayer requests on a daily basis without listening to what He has to say. Communication—talking and listening—is essential when you are developing a lifestyle of prayer.

Now, if you have the luxury of a set time to pray in the morning, that's fine. The schedule that we kept over our years in the ministry made it very hard to have a set prayer time, because we never knew when we were going to bed or would be waking up. Jet lag and being on the wrong side of the clock definitely changed our habits. Climbing into bed at 6:00 in the morning after an overnight flight made it hard to have an early-morning prayer time.

So, I learned to stay in an attitude of prayer, keeping myself in a listening place, hearing as He talked to me, and being able to talk to Him. It doesn't matter where you are—you can be in an attitude of prayer all the time. You can talk to the Lord when you lie in your bed or when you shower. You can talk to the Lord driving down the road in your car. You talk to other people as you are driving, don't you? How do you talk to people on your cell phone? You press the send button, they answer, and you speak to them. It is the same thing when you want to talk to the Lord. Just call on Him and He will answer.

Start now—begin to develop a lifestyle of prayer. When you don't know what to pray, then pray in the Holy Ghost. If you are frustrated about something, don't try to put flowery words to your prayer to impress God. You don't have to pray: "Oh, God, thou knowest my great love for thee, and I knowst." That doesn't impress God. Just get real with Him. Tell Him, "God, I'm really upset about this right now. I'm frustrated, and I need an answer." He knows what you are thinking, anyway. Get specific with Him. Learn what Jesus said about prayer. Learn about the different kinds of prayers—prayers you know He hears and the prayers you can't expect Him to answer, so you know the difference.

Many people in the Body of Christ have been distracted in their prayer life. Instead of their prayers being directed toward the Lord, and in relationship with Him, their entire prayer focus has turned to fighting the devil. There is a time and place for spiritual warfare and intercession, but it's been so overemphasized in many circles that all they want to do is be involved in warfare. In some churches and study groups the people meet to pray, but all they do is fight the devil, and it gets so tiring that nobody wants to pray anymore. They don't want to just go talk to the devil again.

First of all, we don't have to go rescue God in order to have revival. He is not a captive in His own heavens. He's not a prisoner behind bars in Heaven, needing us to pray and break Him out so He can do His job. He is not some weak little entity sitting in the heavens. He knows what is going on. He knows everything. God is going to move whether you pray or not. He is just not going to do it through you. Remember, He didn't need your help to save you.

You don't have to spend all your time fighting the devil. Jesus already defeated the devil. We just enforce that defeat and make it a reality in our own lives. God has it under control. There are hungry people who are praying and pressing in to God, and He's going to move to wherever they are. God always comes to where there's faith and fervency in prayer.

So many people in the Body of Christ have gone totally overboard in this whole matter of warfare. We saw this happen in Turkey a while back. We went in there and helped Pastors Corey and Rose Erman start a church, The River Istanbul. What joy we had, shopping for sound systems and equipment, planning all the details for establishing the church, and bringing in the people. We had gone to Turkey to do what Jesus said in Mark 16:15: *"Go ye into all the world and preach the Gospel to every creature."* We became aware of certain other groups who went into Istanbul and rented an arena to do battle against the "queen of heaven." They brought in many Americans to rent a plane and fly over the city and help them bring down this queen of heaven. It was nothing more than "ignorance gone to seed." They glorify the devil and make out that he is bigger and more powerful than he is. Jesus told us to preach the Gospel, not preach on what the devil may or may not be doing. The Gospel is the good news that changes hearts, minds, and nations.

You know, this type of thing has been a real burden to me, because I find so many good, sincere people who get side-tracked and all-caught-up in whatever it is they're doing. But what they're doing really amounts to nothing. Nobody's getting saved, nobody's getting healed, and nobody's getting set free. When I have a meeting, I pray, of course, but then I go preach and proclaim the Gospel. The power is in the proclamation of the Gospel.

Jesus never said to just go into all the world and pray against demons. He said to go into all the world and preach the Gospel. You must pray—that's your personal relationship with the Lord. Right now, our church, The River at Tampa Bay, is praying like never before. We're praying for the United States and the government, praying that God would give this land a stay of execution, a last-minute reprieve and another Great Spiritual Awakening. But we are still preaching the Gospel and seeing souls set free.

We have a choice. We can go into a city to pray and do warfare, or we can go in and have a crusade where we see souls saved, we cast out devils, and we get people healed. That's the warfare we are called to do. The warfare we are called to do is not carnal but is meant to pull down strongholds. And what are strongholds? Look in 2 Corinthians 10:4-5 for the Apostle Paul's description: *"For the weapons of our warfare are not carnal, but mighty through God to the pulling down of strongholds; Casting down imaginations, and every high thing that exalteth itself against the knowledge of God, and bringing into captivity every thought to the obedience of Christ."*

The strongholds we should be warring against are the thoughts and imaginations in our minds, not in the heavenlies. There are many discussions about "open heavens" or "closed heavens." In Matthew 3:16–17 we read: *"And Jesus, when he was baptized, went up straightway out of the water: and, lo, **the heavens were opened unto him,** and he saw the Spirit of God descending like a dove, and lighting upon him: And lo a voice from Heaven, saying, This is my beloved Son, in whom I am well pleased."* (Emphasis added.)

We see in that passage where the heavens opened, and there is no record in the Bible that says they ever closed again. Your prayers are never hindered by a closed Heaven. There are those who believe there are principalities and powers, clogging up the heavens so your prayers never reach God. That is just total rubbish! God controls the heavens, not the queen of heaven, or anything else man can invent in his mind. It's not the strongholds in the heavens that are the problem. It's the strongholds in the *heads*. Please read my book, *This Present Glory, A Practical Handbook on Spiritual Warfare* as it goes into this in great detail.

How is it possible that we've been able to take our ministry into nations—where everybody else has said the heavens were closed and a move of God was impossible—but we had Heaven break loose? The move of God was strong, people were saved, healed, and set free. Certainly not because we did all the mumbo-jumbo some others did—without results, I might say. Then when we left, some of those people went back in and tried to pull down strongholds in the heavenlies again. People went right back into bondage again, when they could have operated in the freedom we had in the Word of God.

We teach our people about true intercession, travailing in prayer.

We allow the Spirit of God to pray through us the perfect will of God. We are not interested in showing our eloquence in the English language. Why would anyone want to interfere with the Holy Ghost? Romans 8:26–27 says: *"Likewise the Spirit also helpeth our infirmities: for we know not what we should pray for as we ought: but the Spirit itself maketh intercession for us with groanings which cannot be uttered. And he that searcheth the hearts knoweth what is the mind of the Spirit, because he maketh intercession for the saints according to the will of God."*

So, just pray and let it come forth, no matter how long it takes. It may take an hour, two hours or longer, but pray it through. Don't try to put your own interpretation on what you are praying. The Lord doesn't tell you everything you are praying in the Spirit, because you would try to interfere with it. When you are praying in the Holy Spirit, you are praying the perfect will of God. Trust the Holy Ghost. Follow His leading in all things. Pray till you feel His peace and joy. Always end on a note of victory. People who pray and intercede a lot, should be filled with joy, not walking around depressed and oppressed.

Develop a life of prayer—a lifestyle of prayer—and there will be seasons of prayer when you will be moved by the Spirit of God far beyond what you have experienced. There may be times when you sit down at the table to eat and suddenly a spirit of prayer hits you so hard you can't eat. You have to leave the table to go pray. Be sensitive to the leading of the Holy Ghost.

There is a spiritual famine in America today because of the lack of prayer. So much junk has been accepted as prayer that is not prayer at all. Fighting devils morning, noon, and night is not prayer, but many people have been deceived into thinking they are great prayer warriors, when really they are just misled, frustrated, religious people. Some people are constantly harassed—some of it is because they have opened doors to the devil, through sin. Until they clean up their act, they will never be totally free. Keep your heart and life right and thank God that you have the victory!

It is time for everybody who claims the Name of Jesus to develop a lifestyle of prayer. Give yourself to spending time with the Lord, praying in the Holy Ghost. Allow the Lord to use you in intercession for others, praying through you to show forth the perfect will of God. Trust Him to work in you, even when you don't know what He is praying through you. When He stirs your heart to pray, don't be too inquisitive as to what you are praying in the Spirit. You might not like the answer you get from Him. He may have been interceding for you.

If you knew in English what you have been praying in the Spirit you might stop your prayer, because you may not want to hear it. The Holy Spirit may be telling the Father how stubborn you are. "Father, I have told this person time after time to make some adjustments in his life, but he just won't listen and keeps going the wrong way. Father, please move in his life." If you knew what He was saying, you may not keep praying. The Holy Spirit is trying to "sort you out" so just leave it alone. God will tell you what the Holy Spirit is praying for you if He wants you to know. The Holy Spirit is praying through you for God's perfect will in your life. If He wants to show you something concerning your prayers, then He will. You need to trust Him enough just to pray and leave the rest to Him.

Sometimes the Holy Spirit will reveal things to you that are not for publication. He doesn't show you things about people's private lives so you can run around telling it. That's gossip. If you tell a friend in confidence, they will tell a close friend (in confidence, of course) who will tell another friend, who tells *Charisma Magazine*. If you share all the secrets God shares with you, He will stop telling you things, because He can't trust you. God shares with you about someone or situations so you can pray, not so you can prove how spiritual you are or how prophetic you are.

The great soul-winners in the world do not spend their time and efforts in such religious practices as we have mentioned. They spend great amounts of time in the presence of the Lord. When the anointing of God comes on a man or woman, they will want to spend their time in prayer, fellowshipping with the Lord on a daily basis and ministering out of an overflow of that communion with Him. Your anointing will increase as you learn to communicate with the Lord.

A LIFESTYLE OF WORSHIP

The importance of worship in a believer's life cannot be stressed too much. Acts 13:2 says, *"As they ministered to the Lord, and fasted, the Holy Ghost said, Separate me Barnabas and Saul for the work whereunto I have called them."* As they ministered to the Lord, the Lord began to speak to them. We need to spend at least as much time in worship, as we do in prayer.

If you're not a worshiper, what are you? I am not talking about public worship; anybody can do public worship. Many people don't even do that and, I am sorry to say, many preachers do not worship God. It's not what you do publicly—it's what you do privately that is important. Sometimes when I want to worship Him, I'll sing—just sing my praises to Him. One of the things I love about my wife is hearing her sing praises to the Lord. She's always singing. She goes into the shower and it's like an echo as she sings. Her songs are meant for the Lord, but I just listen and thank God for her. Our daughter, Kelly, was like that, too. She just sang all the time. There was always a praise song coming from Kelly.

I remember once driving down the road with a worship tape playing. The power of God hit me so strongly I started weeping. I could hardly see the road for the tears. I said, "Lord, you bless me so much." The Lord said to me, "You bless Me so much." My immediate response was, "No, I don't. How do I bless You?" He said, "You bless Me when you spend all your time traveling around the world telling people how wonderful I am and how awesome I am. And you worship Me. You bless Me." Then the scripture came to me, from David's words, *"I will bless the LORD at all times: his praise shall continually be in my mouth"* (Psalm 34:1).

My heart was so grateful because I don't *have* to bless the Lord—I *get* to bless the Lord. Verses began flowing through my mind, such as David uttered in Psalm 8:4: *"What is man, that thou art mindful of him? and the son of man, that thou visitest him?"* I often say, "Lord, you are so great and my words feel so inadequate when I worship you." Even so, I will continue to worship Him—with psalms and hymns and spiritual songs (Ephesians 5:19). Look with me at Psalm 150:1–6:

> Praise ye the Lord. Praise God in his sanctuary: praise him in the firmament of his power. Praise him for his mighty acts: praise him according to his excellent greatness. Praise him with the sound of the trumpet: praise him with the psaltery and harp. Praise him with the timbrel and dance: praise him with stringed instruments and organs. Praise him upon the loud cymbals: praise him upon the high sounding cymbals. Let everything that hath breath praise the Lord. Praise ye the Lord.

Praise the Lord for who He is, for what He has done and is doing in your life. Worship Him when you feel like it and when you don't feel like it. He is worthy of your praise and your worship. I have heard many testimonies of people who have experienced breakthroughs in periods of grief and depression. As they began to worship the Lord, even in their darkest times, their joy returned, their hearts were strengthened, and they were able to enjoy their life and continue serving God.

I worship Him in my going out and my coming in, my rising up and my lying down. I live, eat, sleep and breathe worship. I worship Him when I am walking or when I am resting.

Jesus spoke of worship in John 4:23–24 when He was talking to the woman at the well and confirmed that He was the Messiah they were looking for: *"But the hour cometh, and now is, when the true worshippers shall worship the Father in spirit and in truth: for the Father seeketh such to worship him. God is a Spirit: and they that worship him must worship him in spirit and in truth."*

If you live a lifestyle of worshiping God, you will begin to see Him in all His creation and will want to worship Him more and more. As you praise Him and worship Him, you will feel His constant presence with you. The result will not only be a more intimate relationship with the Father, but a greater anointing, as well. After all, worship is the highest form of prayer. Fill your life with worship, don't spend time asking for anything, just tell Him how much you love Him and how awesome He is and give Him praise and adoration.

4

INCREASING THE ANOINTING

Through the Word and Hearing His Voice

There is no doubt that communication is one of the most important parts of any relationship, whether it is business, personal, or spiritual. As we saw in the last chapter, the anointing on your life is dramatically affected by the quality of your communication with the Lord—in worship and prayer—or by your lack thereof. We often think those are the only ways we can hear from God, but as you will see, there are several more things we need if we are to have a full relationship with Him.

STUDY THE WORD OF GOD

The study of God's Word is essential if you want to increase your prayer life, your relationship with God, and the anointing on your life. The lack of consistent study of the Word of God will hinder your relationship with the Lord. Many people spend very little time in their personal study of the Word, so they are lacking in that area of communication with the Lord. Sadly, many ministers only study when they need a message, so they must run to their Bible when they are looking for something to preach. Personally, I do not study the Word looking for a message—my messages come out of my study of His Word.

When you are living a lifestyle of prayer, and pursuing a consistent study of the Word, you are allowing the Lord to speak to you through His "communication system." If I am going to call you in Texas, I'm not going to stand outside my home in Florida and shout your name; I'm going to get on the telephone and call you.

So, let's use the communication system set up by the Lord. How does He speak to us? In prayer and through His Word. If you're not in prayer and the Word, you are probably not going to hear the voice of the Lord. You may think you have found a better way, but Proverbs 14:12 says: *"There is a way which seemeth right unto a man, but the end thereof are the ways of death."* Lack of study in God's Word is definitely the wrong way. Every believer should have a good, workable knowledge of God's Word. One of the problems we face today is that far too many Christians do not even have a basic knowledge of the Word. God's people are not walking in the victory and power God has provided because of a lack of knowledge. Because of this, the devil is able to deceive them and rob from them (Hosea 4:6).

Scripture says that many are walking after the doctrine of men, *"having a form of godliness, but denying the power thereof…"* (2 Timothy 3:5). That is why Paul admonished Timothy to, as follows: *"Preach the word; be instant in season, out of season; reprove, rebuke, exhort with all longsuffering and doctrine. For the time will come when they will not endure sound doctrine; but after their own lusts shall they heap to themselves teachers, having itching ears"* (2 Timothy 4:2, 3).

2 Peter 1:20 says: *"Knowing this first, that no prophecy of the scripture is of any private interpretation."* Don't try to put your own interpretation on scripture. In 2 Timothy 2:15–16 Paul tells us: *"Study to shew thyself approved unto God, a workman that needeth not to be ashamed, rightly dividing the word of truth. But shun profane and vain babblings: for they will increase unto more ungodliness."*

Remember, there's a right way to divide and there's a wrong way to divide. First of all, you must take God at His word. Don't look for alternate hidden meanings. God said what He meant, and He means what He says. Then, you must understand the difference between the old covenant and the new covenant. There are certain things that applied under the old covenant that do not apply under the new covenant. You cannot take old covenant principles and apply them to the new covenant, because the old has been done away with, and the new has come. There are things in the new covenant that have totally overwritten the old covenant.

There are people today who have a little bit of the old and a little bit of the new all mixed into their own covenant. They are going from law to grace and back to law again. They are like schizophrenics. They don't know who they are or where they are going. One minute they are under the law, and the next minute they are trying to operate under grace. They are not walking in the freedom that Jesus purchased for them at Calvary. Some pastors are still trying to put their people back under the law—under bondage.

There are absolutes in theology and doctrine that we are not going to argue about—they are not even negotiable. The Deity of Christ, His Virgin birth, the Blood of Jesus, the Cross of Calvary are absolutes that we will stand firm on, because the Word of God is firm on them. But there are things people fight about that are not absolutes. For instance: "Let the women be silent in church." Some pastors preach that like it is an absolute. They don't understand that in the early church the men sat on one side, and the women sat on the other side. When a woman didn't understand what something meant, she would lean out and ask her husband, "What did he say?" She was thus interrupting the message and interfering with the service. So, Paul wrote to them in 1 Corinthians 14:34-35 as follows: *"Let your women keep silence in the churches: for it is not permitted unto them to speak; but they are commanded to be under obedience, as also saith the law. And if they will learn any thing, let them ask their husbands at home: for it is a shame for women to speak in the church."*

This did not mean that women cannot take any part in the church services, but many still teach against women preaching or teaching in the church. Well, perhaps God didn't know that when He anointed Maria Woodworth-Etter who answered the call to "go out in the highways and hedges and gather in the lost sheep." She became known as the "Grandmother of the Pentecostal Movement." Did He make a mistake when He anointed Aimee Semple McPherson, who built one of the greatest denominations of her day, the Foursquare Church? Oops! And what about Kathryn Kuhlman and Joyce Meyer? The issue of women in ministry is not an absolute, but is the subject of many heated discussions among differing denominations: *"Whose adorning let it not be that outward adorning of plaiting the hair, and of wearing of gold, or of putting on of apparel; But let it be the hidden man of the heart, in that which is not corruptible, even the ornament of a meek and quiet spirit, which is in the sight of God of great price"* (1 Peter 3:3-4).

This scripture generates numerous arguments, but if you read it right, you will see that Paul is not forbidding these things—he surely would not want the women to leave off their apparel! But he is admonishing them to work on developing a beautiful inside, rather than merely a beautiful outside. Now, according to the Word, it is important for Christian women to dress modestly, but outward things don't make you holy or unholy. Wearing drab clothes and no makeup isn't going to make you more holy than someone wearing makeup and a pretty outfit. But beauty from within—a sweet, kind, loving spirit—looks good on everybody!

These things are not absolutes, but the devil will try to trap you in a non-absolute because he knows there is no power there. It's the absolutes that carry the power. When you stay with the absolutes, you'll release the power which will, in turn, increase the anointing upon your life. Do not be sidetracked by the enemy into arguing about what color robes the priests wore, or what kind of thread they used on them. Much time has been wasted in trying to prove what the Urim and Thummim were and why they were used by the high priests. Spend your time on learning more about the One who gave His life for you and find His will for your life. That only happens when you study His Word.

The gospel is simple. In fact, I'm going to go a step further and say that the most powerful ministries in the world today are the simplest. The more you complicate the Gospel, the "good news," the more the anointing is hindered. People will try to convince you what great theologians they are, and try to engage you in long theological conversations and/or arguments, just to impress you. But they make them so complicated that even they don't know what they are talking about. They are puffed up about their knowledge of the Word but have no idea how to use that knowledge for the Kingdom of God. Knowledge by itself is not going to bring results. 1 Corinthians 8:1 tells us that mere knowledge causes people to be puffed up, but love edifies and builds up.

I was sitting at lunch with a theologian just before going to see *The Passion of the Christ*, the movie about the last twelve hours of Jesus's life. He remarked, "I hope when it is over someone gets up and explains to the people what just happened." I answered, "God forbid you should need an explanation!" Surely, the message of the Gospel has been simply and clearly laid out for anyone to hear and receive!

That's where the church has gone wrong, folks. The Gospel is not powerless—rather it is the power of God unto salvation (Romans 1:16). Paul says, *"And my speech and my preaching was not with enticing words of man's wisdom, but in demonstration of the Spirit and of power: That your faith should not stand in the wisdom of men, but in the power of God"* (1 Corinthians 2:4-5).

We need to get an education in the Word, and that comes with study. It doesn't matter that your head is full of knowledge if there is no practical outworking of it in your life. I am not interested in what you know if you aren't using it. And don't be so religious that you only study certain subjects. That's the problem with the different camps in the Body of Christ. You get involved with one camp, and you only see things through their persuasion. God did not set in the church just one group of people.

Back in 1980, I worked with Youth for Christ, and my co-workers came from many different denominations. The Lord gave me respect for people, no matter where they came from or what their backgrounds may have been. He has given me the ability to be open to people from other persuasions. I love Jesus, and if they are born-again, washed in His blood, even though they are not from the same denominational background that I came from, I can still fellowship with them. When you are working with other people, you have to open your heart to them. We may not always agree on every matter, but we are to love them because they are our brothers and sisters.

Just remember: when you are studying the Word, try not to get sidetracked away from the simplicity of the Gospel. Do not run off on a tangent into something that does not produce life. You will always know when you are into false doctrine, because you will begin to lose your joy and your peace. Let peace be the umpire (Colossians 3:15 AMPC). *"In thy presence is fulness of joy; at thy right hand there are pleasures for evermore..."* (Psalm 16:11). The letter kills, but the Spirit gives life: *"Who also hath made us able ministers of the new testament; not of the letter, but of the spirit: for the letter killeth, but the spirit giveth life"* (2 Corinthians 3:6).

Allow the Holy Spirit to lead and guide you in your study of the scriptures. Remember: He is your teacher. He will take God's Word and make it alive for you. *"But the Comforter, which is the Holy Ghost, whom the Father will send in my name, he shall teach you all things, and bring all things to your remembrance, whatsoever I have said unto you"* (John 14:26). The Holy Spirit and the Word agree. The Holy Spirit helps us to understand God's Word and gives us revelation concerning it. He will **never** contradict the Word or tell you something that is contrary to it. Jesus said,

> "I have yet many things to say unto you, but ye cannot bear them now. Howbeit when he, the Spirit of truth, is come, he will guide you into all truth: for he shall not speak of himself; but whatsoever he shall hear, that shall he speak: and he will shew you things to come. He shall glorify me: for he shall receive of mine, and shall shew it unto you" (John 16:12-14).

LISTEN FOR HIS VOICE

Hearing His voice is essential if you are seeking His will in your life. *"My sheep hear my voice, and I know them, and they follow me"* (John 10:27). Listen only to Jesus, and stop listening to strangers.

> And when he putteth forth his own sheep, he goeth before them, and the sheep follow him: for they know his voice. And a stranger will they not follow, but will flee from him: for they know not the voice of strangers (John 10:4–5).

Is it your desire to have an intimate relationship with Him? Read Revelation 3:20 and know that He is talking to *you: "Behold, I stand at the door, and knock: if any man hear my voice, and open the door, I will come in to him, and will sup with him, and he with me."* Some people don't really want to hear His voice just to be close to Him—many times they are only seeking a new revelation so they can pioneer a new movement.

"For as many as are led by the Spirit of God, they are the sons of God" (Romans 8:14). You can trust the voice of the Spirit if you're walking in the Word and prayer, but you cannot trust the voices you hear if you are living a life of sin. *You will be deceived.* If you want to follow the Lord and hear His voice, you cannot tolerate sin in your life in any form or fashion. Do not tolerate it in thought, word, or deed. I often quote Ephesians 4:27, because it is so crucial that we remember in our

everyday life: *"Neither give place to the devil."*

When you sin, you are giving the devil access to your life, and you give him a foothold in your mind. The more you yield to sin, the more you yield to the devil. You open the door to deception and familiar spirits who masquerade as the voice of the Spirit but are really of the devil, and will lead you astray. Be careful what voice you are listening to and obeying.

I believe, of course, that a lifestyle of prayer is essential if you want to hear the voice of God, but you must understand that prayer is not just talking—it is listening, as well. As I have stated before: half of your prayer life should be listening to what *He* has to say. It is the same when it comes to your time in the Word: you read the Word, and you listen. First Samuel 3:1–10 (AMPC) tells a powerful story of hearing and recognizing the voice of God:

> Now the boy Samuel ministered to the Lord before Eli. The word of the Lord was rare and precious in those days; there was no frequent or widely spread vision. At that time Eli, whose eyesight had dimmed so that he could not see, was lying down in his own place. The lamp of God had not yet gone out in the temple of the Lord, where the ark of God was, and Samuel was lying down When the Lord called, Samuel! And he answered, Here I am. He ran to Eli and said, Here I am, for you called me. Eli said, I did not call you; lie down again. So he went and lay down. And the Lord called again, Samuel! And Samuel arose and went to Eli and said, Here am I; you did call me. Eli answered, I did not call, my son; lie down again. Now Samuel did not yet know the Lord, and the word of the Lord was not yet revealed to him. And the Lord called Samuel the third time. And he went to Eli and said, Here I am, for you did call me. Then Eli perceived that the Lord was calling the boy. So Eli said to Samuel, Go, lie down. And if He calls you, you shall say, Speak, Lord, for Your servant is listening. So Samuel went and lay down in his place. And the Lord came and stood and called as at other times, Samuel! Samuel! Then Samuel answered, Speak, Lord, for Your servant is listening.

I need to emphasize again: I believe that hearing God has been the source of the success of our ministry. I strongly believe that the Lord has helped us through the years because we've endeavored to listen. At times I have been in a room full of people, but I would still be listening for His voice. Sometimes I would have to ask a person to repeat what they just said, because I was listening to the voice of the Lord. You need to develop this listening ear. Even though your ears are on the side of your head, your listening center is in your spirit.

God speaks to me through the inward witness, accompanied by a peace in my heart. He speaks to me through His Word, and through the still, small voice. He has also spoken in an audible voice, and through dreams and visions. When I am looking for His purpose and plan for my life I often find myself meditating on a passage of scripture that stays with me for days. Every time I pick up the Word to read, that same passage comes to mind, and I just keep it in my spirit and meditate on it. By "meditating," I mean I mutter it quietly to myself, over and over, even throughout the day—until it becomes so real to me. Repeating the Word of the Lord to yourself and praying about certain things will involve both praying and listening. I pray in the Holy Ghost and then listen for His voice.

Sometimes we are asked to make a decision that we are not ready to make. Often, we have not had sufficient time to think the situation through or pray about it enough to hear God's mind on it. There are times when we are too tired to think a matter through. That is why rest is so important. When our bodies are tired, our minds do not work at their best. When I really do not know what to do or haven't heard from God, I find my best answer to be, "Please, let me sleep on it." Sleep shuts our mind down and gets it out of the way. I have found that the Lord will speak to me in that moment when I'm not awake, but not still fully asleep. My mind has not yet kicked into full gear and the voice of the Lord will be so much stronger in my ears and my heart.

There have been other times He has spoken to me through dreams, giving me direction for the ministry and warning me of things that are coming. The dreams are so vivid, I never question them or argue that what He spoke might not happen. I know from so many years of experience that yes, it is going to happen. I simply tell my wife, "I had a dream, and this is what the Lord said."

I get my messages the same way. Before I go to sleep, I meditate on the Word, filling myself with His words. I go to sleep, and as I am waking up I hear the title of the sermon, and the main points come to me, almost like receiving an email. As it drops into my spirit, I get up, go sit down, and take twenty minutes to write out the points as He gave them to me. Point one is always the title, point two is a scripture, point three is another scripture, and so on, as I put down on paper what He has disclosed to my spirit. Titles, series, messages. That's how I function. I'm very reliant upon hearing God's voice for direction.

The thing I value most in my life is the ability to hear from God. If I knew I could only keep one thing in my life I would say, "Please, do not take away my ability to hear His voice. It's the most valued, prized possession I have on the earth. You can have everything else, you can take it all, but do not take the ability to hear the Father's voice." As long as I hear His voice, I know I am safe. If I can hear His voice, it matters not what comes my way or what people say. It may take several days before I receive the direction I need from Him, but His presence is always with me.

Back in 2001, I went through a time of such exhaustion and stress, that I was too tired to distinguish His words on specific things. I was so physically tired I couldn't hear Him. That is why I stress that it is so important to get the rest your body and spirit need. I didn't realize at the time how bad things were. We had poured out every bit of our lives for the ministry and were at a place where it was only the anointing that was sustaining us. The anointing on your life may keep you going, but your body—your physical strength—can only live so long like that, before it expires. During that time, I was pushing my body to its limits—sixty different cities a year—all around the world, with three hours or so of sleep each night. When you do that for fourteen years, something is going to give somewhere.

When you're not hearing God's voice clearly, you need to take some time off to rest and shut down the other voices. Don't just take time off to sit around and watch television or go the movies. Don't go somewhere to visit with people, because then you will still be hearing voices. Often, you rehearse your problems by talking about them with other people, and you're not going to get answers by talking about your problems. You have to take control and shut off all the voices. It doesn't matter what people are saying; separate yourself, shut off your phone, your email, the television, and just get away.

It was on a hunting trip in December 2001, when the Lord gave me the direction I needed. Going to the bush on a hunt always works for me. You can't have a conversation with the animals, so ten days in the bush gets really quiet. After three or four days, I realize how quiet it actually is. When you spend twelve or thirteen hours a day tracking an animal through thick thorn bushes in Africa, it is just you, your tracker or guide, and the animals. You have to be quiet so you don't scare the animals, and the hours of quiet begin to calm your spirit. *Then* you hear the Lord speak.

You may think that you are too busy to take the time to rest, but you must! Your life depends on it. You need to shut it all down, shut out all the other voices. Take time to shut out everything so you can clearly hear the voice of the Lord. Don't turn on the television, don't check the news, and don't communicate with anybody. When you eliminate every other voice, then you know it is the voice of the Lord speaking, and Him alone. You may say that you can't stop everything, but we are talking here about the anointing. When you seriously want to increase the anointing in your life, you will take the time—you won't say you're too busy.

I'm talking in hindsight. Do you know what "got to me" and nearly took me out of the ministry? Outwardly, I am an extremely bold person, especially when it comes to what God has called me to do. If He told me to do it, I would charge Hell with a dry water pistol. But inside myself, I didn't really feel that I was anything—I just felt inadequate.

I have had to overcome some major obstacles in my life—giants, such as insecurities and fear over the years. Most people deal with the same problems, but few will admit they do.

As I said before, when God first sent us to America from South Africa He said: "Find out what everybody else is doing (their methods). You do the opposite, and it will be Me." As we got the mind of God and revival broke out, we took off running. As the ministry grew, God started taking us around major ministries and although we didn't notice it at first, we soon began to be influenced by them. We didn't intend to be led by their suggestions, but during the next five or six years, the practice increasingly hindered what God was telling me to do.

I became concerned about who was speaking into my life. Who was speaking into the life of the person speaking to me? And who was speaking into the life of that person? It always amazes me that when someone speaks into your life, they suddenly feel it gives them license to direct both your life and your ministry.

Well, I'm sorry, but that is not how it works. That was not what God had told me to do. Someone told me I should meet certain people, and get them to go to lunch with me, because they could open doors for me. The Lord had said: "Don't do that. Don't put your eyes on man. Don't be directed by people." We have never done that in our ministry. We don't run after other ministers, trying to pull strings to make something happen.

Yes, we have people we allow to speak into our life, but we know their heart. We know they are people who have a deep respect for God and His Word, who have been touched by revival, who also seek to hear God for themselves and are not manipulative or self-serving. We meet many people who want to speak into our ministry, but I sift through them, to see who is genuine and who is not.

Equally as threatening, to both our ministry and personal life, were those who wanted to be a part of our ministry just because it was the latest thing happening. They wanted to latch onto the next wagon riding into whatever was happening. Everybody has an opinion, but you need God's opinion over all the others. It's not great to be criticized, but flattery can be even more dangerous to you. We have a saying: "Never believe your own publicity!" Don't allow pride to direct you. Stay humble. Stay small in your own eyes. Don't do things to please or impress people.

When people come around and start influencing you away from the purpose and plan of God for your life, you have a problem. That's when you realize how important hearing the voice of God really is, if you are going to protect your anointing. People will hang around you when you're popular, but when you become controversial, they scatter—always get away from all that distracts and stay with your primary purpose.

The final straw for some people—in 1999—the one that broke the camel's back...was the crusade at Madison Square Garden in New York City. That was a time of separation, not only for our ministry, but personally for our family, as well. People thought we were crazy to try to hold a meeting in Madison Square Garden for six weeks and tried to convince us that it would only bring reproach on the Gospel. Preachers who were sure we were going to fail began to separate themselves and their ministries from us.

I am a very relationship-oriented person, so I took it all personally. I felt unloved and rejected by everyone I knew. I had carried the message of joy all over the country and had rescued many pastors from failure when their church was about to close because of finances. Many of the churches had doubled or tripled in size because of our ministry there, and their finances grew to a level where they were able to do the work the Lord had called them to do. Pastors who were struggling to make ends meet personally were then able to live in better homes and drive nicer cars. But now, when I needed *them*, they would not even answer my phone calls.

I took it all so personally that it caused a lot of hurt in my life—so much so that I wanted to quit the ministry and walk away from it. The Lord, however, was gracious and kind, keeping me safe in the palm of

The ANOINTING

His hand. But it came close…that's all I will say…it came close.

Then when our daughter Kelly died on Christmas Day in 2002, we were overwhelmed by the phone calls and love that began to come in from all around the world. Many ministers and other people who called hadn't spoken to us in five years. They called just to say: "We love you. We are praying for you." Over the next four days, despite the loss of our precious daughter, we were greatly encouraged by experiencing the love coming from these people. Many who called were people whose friendship we felt we had lost along the way, but now was restored. It was a time of great healing for us and our family.

Regarding relationships in the Body of Christ, we have found that problems often come when we align ourselves with those the Lord never intended us to be linked with at all. Many times, all we want is His presence and His anointing on our lives, but those we are connected with have totally different motives and agendas for their ministry. If we are not careful, we will begin to go in a different direction than what the Lord intended for us. Problems could often be avoided if we would stop long enough to pray and hear His voice before aligning our lives and our ministries with these people. If the Lord does not put the relationship together, do not try to force it. As in everything else in your life, there should be a peace and a flow.

At that time, I made a decision to stay away from certain people—some whom I love greatly—because they had a detrimental effect on me. I knew they loved me and believed in our ministry. But they questioned everything I did, and I would think about it for days, instead of focusing on what God had told me to do. I have learned over the years that "voices" will sidetrack you. They will bring you out of your anointing and what God has for you, but the voice of the Lord will never fail you. Look again at the words of Jesus in John 10:27: *"My sheep hear my voice, and I know them, and they follow me."*

In the parable of the good shepherd and his sheep, in the first part of the chapter, Jesus explains why we are to listen only to His voice:

Verily, verily, I say unto you, He that entereth not by the door into the sheepfold, but climbeth up some other way, the same is a thief and a robber. But he that entereth in by the door is the shepherd of the sheep. To him the porter openeth; and the sheep hear his voice: and he calleth his own sheep by name, and leadeth them out. And when he putteth forth his own sheep, he goeth before them, and the sheep follow him: for they know his voice. And a stranger will they not follow, but will flee from him: for they know not the voice of strangers.

JOHN 10:1-5

Learn to have a listening ear. Make hearing His voice the most important thing in your day. You will notice a difference in the anointing on your life.

5

INCREASING THE ANOINTING

Through Building Your Character

The American culture today wants to lift up a man, put him on a pedestal, and then see how fast he can be knocked off the pedestal. They get joy and pleasure from watching people fall, because it makes them seem higher in their own eyes.

Don't ever be guilty of putting a man of God on a pedestal. Respect God's ministers, but worship only Jesus. We need all the godly men God has anointed for His service, and God is not honored and glorified when one falls.

I tell the people at our church, The River at Tampa Bay: "You should only follow me as I follow the Lord, but you *must keep your eyes on Jesus.*" You might be fond of me and like the anointing on my life, but look only to Him. Look to Jesus. Look *only* to Jesus. He is your security. Focus your eyes on Jesus and continue in what He has given you to do, and don't depend on man for your directions.

Be very careful about people who try to draw others to themselves, wanting people to follow them as though they are some great prophet, seer, leader or whatever they claim to be. Keep your eyes on Jesus, because if something happens to that person and your faith is in them, your faith will be rocked. Your faith will be set back, and you may never do what God wants you to do.

People come up to me all the time and say: "I can't believe what 'so and so' did. We were following him, but he fell. He failed us." You know, it's wonderful to receive from the anointing, on different ministries, when the Lord's using people, but you should always keep your eyes on Jesus. Remind yourself: "I must not set my eyes on a man or a woman. I must keep my eyes on Him alone; I must follow the Master; I must hear His voice."

How will you know if a person or ministry is following Jesus? Do their words speak to your heart? Are they glorifying Jesus? If my words are speaking to you about the Spirit of God and His anointing, then you should hear the voice of the Lord coming to you through my words.

Don't follow miracles: follow Jesus. Don't follow manifestations: follow Jesus. He is the One who is the manifest presence of God. Many people in the Body of Christ run from a flag-waving service to gold-dust manifestations to "God only knows what." None of it is scriptural. None of it is edifying. None of it draws people to Jesus. Judge it by the fruit. How do I know that I'm following the ministry of Jesus? Because the number one emphasis in my life after I got saved was souls—the harvest—bringing people to Jesus. If your ministry doesn't produce the fruit of souls saved, then you are not preaching or demonstrating the Gospel.

There are many ministries in danger of becoming merely success motivators, but they call what they are preaching "the Gospel." Their message has elements of the Gospel, but they are not preaching the whole gospel. He came so that a lost and dying world could be saved. We are to get people saved, healed, and delivered; we are to teach them the Word and make disciples of them. Anything else is just peripheral, if you genuinely want to follow the ministry of Jesus, because that's what He came to do.

How do you follow His ministry? Go where the anointing is poured out. **The anointing is not taught...it is caught.** If you are seeking an anointing, sit under anointed teaching/preaching. Sit under the ministry of people who exalt the Name of Jesus, who are on fire for Jesus, who flow in the Holy Ghost, and who have sound doctrine and godly character. We need to be imitators of God, as dear children. We need to be submitted to His Word. When we do what the Word tells us to do, He will anoint us.

Immerse yourself in the Gospels; don't just treat them as books for newborn believers. Bathe yourself in Matthew, Mark, Luke and John: go to crusade meetings, watch how He functioned and listen to what He said. Do some studies on the sayings of Jesus. Watch how He prayed—how He talked. Pay close attention to how He dealt with people. Meditate on Jesus's sayings—even the ones that are not as popular—the ones you don't always hear people preaching on—and start meditating on them.

Be faithful to the call of God, whether it looks like you are a success or not. In Jesus's parable of the talents in Matthew 25:21, we read the following words of the master to his faithful servant: *"His lord said unto him, 'Well done, thou good and faithful servant: thou hast been faithful over a few things, I will make thee ruler over many things: enter thou into the joy of thy lord.'"* It should be our goal to stand before our Lord and hear Him say those words: *"Well done, thou good and faithful servant."*

Don't judge yourself in the light of another servant of God. When you observe their ministry, you may think that they are so much more blessed than you are, which makes you feel that you don't have what it takes. Don't compare yourself—just find out what God requires of you and do it faithfully. In the early days of my ministry, back in 1981 and 1982, there were probably those who thought that we were failures and losers. Some people would even intimate that. I would come back from a crusade, excited about the great meeting we had, until someone asked how many people came. I told them: "We started with twelve, and by the fourth night the crowd had grown to forty, but God moved in an awesome way and two people got saved. A lady with one deaf ear was healed." I was so excited about the results, but people would look at me with astonishment and say: "Boy, if I were you, I would just give up." But I didn't quit. I didn't give up. I just kept on doing what He told me to do.

DON'T DESPISE THE DAYS OF SMALL BEGINNINGS

I recently went into my basement and pulled out some of the archives from those early years. As I looked at all of the sheets with our monthly income, I just shook my head in awe at how God has worked in our lives, and the journey He has brought us on. In the eyes of man, the years from 1980 through 1988 may not have looked like much was happening, but we were still faithfully doing what He had called us to do. Souls were saved, the sick were healed, people's lives were changed. The Lord was preparing us and equipping us for what He was going to do and where He was going to take us.

In 1996, we started The River at Tampa Bay and, in 1997, added the Bible School. People thought we were stepping outside our calling, but it just goes to show that people judge after the flesh and have no idea of the calling on a life, or what God is capable of doing through a person. People told us that we were not called or anointed to do it and that we would fail, but we weren't working our own plan. We were working God's plan! Man's plans will fail, but God's plans—followed and obeyed—will always succeed.

Then came the dream for the New York Crusade...with all the criticism that brought. In the sight of our critics, renting Madison Square Garden for six weeks was a terrible mistake. They tried to talk us out of it—or they told us to only do two weeks. They were sure we'd fall on our faces—and we would have if it had been our own plan—but we were following the plan of God. It cost us $6.7 million to do it and the Lord paid every bill. Right on the heels of that, we went to Shreveport for a crusade, and we made the choice to mortgage our home to put $300,000 into the crusade.

A pastor once told me we had failed horribly in the Shreveport crusade, because we borrowed money to do it. I told him that he must have failed when he built his new building, because he had borrowed money to build it. I said: "How can you borrow the money for your new building and call it a success, but when I borrowed money to win souls then suddenly it's a failure?"

No, it wasn't a failure—it was a test to see if we would be faithful. I went to the Lord and asked Him: "Am I a failure? Have I failed in doing this? Because, Lord, if I'm failing after winning 59,000 souls, then may I fail every day of my life."

Those same people who were calling me a failure would have determined that the actual cost of the "event" at Calvary proved it was a failure, because only the thief on the cross…and possibly the centurion… got saved. If you were going to stage an event that would shake time and eternity, then you should surely have had the whole of Jerusalem saved at the time. But, the Cross was not a failure: it was the devil's defeat and our victory!

Because people are so into numbers and graphs and charts, most people don't know how to judge what is a success or what is a failure. Don't judge yourself by other people. What has God called you to do? Do only what He's called you to do. You can't do anything more than He has called you to do. Don't take your guidance from other people to determine if you're a failure or success. Is the anointing with you? Are you bearing good fruit? Then you are not a failure. Success is doing what God has called you to do.

People tell me, "Well, Brother Rodney, we are having some problems financially." My answer is usually: "Oh, you mean you are having to believe God? Wonderful." Does that mean you are a failure because you're having to believe God for finances? It is surprising how many Christians don't want to be in a position to have to trust God. It's too much of a strain on their flesh. Having to stay on your knees will keep you humble. Some people want to use their faith to get enough money so they can rely on that money and not have to trust God anymore. I have news for you: if you are going to walk with God, you are going to have to trust Him. Walking with God is a faith walk. You start out small and the things you believe God for just get bigger and bigger as your faith grows. You can never get comfortable if you want to see the supernatural manifest through your life and ministry.

People promise the Lord: "Lord Jesus, if you will just get me out of this mess I'm in, I won't step out so far next time." When that is your attitude, you are always going to operate from your comfort zone and you'll never do anything for God, because you will never stretch yourself beyond yourself and what you can do. Trust God. Obey Him. Be faithful—be faithful!

When you are doing what God has called you to do, trusting that He is leading your steps, you will not have to compare yourself with anyone else. David looked like the forgotten son on the back hills of nowhere. His own family didn't believe in him, but he was the one chosen when all of the sons stood in front of the prophet. Read the story in 1 Samuel 16:6-13:

> And it came to pass, when they were come, that he looked on Eliab, and said, Surely the Lord's anointed is before him. But the Lord said unto Samuel, Look not on his countenance, or on the height of his stature; because I have refused him: for the Lord seeth not as man seeth; for man looketh on the outward appearance, but the Lord looketh on the heart. Then Jesse called Abinadab, and made him pass before Samuel. And he said, Neither hath the Lord chosen this. Then Jesse made Shammah to pass by. And he said, Neither hath the Lord chosen this. Again, Jesse made seven of his sons to pass before Samuel. And Samuel said unto Jesse, The Lord hath not chosen these.

And Samuel said unto Jesse, Are here all thy children? And he said, There remaineth yet the youngest, and, behold, he keepeth the sheep. And Samuel said unto Jesse, Send and fetch him: for we will not sit down till he come hither. And he sent, and brought him in. Now he was ruddy, and withal of a beautiful countenance, and goodly to look to. And the Lord said, Arise, anoint him: for this is he. Then Samuel took the horn of oil, and anointed him in the midst of his brethren: and the Spirit of the Lord came upon David from that day forward. So Samuel rose up, and went to Ramah.

Be faithful. God knows where to find you. You're not a lost number out there somewhere, and you're not missing in action. He knows where you are. He knows your name and He knows your telephone number.

There are no shortcuts. Be faithful and He will promote you. Success is doing what God has called you to do, not what other people think you should do. And don't forget where you came from, or you might lose your way.

Several years ago, I went back to South Africa, and I felt led to play golf on a particular course. Years ago, Adonica and I had actually lived in a townhouse right on one of the sides of this course. You might wonder why the Lord would lead a person to play golf at a certain place, but He had a plan to show me something. So, I went. As I was coming up on the thirteenth fairway, I saw the apartment where we had lived. After I hit the tee shot, and, as I was walking along, suddenly the Lord took me back to the year 1986 when I was walking that same fairway. I was under major persecution even then, and it just looked like that was to be my lot in life. I really didn't have to do much to be criticized; I was persecuted just for showing up. If I stuck my head in the door, I was persecuted for sticking my head in the door. That's just the way it was. I felt like I had a bullseye painted on me.

I remembered walking that same fairway, crying out to the Lord: "I know that what You've given me is not just for me, but it is for the nations. Lord, I promise You: if You will get me out of this place I am in right now, I promise You I'll go to the nations." Now here I was, walking on that same fairway, and the Lord reminded me of that prayer. I looked over and I saw the townhouse, and then, suddenly, in my mind I saw all that the Lord had done since then—taking us to America—taking us around the world to many, many nations. I thought of the great move of God we had seen over the years and I was so thankful. I was almost in a state of shock. The Lord said, "I heard your prayer as you cried out to Me. Be faithful—be faithful, because as you do, this anointing will increase in your life."

Some ministers go on a forty-day fast to increase their anointing, but they haven't increased their godly character to go along with the anointing. You must have the character to match the anointing, otherwise you won't be able to do what God has called you to do. So, what does it matter if you can heal the sick and raise the dead, but are not faithful to your wife? What does that tell you? It says that you pressed in to God, and received a gift from Him, but you have not allowed Him to do a work in you, personally—you are not personally submitted to Him. You preach the Word, but you don't apply it to your own life. And, like Samson, you could end up losing your ministry, your life, and everything you have.

BUILDING YOUR CHARACTER

Far too many people only want the anointing, but they don't want to develop the character to go along with it. But, if you are going to get things done for God, you have to have the character as well as the anointing. How does that character get developed? By obeying God's Word—being a doer of the Word—even through the hardships and challenges that life throws at you. Character is birthed in the Fire.

You take a piece of raw metal and put it into the furnace, then you put it on the anvil, take a hammer and start beating it, and that piece of metal is going to shout "ouch." But the heat and the pressure of the hammer are necessary if something useful is to come from the metal.

Most Christians want to be used of God, but they are not willing to allow themselves to be shaped into something beautiful and useful for the Kingdom of God. If you are not submitted to His will and refuse to be shaped into something new, you will be like that purposeless blob of metal. Nothing will come of your desire to be used of God. Many people try to take the easiest route to get to their comfort zone. If anything gets uncomfortable for their flesh, they think it must be the devil…and are sure that it is not God. These are the people you see running from church to church, looking for a place where the message fits them better. Where they don't have to pray or win souls, and nothing is said about living a holy life. Above all, no one is telling them to give, give, give.

Some people try to do the will of God by the arm of the flesh. Years ago, I spent some time with a group of pastors and men who were very involved in the right-to-life and anti-abortion movement. Remember, that was quite strong back in the 1990s. Groups were blocking abortion clinics, getting arrested, and even pastors were going to jail. I was against the movement because it was promoting civil disobedience and urged them to go to Washington and lobby to change the powers-that-be in the government. I felt the efforts of believers were misplaced.

Several of the pastors I was talking to had been arrested many times, fined, and had marks against their name by the government as people who needed to be watched. I asked them why they stopped protesting. Their answer was simple. Sitting in a cell, locked away from their families, they began to ask themselves: "Is this really what I'm supposed to be doing? What have I really accomplished?" Several of them had close friends, Pentecostal pastors, who were plotting to burn down abortion clinics, and had even made statements that they wished there had been people in the ones they had burned.

The pastor telling me this story said that he realized he had given himself over to the wrong spirit. He had been motivated for a cause that he thought was righteous but knew in his heart that he had gone about it the wrong way. The Lord put it on their hearts to begin to work at a higher level in legislation and in areas of the government, with a better result. There are people still ministering outside abortion clinics, around the nation, and through love, kindness, and prayer are saving many babies and reaching the workers with the truth. Even so, much good has been accomplished through changing legislation. Don't let the devil draw you out of your call. Be careful about the cause you pick up, because as righteous as it might seem, you may be moving under a spirit other than the Holy Spirit. Success is not built on doing things that are not led by the Spirit of God. Some people's "success" is really built on the works of the flesh.

A PERSONAL RELATIONSHIP WITH GOD

Relationship with God has been the platform for our ministry for all these years. Obviously, you have to work with what's real to you, but if you want to be a success, you must be led by your relationship with the Lord. If you don't have a relationship with Him, develop one! And don't pattern it after someone else's. You must have your own, and it has to grow out of your faith in Him. Don't feel that your faith is too small. Remember the words of the Apostle Paul in 1 Corinthians 1:27: *"But God hath chosen the foolish things of the world to confound the wise; and God hath chosen the weak things of the world to confound the things which are mighty."*

Again, we read in Mark 12:10: *"The stone which the builders rejected is become the head of the corner."* You may feel weak and you may be looked upon as a failure, but He loves you so much. There is nothing you can do for Him that will impress Him. Even your salvation was provided by His grace and His love. But you can still get His attention. Not because you have a big ministry or are the best singer in the choir. You may be the biggest giver in your church, but it is your heart that He wants first. He wants a relationship with you. Listen for His voice.

The anointing of the Lord is so wonderful and so necessary in a ministry. Sometimes, people wonder why, in a service, I just stand quietly and wait, not doing anything. The answer is simple. I don't want to mess anything up by doing something before I hear from God. When I hear from Him, I do as I'm instructed. Sometimes the Lord is moving on the congregation, without anyone doing anything, or needing to do anything—and when the Lord is moving and touching people—there isn't anything we need to say, anyway. Preachers are often the biggest hindrance to the move of God. They do things in their own strength. They are not sensitive to—or submitted to—the voice of the Spirit. They ignore the Holy Spirit and speak right over Him, even as He is trying to move. They take the service from the hands of the Holy Spirit into the opposite direction and wonder why they never see a move of God.

YOUR FULFILLMENT IN LIFE MUST COME FROM GOD

Your fulfillment must come from God and not from other people. It's not found in having a big ministry, because you might find that when you do get what you want, it's not really what you wanted after all. If you can't learn to be content where you are now, you won't be content where you're going. If you can't enjoy your life where you are now, you will definitely not enjoy it where you are going. Even if you obtained the whole world, you would still be of all men most miserable, until you realized your joy and fulfillment is found only in Him. Our joy should be in obeying Him—in seeing people's lives touched and changed—not in the outward indications of success.

You may be a pastor and are thinking: "Oh, if only my church could run a hundred people." Then, when you reach your goal, you say: "If only I could have five hundred, I'll be happy." If you had five hundred, you would still be miserable. "If only I can have one thousand, I'd be totally happy." No, you'd be miserable. Many pastors have a burning desire for a new building. I meet pastors all the time who tell me, "Well, if only my ministry could grow, I could get on radio or television." Next, you want to write a book. Publish several books and what do you have? A miserable book writer—that's all. Perhaps you want to go to the mission field. Listen to me: those poor people don't need you on the mission field, miserable in your discontent. They have enough misery without having you bring another burden to them. The last thing they need is another miserable American missionary, peddling religion and tradition.

What you really need is to be free. He must be your Number One—

your all in all. Your joy should be found in your relationship with Him.

I'm fifty-seven years old now, and one of my biggest challenges happened when I was thirty-five. I realized I had met all the goals that I had set for my life. If you think failure is a problem, try success. Success can be the biggest and most difficult thing to deal with, because you've reached your goals and you don't have anything else to shoot for. I thought that maybe my ministry was finished because we had achieved all we had set out to do. So, what now? What do you do when it is all done? When you're done, God is just getting started.

I can't speak for everyone, but I realized my ministry is not just about reaching goals. Many people, after they have worked hard and achieved some success, want to sit back and relax. Like David, that's when many of them stop fighting the battle, and their eyes go off of God and onto their own personal desires. They feel like they've earned the rest and relaxation. God isn't against rest, but when we take our eyes off of God, the devil is waiting to distract us and take us off course.

God has greater plans than we have. You're not done till you're done. Just keep obeying Him. Keep preaching and demonstrating the Gospel.

As you read this, you may be looking for greener pastures. You think surely the grass is greener on the other side. If you can just get there, you will be like a happy cow eating green grass. Believe me, you will only be a miserable cow, giving sour milk. If you are not happy now, you won't be happy then. You will find your problems have just multiplied. Because you take yourself with you wherever you go. People don't do a good job of the position and task they've been assigned, because they are always looking out for another, better opportunity. As a result, they are never satisfied or fulfilled, no matter where they go. Do—and give—your best, wherever you are. When it's time for you to move on, God knows where to find you, and He will open the doors. At all times, be content. *"But godliness with contentment is great gain"* (1 Timothy 6:6).

People are like the donkey with a carrot on a stick hung out over him where he can't quite get to it, but he keeps moving forward chasing the carrot. One of the devil's tactics with us is to tempt us with something just out of our reach. We may spend years chasing a "carrot" around the greener pastures on the other side of the fence, only to find we have wasted the gifts God gave us to win souls and expand His Kingdom. Your "carrot" is just a distraction. Look up, beyond your own desires, and see what's really important. What has significance in eternity? Make that your focus.

Have you ever heard someone say, "I need a husband to make me happy"? I've met many women, who have husbands, but they're miserable. I have also heard men say the same thing. "I need a wife to make me happy." I know many men who have a wife and they're unhappy. So, that can't be the solution for you. They say, "If I had the finances I need, then I'd really be happy." I've met people who are worth millions, even people with several billion dollars, and they're *still* miserable. They have homes on every continent, but not enough time to enjoy them. I sat and talked to them, and it was obvious they are not happy. So, money can't be the solution.

I hear people all the time talk arrogantly about themselves and their ministry. I tremble for them, because they are so sure of themselves. I know they are setting themselves up for a fall. As long as your assurance comes from the Lord you are fine, but be careful about opening your big mouth and spouting about what *you* think. You may have all the formulas and think you know what's going on, but it doesn't work that way. You are either lifting yourself up or you're lifting Jesus up. Paul said: *"For we are the circumcision, which worship God in the spirit, and rejoice in Christ Jesus, and have no confidence in the flesh"* (Philippians 3:3). If your ministry is all about you, and not about Jesus, then it's something, but it's not a ministry.

I have one passion right now: I want to see one hundred million souls saved, and one billion dollars put into world missions—to fulfill the vow I made when I placed my daughter Kelly on the altar the night she went home to be with the Lord. I have no other desire—no other dream. My job is to "catch fish." Whatever it takes, I am willing to do. I have no other dream, and if I can't do that, then I must go on to be with the Lord.

We must learn to discern if the dream we are longing for is really from Heaven, because there will still be challenges along the way. We will still need to trust in the Word of the Lord and we still need to exercise our faith to see it come to pass.

Jesus didn't say that we would never have problems—we are not in Heaven yet—but He always provides the answer to, or the way out of, any situation. Psalm 34:19 says: *"Many are the afflictions of the righteous: but the LORD delivereth him out of them all."* The whole thing comes down to trust.

When you are going through the heat of the storm, there are always people who are happy to have a word for you. If the word is just man's opinion, my word to them is, "I don't want to hear it." The night before our daughter died, what helped me most was the Word of the Lord. He asked me: "Do you trust Me with your life?" Of course, I said, "Yes." He asked two more times, "Do you trust Me with your life?" and each time my answer was, "Yes, Lord, I trust You with my life." Jesus carried us through that challenging time and it became a testimony of His goodness and grace. He never fails us.

LEARN TO DO IT ALL IN HIS ABILITY

I realize now that when the Lord was blessing the ministry and things were exploding internationally, I was so busy having meetings and traveling constantly that I really didn't enjoy what I was doing. I didn't take the time to stop and enjoy anything. I ran so long and so hard, without letting up. I was under so much pressure, mentally and physically, I told the Lord: "I am so sorry, but I can't do this anymore." I thought He would berate me, but instead He told me to stop, come off the road, rest, and call in the harvest. I did as He said. It took me months to even start feeling normal again, but that rest saved me physically and mentally. Even though I wasn't traveling, He provided for us financially everything we needed. We didn't miss a beat.

The Lord rescued me from that and I'll never go back to it again, but now I see the tell-tale signs when I see other pastors doing the same thing. We have to realize we are humans on the earth, and yes, God has given us supernatural powers through the Holy Spirit, but we don't have glorified bodies yet. We need to do it in His strength, not our own. We need to work, and we need to rest.

Learn to do it all in His ability. We have to walk by faith. We have to trust God. Pray like it all depends on Him and then go and work like it all depends on you.

Each of us has to talk to the Lord for ourselves. No one else can do it for us. The Lord says to us in Isaiah 1:18: *"Come now, and let us reason together…"* You don't have to leave a voice message for Heaven. He is listening, so pray as if your life depends on it.

This is not about your comfort. If you're looking to be comfortable, you're looking for the wrong thing. It's not about your comfort. How would you pray if you were hanging over a cliff? Get with it! Earnestly, tell the Lord right now you only want what He wants for you. Jesus prayed that way in the Garden: "Not my will, but Thine." Learn to pray: "Have thine own way, Lord."

But know that when you pray a prayer like that, you are giving God permission to change and move things around according to *His* will, not yours. You can't back out and then complain about the way things are going. You just told Him to have His will in your life. When the Spirit of God starts shaking your life, He's going to shake loose everything of the world and of the devil in your life. Let Him do it. The flesh and the carnal mind rebel against and resist the Spirit of God. They have a hard time yielding. Don't let them win. Don't let them drag you backwards. The work God begins in you, needs to be taken through to its completion.

You may be in a hard place but, if you don't trust Him and follow His leading, nothing will come of your life. You will abort all your own hard work. When you have a chicken sitting on an egg to hatch it, don't crack open the egg prematurely or you won't have a baby chick. The chick will be born when it's ready and not before. **Success doesn't come overnight; it is forged in the fires of life, through the hard**

things we face and come through. Those who rise overnight usually fall before daylight. God has His plan for you, so don't jump back into your own plan. If the grace of God didn't lead you where you are, the grace of God cannot keep you there.

6

INCREASING THE ANOINTING

Through Yielding to Him

I am often amused when I hear preachers talk about *their* anointing. Remember, when we were saved and filled with the Holy Spirit, He came to dwell in us, so we have had the anointing in us since that time. But, it is not *our* anointing, it is *His* anointing. Again, the anointing is the manifest presence of God. We only yield to Him.

As we travel around the world and see different ministries, we notice that certain ministries seem limited. It's not that the Lord limited them… they have limited themselves. They have not learned how to flow in the anointing. They are not yielding to Him.

YIELDING TO THE LORD

Many people want to yield in their place, or area, of comfort. It is comfortable for them to yield in one particular gift of the Spirit, so that's all they use. For example, let's use the revelation gift "Word of Knowledge." A minister God uses in the area of the Word of Knowledge gets comfortable yielding in that area, so that's what he does, but he never steps into another area of anointing. Meanwhile, the Lord may have wanted to use other gifts in him, so that he could grow in those gifts, but he wouldn't step over into them because it would demand another level of faith in that area.

So, people find that they are limited in the anointing—they have a narrow view of what the Lord wants to do through them. There's only so much they can do, they think. Maybe it's because I was born in Africa, but when I went out to minister I was it—just me. I had to yield to His anointing, because if I couldn't do it there was no one else I could call up to the platform to do it for me. There were times I would have liked to have someone else and their higher level of anointing, but I was it. I had to depend on the Lord and yield to Him. When you're in the bush in Africa, you're "the one." You need to be "the one" wherever you are.

Pretty much every challenge is going to be thrown at you at one time or another, so you will have to trust the Lord and step into an anointing that may not be in your comfort zone in order to demonstrate the power of the Gospel to meet the needs of people.

Obviously, we understand about the grace of God, and that where He places us has to do with His calling and His grace. I am not disputing that for one little moment. However, unless you are placed in a position for the anointing to be used or where a demand will be placed upon that anointing, you will not see much happening. For example, if you want to see miracles, then start lining people up and praying for them.

Somebody once said to me: "I have never seen deaf ears open." My answer was: "How many deaf ears have you prayed for?"

"None?" Well, that figures. You have to start praying for them to put yourself in the position to see the healing take place. That means you have to stand up and say: "I'm going to pray for the deaf so, if you are deaf, come up here." Until you put yourself out there, you'll never see the anointing of God manifest. Someone else said, "Well, I have never seen devils come out of people." If you are not prepared to pray for them, then you probably won't see it happen.

It's all about pushing in and pressing in—touching the hem of His garment. You touch Him, and He touches you. He'll touch you in a lot of areas if you will put yourself in a place to be used. The thing that has always been a comfort to me is knowing that the Lord has given us a wide variety of gifts. He gave us many arrows in our quiver, so that we were not limited to what we could do with the Gospel. You may think your ministry is just mainly teaching. Yes, it may be. But you can see God confirming His Word with signs following if you just step out in faith.

YOU DON'T HAVE TO BE LIMITED TO JUST ONE GIFT

Paul told Timothy, the pastor, to do the work of an evangelist as well. Develop and grow in the anointing. You can develop. You can grow. You can mature. And you can move into other areas of the anointing. Don't say, "Well, that's not my anointing." You might not be anointed to sing, and when you open your mouth, we may agree with you. But don't ever say that's not your anointing—none of it's *your* anointing. It's all His anointing and you are just the vessel. You are a container that He pours into and pours the anointing out of for His glory. Rather say, "This is the way I yield to the anointing in this area," because when the anointing comes into the room, it comes in for a purpose. It comes in and whoever yields, will hook up with it.

If you yield in the area of prophecy, you'll hook up prophetically. The same anointing that brings prophecy brings healing; the same anointing that brings the joy brings deliverance. People come along and say, "Oh, I have a deliverance anointing." No, it's all *His* anointing. Some say, "Well, you have an anointing for joy and I have an anointing for healing." Rubbish! It's all the anointing to do the ministry of Jesus.

I knew when I started out in the ministry, I had to be developed and I had to grow by Jesus's guidance. The only way I could do that was to have daily meetings, putting myself in a place to minister every single day, so that I could become a minister who would yield to the Spirit of God. And you know, when the ministry grew and the crowds grew, we weren't doing anything different than we did when we had ten people in the meeting. We were doing exactly the same thing—just more people showed up. I've learned over the years it doesn't matter how many people are there—we are going to have a move of God.

Not everyone who comes to our meetings will come to every service. Some people leave early, and some just don't come back. Jesus cleared the room before He raised the dead. (*See* Luke 8:51.) Sometimes the best miracles will happen when some people have gone home. Sometimes you may need to run certain people off. Don't be afraid of that. People think you are supposed to have this nice anointing that keeps everybody happy. They're reading the wrong Bible. I read in Matthew, Mark, Luke and John, and the Book of Acts that when God starts to move, some people are going to be stirred up—and not in a good way.

Look at the meetings Jesus had. If you are preaching His Word, you never know what He will do. There could be a whole herd of swine running down the hill into the sea. There may be a roof ripped up and somebody coming down through the roof. You never know what's coming. But there will never be a dull moment; that's for certain. If you are hanging around the anointing of God, it will always be interesting. There won't be "yawns and snores, and oh, how boring." No, no! It will be a "sit on the edge of your seat" meeting. "What's going to happen next? I don't want to miss this, because Jesus is in the house. Something's going to happen."

DIFFERENT ANOINTINGS

You must learn about the different anointings so you can recognize them. You need to train yourself to "read" a service, so that you are able to pick up the flow of the Holy Spirit. If people learned to pick up the flow of the service, they wouldn't do some of the dumb things they do—always at the wrong time. When you are in the flow, you will know when the altar call should be. Or you'll be sitting there and begin to feel that somebody's going to be healed right now. Yes, you can feel it.

When the anointing is flowing, whoever is in charge of the meeting must follow the flow. That is not the time for everyone to do their own thing. Anything without a head is a monster, and if it has two or more heads, it is a freak. Some people think a meeting is a free-for-all, so everyone should do his own thing. No, not around the altar. There is a price to pay to come around the altar. We will cover this more later.

If you allow it, there are times when someone may want to get up and take charge of the meeting. They want to lay hands on people. But we don't even know them or where those hands have been. Five minutes before, they may have doing something they shouldn't have been doing, and now they want to lay hands on people's heads. Absolutely not! These are holy things that we are seeing when the anointing is flowing. It's not a game.

There is a saying: "Some people are called and some are sent; others just bought a microphone and went!" It's not your physical equipment that makes you a minister—it's your *supernatural* equipment. The anointing is the equipment to get the job done. It's a supernatural ability, and when God anoints you He can drop you anywhere on the planet and your anointing will produce fruit. You can be dropped in the desert, and when they come to find you a year or two later, you will have an oasis growing with palm trees and plenty of water, figuratively speaking.

Now, there are many different anointings or graces of the Lord, and not all of them have something to do with public ministry. The problem in the church is that people think the anointing is only for public ministry. That's not the case. You do not have to be a preacher to be anointed by the Lord for ministry. There are many in public ministry, without an anointing to preach, and just as many who are gifted by God and should be in the ministry. I have seen some people in ministry who should be selling cars—and others selling cars who belong in the ministry.

But let's just focus now on public ministry. There is an anointing to preach and there is an anointing to teach, but not all preaching and teaching is anointed. Of course, the anointing is on the Word of God, but the minister of the Word is the conduit that the anointing flows through. If the Word of God is dead in your heart, it will be dead on your lips. If it's alive in your heart, it will be alive on your lips.

There is an anointing to sing. But many people who sing don't have that anointing. Don't confuse professionalism with the anointing. There is a difference—a big difference. And, bless their hearts, many people don't know the difference. Professionalism might be pleasant to listen to, but it does not have power to touch and bless and heal like the anointing does. The singers need to live pure lives and be surrendered to the anointing as much as the preacher. The problem with many singers is that they rely on their gift, rather than on the presence of the Lord. They will never know the privilege of being used by Him.

You know you have an anointing to preach when God puts a fire in your belly and a fire on your lips to proclaim the Word of the Lord. When you release that anointing through the words of your mouth, it is like your words are little Holy Ghost "bombs." They go out into the air and explode. Then revelation flows and captives are set free. People are delivered right where they are, in a meeting or through the television and radio waves, because the anointing is on you to preach.

Remember some of the messages you have heard in the past. They had no power. They were flat—no substance, because there was no anointing on them. The Apostle Paul said in 2 Corinthians 5:11: *"Knowing therefore the terror of the Lord, we persuade men; but we are made manifest unto God; and I trust also are made manifest in your consciences."*

AN ANOINTING TO PREACH

Preaching is persuasion. It must move people. Preaching must take them on a journey, not leave them nonchalant and indecisive. It must convict them of sin and bring them to the point of a decision.

"Preach the word; be instant in season, out of season; reprove, rebuke,

exhort with all long-suffering and doctrine" (2 Timothy 4:2). Remember these key words:

- Be instant in season and out of season
- Reprove
- Rebuke
- Exhort

Notice Paul's final words. We are to do it with "all long-suffering and doctrine." The word "long-suffering" means patience, endurance, constancy, steadfastness, and perseverance. We are to patiently, consistently, and steadfastly endure and persevere in our preaching of the Word. Preach to see a change, not to keep things as they are.

Too many people just want to exhort—they don't want to rebuke or reprove (because it's not as popular). But, two-thirds of preaching is reproving and rebuking. You can tell by the look on some people's face when they are not receiving the word. They may say: "Now he has quit preaching and gone to meddling."

That's what preaching is! Preaching finds the problem and deals with it. Jesus knew what was in people's hearts and He confronted wrong thoughts and attitudes. When you come to my meetings, you will never leave the same way you came. You will not be able to be complacent—you will either get mad, sad, or glad—but at least you will get something. My messages are meant to do just that.

When you are in one of my meetings you will have to make a decision. A good preacher "closes the sale." Not all preachers are alike; they all have different flows and different ways to preach. Compare that to a car salesman, for example. He doesn't meet you on the showroom floor, show you a few cars and go off somewhere to let you decide if you want to fill out the necessary forms needed to take the car home. No, he *persuades* you until you are ready to sign on the dotted line.

AN ANOINTING TO TEACH

Now let's take a look at the teacher. He takes the Word of God and breaks it down into pieces so you can handle it and have a clearer understanding of the Word. However, sometimes a teacher will finish teaching, having left you more confused than you were when he began. You wonder: "What in the world was that person talking about?" The longer some people teach the more confused you get, because they are just speaking words from the head, without the anointing from God.

Over the years, I have seen people attend conferences, listen to the speaker and take notes on his message, while others are drawing cartoons across the page. Many are doodling on the page because they don't understand what he is saying. Often you get the idea that even the speaker isn't sure what he is trying to teach—even he seems confused. But when he sees all the people writing on their notebooks, he thinks they must be enjoying what he is saying, because they are taking notes. That spurs him on, so he goes on speaking while his audience wishes he would just shut up.

The bottom line is you have to *keep it simple*. Don't complicate it. Don't try to impress. Don't try to make your message so deep they can't understand it. A shepherd leads his flock of sheep to food that is easy for them to eat and digest. But spiritually speaking, when a shepherd tries to get too deep, the sheep can't eat or digest the food and are still running around hungry. Don't ever preach or teach deep, difficult lessons just to impress other preachers while your sheep are dying of hunger.

We would have conferences with hundreds of ministers in attendance. I followed the anointing and preached the simple, basic things that would touch those who had come to hear the plain truth of the Gospel. I loved to watch the look on some of the other preachers' faces as they sat there, wondering why on earth I was preaching such simple things. And then the anointing would hit the place, and the altar would be full of people wanting Jesus. One night, a preacher actually got up out of his seat and went to the platform to look at my notes to see what I was preaching. He couldn't understand why the anointing fell with such simple words.

The Gospel is simple and it's powerful. Keep the message simple. If you're a preacher, keep it clear and simple; the great preachers were and are simple preachers. The same is true with great teachers; they are simple teachers. They simply teach the truth, right out of the Bible. Whether you preach or you teach, when you come to the end of your message, you have to give God an opportunity to perform what you just said He would do. Otherwise, your message is a waste of time. So, preach something that God can confirm. God only confirms His Word—not your theory, your ideas, or your stories—only His Word.

When Jesus preached, He taught, and He demonstrated. There are too many ministers who love to preach and teach, but they don't demonstrate. They think all Jesus did was go around and preach and teach. Yes, He did that, but He also demonstrated what He had just preached. When you preach and teach, if you don't give God an opportunity to confirm His Word, then just sit down and shut up. Some people just talk for the sake of talking, but there is no point to it and no purpose in it. As the saying goes: "If you haven't 'struck oil' after twenty minutes, stop 'boring.'"

DEMONSTRATE

Jesus preached and He taught and demonstrated everywhere He went. Sometimes the demonstration was in the message, and sometimes the message was in the demonstration. Often, His messages were short, but they resulted in something happening. Most of them would not result in a tape series—they were too short. Take, for example, the story of the four men who let the sick man down through the roof of the house. It did not take a long message to result in his healing. Jesus demonstrated and preached a simple message, all in a few words. Look at Mark 2:3–12:

> And they come unto him, bringing one sick of the palsy, which was borne of four. And when they could not come nigh unto him for the press, they uncovered the roof where he was: and when they had broken it up, they let down the bed wherein the sick of the palsy lay. When Jesus saw their faith, he said unto the sick of the palsy, Son, thy sins be forgiven thee. But there were certain of the scribes sitting

there, and reasoning in their hearts, Why doth this man thus speak blasphemies? who can forgive sins but God only? And immediately when Jesus perceived in his spirit that they so reasoned within themselves, he said unto them, Why reason ye these things in your hearts? Whether is it easier to say to the sick of the palsy, Thy sins be forgiven thee; or to say, Arise, and take up thy bed, and walk? But that ye may know that the Son of man hath power on earth to forgive sins, (he saith to the sick of the palsy,) I say unto thee, Arise, and take up thy bed, and go thy way into thine house, and immediately he arose, took up the bed, and went forth before them all; insomuch that they were all amazed, and glorified God, saying, We never saw it on this fashion.

Another message and demonstration of Jesus's preaching is found in the words spoken to the thief on the cross: *"And Jesus said unto him, 'Verily I say unto thee, Today shalt thou be with me in paradise'"* (Luke 23:43). Jesus was anointed to preach, teach, and demonstrate. Acts 10:38 says: *"How God anointed Jesus with the Holy Ghost* **[there's the Godhead in operation again]** *and with power: who went about doing good, and healing all that were oppressed of the devil; for God was with him"* (Emphasis added).

So, the ministry of Jesus will bring healing. Often people will say: "But, we don't move in healing around here." Well, then you're not hanging around Jesus. Do you want a ministry like Jesus had? Then look at what He did. He preached, He taught, and He demonstrated. You know when you do what He did, you are following in His footsteps. We'll get to this in another chapter, but let me just mention that part of His ministry included laying hands on the people. He finished preaching or teaching by laying hands on them—healing the sick and transferring the anointing.

At times, you may lay hands on someone to transfer the anointing, but they don't receive it. They put no demand on the anointing. Maybe they don't know it is available for them, so they aren't expecting it. When you tell a little child that you are going to bring some candy when you come home, they will be running around wanting to know where the candy is. They were waiting in anticipation for it. When you transfer the candy from your hand to the child's hand, it will go straight to his mouth. A transfer takes place, because there is an expectation.

When people come around the things of God, if they don't expect anything, that is exactly what they will get. Nothing. They should leave happy because they got what they wanted. That was what happened when the woman with the issue of blood touched Jesus and was healed. There's no record of anyone else in that crowd, who were jostling and touching Jesus, receiving a healing, because even though they were touching Him, they had not placed a demand on the anointing that was on Him.

There were only two things that made Jesus marvel: **great** faith/expectation and **no** faith/expectation. Peter and John saw a lame man at the temple who was ready to receive, and with just a word and a touch from Peter, he got what he needed—his healing. Only one man received his healing from Jesus at the Pool of Bethesda, even though He had the power to heal them all. Even Jesus could do no mighty work in His own hometown, because they did not respect the anointing on His life. You must be in a place to receive, and place a demand on the anointing in order to receive that anointing.

> And Jesus answering saith unto them, Have faith in God. For verily I say unto you, That whosoever shall say unto this mountain, Be thou removed, and be thou cast into the sea; and shall not doubt in his heart, but shall believe that those things which he saith shall come to pass; he shall have whatsoever he saith. Therefore I say unto you, What things soever ye desire, when ye pray, believe that ye receive them, and ye shall have them.
>
> MARK 11:22-24

FAITH IS RELEASED BY THE WORDS OF YOUR MOUTH

That passage from Mark tells me that you place a demand by the words of your mouth. You release your faith by the words of your mouth.

Before you leave your house to go to church say: "I'm going to the meeting tonight, and I'm going to receive something." What are you doing? You are releasing your faith by the words of your mouth. Let me repeat that: *Faith is released by the words of your mouth*, and something's going to happen!

For years, I have released my faith that way. I do it automatically whenever I fly to another city to preach. While I am on the plane, I'll say to myself, "The moment my feet touch the tarmac I will receive an anointing for that city." Then I get off the plane, lift my foot, and as I plant it solidly on the ground I say, "By faith, I believe I receive the anointing from Heaven that I need to do what God wants to do in this city." The moment my feet touch the ground, I receive an anointing for that city. It never fails. I may be worn out from traveling or from speaking in other meetings, but when the anointing comes, I am energized and ready to go.

You have to speak it out of your mouth. That's why the devil tries so hard to keep your mouth shut, because he doesn't want you speaking out in faith. He knows that when you speak, you release the anointing, and people's lives are going to be changed. He wants to shut up the anointing in you. Have you ever started to say something and felt the devil trying to confuse your words or stop you from sharing the Gospel with someone? Of course, because he doesn't want those words coming out of your mouth.

The author of Hebrews wrote:

> For the word of God is quick, and powerful, and sharper than any twoedged sword, piercing even to the dividing asunder of soul and spirit, and of the joints and marrow, and is a discerner of the thoughts and intents of the heart.
>
> HEBREWS 4:12

Preachers are often afraid to speak out and preach the Word of God that He has told them to preach because they are afraid it will offend someone. We can't change the truth of God's Word to appease people. There is an old saying that goes: "If the cat's fur is getting rubbed the wrong way, let the cat turn around." If God's Word cuts cross-grain to your life, then your life needs to change to line up with God's Word. If you preach what God has given you from His Word, you may lose some people who don't want to hear it. But we are not here to water down the message for them. We are sent by God to get results—Bible results.

Remember, the anointing is God's electricity. You are a Holy Ghost power station, bringing light to a city when there is a "power outage." Speak the Word and you will light up the city. *"But we have this treasure in earthen vessels, that the excellency of the power may be of God, and not of us"* (2 Corinthians 4:7). We have a treasure in us that can destroy sickness and disease. It can break the power and chains of sin and destroy every yoke of bondage.

People ask me all the time what my secret is. They wonder how I do the things I do in my meetings. I demonstrate the power of the anointing, people are healed, and their lives are changed in every meeting. I could tell them I go home and stand on my head for two hours and then I drink some strange kind of soup. They would probably believe it, because they think you have to do something weird to get an anointing. But there is nothing weird about the anointing. Just because there are some weird people out there, it doesn't mean you have to be weird, or do strange things in order to have an anointing.

I have seen people trying to pass all kinds of things off as the anointing, but they are not real. When the woman with the issue of blood touched the hem of the garment that Jesus was wearing, she was healed not by the garment itself, but by the anointing flowing through it from Jesus.

As I have said several times earlier, when you are saved and filled with the Spirit, you receive an anointing. The Bible talks about a diversity of anointings. He uniquely anoints each of us—not to do our own thing, but to do His thing. It is like a coat of many colors—like the one Jacob gave to his son Joseph. Just as Joseph's brothers were jealous of his coat, so there are those who will not like the colors of your coat. They could get their own coat from God, but instead they are offended by yours. People will try to get you to get rid of some of the brightness of the coat and all the beautiful colors in it. They will try to take out the color of tongues, and the color of joy. They will want you to take out the color of giving, worship, and your freedom and liberty in Christ. It is their plan to replace your coat with a "religious" color that will not offend anyone. You can't receive from an anointing that you don't respect.

Jesus asked: "Who touched my clothes?" Someone had placed a demand on His anointing. He felt it, and she felt it. Virtue flowed out. Don't ever lay hands on anybody without expecting something to happen.

T. L. Osborne preached at our church when he was eighty years of age and made a profound statement. He said that during all of his ministry he knew that wherever he went, if he preached the Word, as many people as heard him would have their lives changed. He said: "I knew that wherever my voice went, if they could hear me speak, they would never be the same." He had great faith in the power of the Gospel, through his mouth, to save, heal, deliver, and set free.

When you have mass crowds of up to 400,000 people as he did, there is no way you can lay hands on everyone. At that point, you need to release the anointing through your words, like Jesus did. He healed the centurion's servant through the power of His words, because of the faith and expectation of the centurion. I know that when I preach the Word, the anointing rises as people's faith and expectation rises. As the Word goes forth, the Lord begins to touch people. I also know that if I could just lay my hands on people, their lives would be changed—through the anointing on my life. Not my power, but His.

The anointing is the manifest presence of God, and He manifests it at different times and in different ways as we yield to Him. Just keep in mind that it is His anointing—not yours. Give all the glory to God for the things that happen in your life and in your ministry.

7

RELEASE AND TRANSFER THE ANOINTING

Letting it Flow through You

*I*n the last chapter, we looked at the words of Jesus when the woman with the issue of blood touched Him: "Who touched my clothes?"

That seems like a strange statement to make when you are in the middle of a crowd. That's the first thing you will notice in a large crowd of people—someone touching you from all sides. You might experience that when you fly somewhere, people trying to grab their bags and bumping into others in their hurry. When there's a crowd, there's likely to be some bumping and some pushing.

When the disciples looked at Jesus, they were surprised at His question. Peter probably stood there, thinking to himself, "He has been out in the sun too long. Of course, someone touched Him." Thomas may have said, "I doubt anyone touched Him." Judas would have remarked, "Better check your wallet to see if it's still there."

But this was more than just a touch—it was a demand on His anointing. Let's look at the scriptures in Mark 5:25–34:

> And a certain woman, which had an issue of blood twelve years, And had suffered many things of many physicians, and had spent all that she had, and was nothing bettered, but rather grew worse, When she had heard of Jesus, came in the press behind, and touched his garment. For she said, If I may touch but his clothes, I shall be whole. And straightway the fountain of her blood was dried up; and she felt in her body that she was healed of that plague. And Jesus, immediately knowing in himself that virtue had gone out of him, turned him about in the press, and said, Who touched my clothes? And his disciples said unto him, Thou seest the multitude thronging thee, and sayest thou, Who touched me? And he looked round about to see her that had done this thing. But the woman fearing and trembling, knowing what was done in her, came and fell down before him, and told him all the truth. And he said unto her, Daughter, thy faith hath made thee whole; go in peace, and be whole of thy plague.

This woman had undoubtedly heard about Jesus and knew if she could just reach Him and touch Him or even His garment, she would be healed. She had been to doctors for twelve years and they took her money, but none of them had been able to help her. She had spent all she had and was no better, but rather had grown worse.

Since she had an issue of blood, she was not allowed in a public place, so she had to make her way to Jesus surreptitiously. She had to do it unnoticed, because if she approached Him publicly she could be stoned. (Under the law, if you had an issue of blood and were found in a public place, you were to be stoned.) But she thought, "I'll sneak through the crowd, take my healing, and no one will know."

"Jesus knew at once that someone had touched him, for he felt the power that always surged around him had passed through him for someone to be healed. He turned and spoke to the crowd, saying, **"Who touched my clothes?"** (Mark 5:30 TPT). However, she did not count on the fact that the virtue—the *dunamis* power—would flow and Jesus would know what she had done. As she worked her way through the crowd she said to herself: "If I can just touch the hem of His garment I will be healed." That was her point of contact. When Jesus said, "Who touched me?" she was full of fear and trembling, knowing what had been done in her body. She knelt before Him and told Him the truth. He said to her: "Daughter, thy faith hath made thee whole; go in peace, and be whole of thy plague." She had received her miracle.

I want you to notice that Jesus immediately knew in Himself that virtue had gone out of Him. Virtue—that's what anointing is—virtue. It is that special, heavenly tangibility, that heavenly materiality, that heavenly substance. Virtue went out of Him into her. There was a transfer into her of virtue—power, strength, ability, miracle-working power—dunamis—dynamite power.

Virtue is the same word used in Acts 1:8 that says:

> "But ye shall receive power, after that the Holy Ghost is come upon you: and ye shall be witnesses unto me both in Jerusalem, and in all Judaea, and in Samaria, and unto the uttermost part of the earth."

The Passion Translation says: **"But I promise you this—the Holy Spirit will come upon you and you will be filled with power. And you will be my messengers to Jerusalem, throughout Judea, the distant provinces—even to the remotest places on earth!"**

Acts 5:15 says:

> "Insomuch that they brought forth the sick into the streets, and laid them on beds and couches, that at the least the shadow of Peter passing by might overshadow some of them."

The Passion Translation says: "In fact, when people knew Peter was going to walk by, they carried the sick out to the streets and laid them down on cots and mats, knowing the incredible power emanating from him would overshadow them and heal them."

In other words, when we are baptized in the Holy Ghost, we receive the same virtue and power that flowed from Jesus into the woman with the issue of blood. What powerful things could take place if we just have faith in that virtue and power!

HOW THE LORD TAUGHT ME ABOUT THE RELEASE OF THE ANOINTING

The first year that I went into the ministry, I worked with a group called Youth for Christ. They knew, after I filled out the information form, that my background was Pentecostal, so they called me in and told me they knew what I believed, and I was forbidden to talk about the Holy Spirit. There could be no tongues or laying on of hands. I was not to even mention it, or I would get the "left foot" of fellowship.

I asked them what I could talk about, and they said that I could talk about Jesus. I told them that was actually Who I had come to talk about. They didn't know when you talk about Jesus, the Holy Spirit shows up! They didn't know that He said, *"And I, if I be lifted up from the earth, will draw all men unto me"* (John 12:32). And, *"No man can come to me, except the Father which hath sent me draw him"* (John 6:44). It is the Holy Spirit who saves, heals and delivers when the Gospel is preached.

The Lord had touched me with the fire of God in July of 1979, and now here I was in 1980, traveling around with this group, going into Methodist churches, Presbyterian churches, Baptist churches, and Anglican churches, etc. There was a larger group who went around doing Christian musicals. I was in the smaller group, informally called "the-ready-for-anything group." The services we held in the various churches consisted of us singing and then testifying/preaching. Each of us gave a testimony, and we would see one or two saved in most of the meetings. When I went to the training camp, there were about fifty-four young people. Only a few were baptized in the Holy Spirit, so I decided I was going to hold a prayer meeting in the bus. They had a bus parked right there on the field. At night after dinner, I would go down, get in the back of the bus and start praying. Many nights I heard the bus doors open and I could feel the bus move as the young people stepped on to join the prayer meeting. As we prayed, one by one, they began to speak in tongues for the first time.

The power of God was hitting these young people, and they were getting baptized in the Holy Ghost. So, at the end of three months when we started off on tour, forty young people had been baptized in the Holy Ghost. They were never the same. Over the course of that year, as we traveled around South Africa, singing and preaching, the Lord began to teach me more about the transference of the anointing.

As a little boy, I was so hungry for the anointing that you couldn't keep me away from church. At home, I would lie in the middle of the living room, playing with my cars under the table during home meetings and all-night prayer meetings, while people were falling under the power all around me. I was so hungry for God that I had to have a front-row seat—both at home and at church. I can still remember sitting on the pew in church swinging my legs because my feet could not reach the floor.

I watched every little thing that happened—especially when a man of God came in from America. I thought God lived in America, because when anyone came in from there they always seemed to be powerfully anointed. They must have wondered who this little kid was who always sat on the front row and listened so attentively. Most people were interested in everything the American said. I was so hungry that I not only listened, but I also intently watched how he flowed in the anointing.

I wanted to know how the anointing works—how it functions. I wanted everything I could get so I could learn more about the anointing. In those days, they didn't have cassette tapes or eight-tracks yet; they only had reel-to-reel tapes and long-playing records. Even by the age of seven, I would listen to the messages so many times that I memorized them and could preach them "by heart." I wanted to find out what the purpose of the anointing was and what to do with it when you have it. I was full of questions. Is it true there is a distinct difference in your life when you are under the anointing and not under the anointing? What is the difference? How does the anointing flow? If I had the opportunity to ask a preacher a question, it would be a question about the anointing.

In 1979, when I had an encounter with God and the fire of God fell on me, for three days I was beside myself. I was laughing. I was weeping. And I was speaking in other tongues. Everyone I touched was also touched by the anointing. It just takes one person to get hungry for God, to receive the anointing, and many others are touched. I found it's one thing to have the anointing come on you, but it is quite another to have it flow *through* you. Firstly, you have to personally submit to the anointing to allow Him to come on you, and secondly, you need to allow Him to have His way in you, and to clean you out and make the changes in you. Only then is He able to touch others through you.

I'll never forget, as long as I live, the meeting we held in a little Methodist church one day. Before the service, we were sitting in a back room they called a vestry. (That's a holy name for an office, where they hang the garments for those who dress up like Mother, yet we call them Father.) I was just sitting there, minding my own business. I had not just come off a forty-day fast; I had not been indulging in five hours of intensive prayer per day, nor was I doing an extensive study of the scripture. I was just sitting there when one of the young ladies, who was on our team, came through the door, crying in terrible pain. The first thing she said as she came in the door was, "Pray for me."

I got up from where I was sitting and walked toward her, intending to do what the Bible says to do: lay hands on the sick. As I lifted my hand to put it on her head, it only got part of the way there when it felt like the tips of my fingers had come off and my hand had become a pipe or a conduit. It felt much like holding a firehose with a full stream of water flowing out of it. I felt the power of God as it flowed right out of my hand, went through the air, and hit her in the head. She crumbled right in front of me. She had fallen out under the power, but the anointing didn't stop. It was still flowing. It was so strong that it almost felt like an explosion. The fire of God was tangible on my hand and it was tangibly coming out of my hand, even though you couldn't see it. No one in the room was more shocked than I was.

I had seen people fall under the power, but this was different. The Lord was showing me what was actually taking place. I knew He was teaching me that the anointing is tangible, it is transferable, it can be communicated, and you can give it away. Just as you can hand a book to a friend and he can hand it back to you, the anointing can be transferred to someone else. If you have the anointing, and the recipient draws on the anointing, a transfer can and will take place. The laying on of hands is not merely ceremonial—something is transferred. That's why you need to be careful who lays hands on you. Make sure those hands are clean—not merely physically, but spiritually clean.

God's power is real. When you lay hands on people, the power of God should be transferred from you to them, to do the works of Jesus. We are dealing with spiritual things here. It's not our power—it's His power. Not just anybody should be laying hands on people. If you don't have the anointing, you can't give the anointing. You can't give what you don't have.

People who have a spirit that is unclean or impure should not be laying hands on anyone. Simon, the sorcerer, wanted to buy the power to confer the Holy Spirit by the laying on of hands, but his motives were selfish and manipulative (Acts 8:9-13). Paul had to sternly rebuke him. Unfortunately, you can't share these truths with just anyone. These are holy things and not to be taken lightly. Jesus said: *"Give not that which is holy unto the dogs, neither cast ye your pearls before swine, lest they trample them under their feet, and turn again and rend you"* (Matthew 7:6).

I've had the privilege of sitting down with ministers privately and have shown them how the anointing is transferred. Many of them had never flowed in the anointing before, but once they realized what it is and how it works, they wanted it. Many have told me that since I laid hands on them, their ministry is different, and they are now ministering with tangible anointing. Remember, you can lay hands on people, or you can just speak the Word, like Jesus did for the centurion and his servant in Matthew 8.

> And when Jesus was entered into Capernaum, there came unto him a centurion, beseeching him, And saying, Lord, my servant lieth at home sick of the palsy, grievously tormented. And Jesus saith unto him, I will come and heal him. The centurion answered and said, Lord, I am not worthy that thou shouldest come under my roof: but speak the word only, and my servant shall be healed. For I am a man under authority, having soldiers under me: and I say to this man, Go, and he goeth; and to another, Come, and he cometh; and to my servant, Do this, and he doeth it.
>
> MATTHEW 8:5-9

There is nothing fake or made up about this. Even when people have never fallen out under the anointing, or they don't believe in it, we've seen them go down when God's power touches them. Some people have been in church for years yet never experienced God's power. That is just sad. Some people, who never usually fell down, felt a hand touching them and they went down, thinking I pushed them. Their family had to tell them that I was far away from them—it was the Lord who put His hand on them.

FALLING UNDER THE POWER

- Revelation 1:17 – John on the Isle of Patmos—fell at his feet as dead.

- Ezekiel 1:28 – "As the appearance of the bow that is in the cloud in the day of rain, so was the appearance of the brightness round about. This was the appearance of the likeness of the glory of the Lord. And when I saw it, I fell upon my face, and I heard a voice of one that spake."

- Ezekiel 2:1-2 – "And he said unto me, Son of man, stand upon thy feet, and I will speak unto thee. And the spirit entered into me when he spake unto me, and set me upon my feet, that I heard him that spake unto me."

- 2 Chronicles 5:14 – "So that the priests could not stand to minister by reason of the cloud: for the glory of the Lord had filled the house of God."

- 2 Chronicles 7:1-2 – "Now when Solomon had made an end of praying, the fire came down from Heaven, and consumed the burnt offering and the sacrifices; and the glory of the Lord filled the house. 2 And the priests could not enter into the house of the Lord, because the glory of the Lord had filled the Lord's house."

- John 18:4-5 – "Jesus therefore, knowing all things that should come upon him, went forth, and said unto them, Whom seek ye? They answered him, Jesus of Nazareth. Jesus saith unto them, I am he. And Judas also, which betrayed him, stood with them." As soon as he said I am he, they went over backwards and fell to the ground."

- Matthew 28:4 – "And for fear of him the keepers did shake, and became as dead men."

- Matthew 17:5-6 – "While he yet spake, behold, a bright cloud overshadowed them: and behold a voice out of the cloud, which said, This is my beloved Son, in whom I am well pleased; hear ye him. And when the disciples heard it, they fell on their face, and were sore afraid."

- Acts 9:4 KJV – "And he fell to the earth, and heard a voice saying unto him, Saul, Saul, why persecutest thou me?"

- Acts 26:14 – "And when we were all fallen to the earth, I heard a voice speaking unto me, and saying in the Hebrew tongue, Saul, Saul, why persecutest thou me? it is hard for thee to kick against the pricks."

The important thing is not about the falling—it's about yielding to God. Some people are so determined not to fall down, they receive nothing. You can't receive from the anointing with your head. The anointing is not a mental thing. The anointing has nothing to do with your mind. It has to do with your spirit. The Spirit of God does not speak to your head. He speaks to and deals with your heart, the spirit man. Those who remain in the mental realm, when they come for a touch, can't receive. You have to grab hold of it with your heart.

The carnal mind is an enemy of God. It cannot and it will not obey God's Law (Romans 8:7). That's why we have to renew our minds with the Word of God (Romans 12:2). We need to fully submit to God and allow the Spirit of the Lord to change us from the inside out. When we are filled with Him, He will quicken—make alive, bring life to—our minds and our bodies (Romans 8:11).

METHODS

Look at the New Testament to see how people were healed then. Jesus spat on *the ground, made clay and put it on the man's eyes (See* John 9:11). Acts 5:15 says: *"Insomuch that they brought forth the sick into the streets, and laid them on beds and couches, that at the least the shadow of Peter passing by might overshadow some of them."* Jesus spoke the Word and laid hands on people, and they were healed. He touched people and they touched Him.

Some of the methods they used we would never use today. I have never used the method of spitting, at least not on purpose. How did Jesus heal the man by spitting and making clay? Did He religiously and delicately spit a tiny drop of saliva, and mix it with some finely ground sand from the Jordan, in a little silver cup or chalice, off a satin pillow that Peter brought Him, as He made the sign of the cross? No, of course not! He would have had to spit a large hunk of spit to have enough for both eyes. And He mixed it with ordinary sand from under everyone's feet.

The methods they used in the Bible would not be acceptable in most modern-day churches. The things Jesus said and did would empty many churches today. "That crazy preacher spits on everybody. He prays for the deaf, spits on his hands and touches their ears." They would have so many problems with the methods they wouldn't see the results. If they had been in Jesus's day, they would have interviewed the blind man and gotten the real story.

> The neighbors therefore, and they which before had seen him that he was blind, said, Is not this he that sat and begged? Some said, This is he: others said, He is like him: but he said, I am he. Therefore said they unto him, How were thine eyes opened? He answered and said, A man that is called Jesus made clay, and anointed mine eyes, and said unto me, Go to the pool of Siloam, and wash: and I went and washed, and I received sight. Then said they unto him, Where is he? He said, I know not.
>
> JOHN 9:8–12

The man who was healed didn't know who Jesus was or where He had come from, but one thing he knew: "Once I was blind, but now I can see." (*See* John 9:25). He didn't question the method; he just went away rejoicing that he had been healed.

Religious people today would question whether he could see or not, or even if he was blind in the first place. They would want to have the spit sent to a laboratory to be examined under a microscope to decide if it was real or counterfeit spit.

We must understand it is not the spit or the laying on of hands. It wasn't in Peter's shadow as he passed by the people (*See* Acts 5:15). It's the power of God. The Lord wrought special miracles by the hands of Paul, so powerful that they took handkerchiefs and aprons that he had touched and laid them upon the sick, and they were healed. But the power wasn't in the cloth, per se. It was the transference of the power of God—the anointing on the cloth—that healed them. If no anointing goes into it, what good is it?

Now, back to my story of the young lady who had fallen under the power of God in the little church. I stood looking at her on the floor, still feeling the anointing flow through my fingers, and thought to myself: *You had better be careful where you point your hand; that thing is loaded!* As the rest of the team began to come in just before the service, I didn't know what to do with this anointing flowing through my hands, so I went around the room laying hands on everyone, and they all went out under the power of God in the back room of that little Methodist church.

At that point, I began to wonder what I would say if the pastor came back in and saw everyone on the floor but me. He would know I was the culprit, so perhaps I should lie down with them. I decided to go around and get them all back on their feet, but they were all a bit woozy, so I had to shake them a little and try to get them to pull themselves together. I finally got them all up, except for one young lady who had to be propped between two young men and walked out to the service.

As we began to minister, I was thinking, *Lord, if we could only have the same thing happen here that happened in the back room. What a difference it would make in these people's lives.*

I knew I had been forbidden to speak on the Holy Spirit or talk about tongues or the laying on of hands, so what would I do? I was preaching on 1 Corinthians 2:9–12:

> But as it is written, Eye hath not seen, nor ear heard, neither have entered into the heart of man, the things which God hath prepared for them that love him. But God hath revealed them unto us by his Spirit: for the Spirit searcheth all things, yea, the deep things of God. For what man knoweth the things of a man, save the spirit of man which is in him? even so the things of God knoweth no man, but the Spirit of God. Now we have received, not the spirit of the world, but the spirit which is of God; that we might know the things that are freely given to us of God.
>
> 1 CORINTHIANS 2:9-12

I was probably about ten minutes into the message. I had been talking to the Lord the whole time I was preaching. (Actually, in some of the places I go, I have to pray a *lot* as I preach.) I was still wondering if we could have the same thing happen in the service that I had just seen in the back room. The Lord, who knows how to do things right, told me to call for all those who wanted a blessing. They all raised their hands, but their idea of a blessing and my idea of a blessing were two totally different things. Possibly, their idea of a blessing was someone standing over them making the sign of the cross and saying, "I can play dominoes better then you can." My idea of a blessing was them being touched by, and receiving, the power of God through the transfer of the anointing.

So, I told all those who wanted a blessing to come down and line up at the front. As I was about to step off the platform to lay my hands on the first person, the Lord said to me: "Be very careful how you touch them, because some of them will think you are pushing them down. Just take the index finger of your right hand and gently lay it on the forehead of the first person and say: 'In the Name of Jesus.'"

I went down from the platform, and as He had instructed, I walked up to the first person and put my finger on his forehead and said: "In the Name of Jesus." Before I even finished saying His name, they started falling. I went right down the line and the whole row hit the deck. As they fell, they were speaking in other tongues. I turned back to the pastor and said: "It wasn't me. I didn't do it." I was reminded after that incident of a famous John Wesley quote:

> "My fear is not that our great movement, known as the Methodists, will eventually cease to exist or one day die from the earth. My fear is that our people will become content to live without the fire, the power, the excitement, the supernatural element that makes us great."

We had a similar experience later when we were in Hong Kong. During the meeting the people were praying, and it sounded like they were praying in Chinese but they were actually praying in tongues. When we laid hands on them, they fell out under the power, and began speaking in other tongues. My interpreter told me these people had never spoken in tongues before. At first, I couldn't tell the difference, but he could tell it wasn't in their languages—Mandarin or Cantonese. It was the language of the Holy Spirit. Some of the people were stuck to the floor for up to an hour and a half. They were pinned to the floor like they had been super-glued to the carpet. They tried to get up but couldn't.

When they were finally able to get up they came over to me and asked: "What is this?" I told them: "This is that," referring to the words of the Apostle Peter. *"But this is that which was spoken by the prophet Joel; And it shall come to pass in the last days, saith God, I will pour out of my Spirit upon all flesh"* (Acts 2:16-17).

THE TRANSFERENCE OF THE ANOINTING

This means that whatever you are doing in the ministry will be anointed as the Spirit comes on you. If you have been touched by the power of God, when you are playing a guitar or a keyboard, the anointing will come out of your hands onto the keyboard or into your guitar and go out in anointed sounds. As you play, the notes will strike the hearts of the people, and healings will take place. Miracles will take place. Now, get ready—expect miracles when you play. It's not some mystical thing. It's real. You can't *make* it happen. On the contrary, when you yield to Him, He will flow through you.

My wife had an experience with the Lord when we were newly married. We were in church and the worship team was playing the song, "I Love You with the Love of the Lord." As she hugged one of the other ladies, unexpectedly, she felt a powerful surge of the love of God flowing out of her into this lady. It was more like it was pulled out of her than pushed, if you know what I mean. The lady began weeping and thanking Adonica. She replied: "It wasn't me; it was Jesus." If you just make yourself available, the Lord will touch others through you, even when you least expect it. The lady needed a touch from Jesus and she received it.

Many think it is just about laying your hands on someone, but if God puts you in front of a large crowd of 30,000 or more people, how will you touch all of them? You can't lay hands on that many people, so you have to learn to release it in another way. The problem is that some people only know how to receive by the laying on of hands. You have to teach them how to receive when you speak the Word from God. Otherwise, they think they didn't receive because you didn't touch them.

But, as I said, there's no possible way for you to touch them all. Going down into the crowd to pray for people and lay hands on them could endanger your life and the lives of your team. I have almost been crushed several times in different places, and especially in ministry on foreign fields.

I remember the first time we went into Moscow, in the former Soviet Union. The building was filled to capacity, so when it came time to pray and lay hands on the people, I told them to go out to the foyer where we would put them in a line for prayer. But they wouldn't let me out of their sight, so they stayed where they were.

I instructed them again, through the interpreter, but they still did not obey me. So, I walked to the foyer and then they all followed me out. They were not lined up, but were just a massive group of people, watching my every move. I could not seem to make them understand what I needed them to do. They wanted to be right with me.

It turned into what the Bible calls "a press," a multitude of people, such as the press when the four men let their friend down through the roof so he could be healed (*See* Mark 2:4). Or like the crowd, or press, the woman with the issue of blood came through to get to Jesus (*See* Mark 5:27). In the midst of all that, finally, we did manage to line them up and get everyone properly prayed for, even though it was a bit chaotic in the beginning. The point is, of course, that you can lay hands on people, but there are also other ways to communicate the anointing. The anointing can be specifically directed.

I was preaching in a meeting in Texas and happened to look over at one of our pastors. I felt the anointing go straight out of my eyes into him. He felt it as it went into his eyes. As our eyes had met—boom! He was smacked with the anointing. I have experienced that several times.

You can't make it happen. It is the Lord who does it. It has everything to do with hunger and with being receptive.

Again, it was like the woman with the issue of blood. She was determined to get her healing that day because she was desperate to get a miracle. It didn't matter who was around her—she was going to get a miracle *that day*. She had spent twelve years seeing many physicians, not getting better, but worse. She had spent all her money, so her last resort was to get a miracle, and she knew, for that, she needed Jesus.

Jesus knew when virtue left Him. He felt it. I had experienced the same thing when I reached out to that young woman in the little Methodist church. It is the power of God! The Apostle Paul put it this way: *"But we have this treasure in earthen vessels, that the excellency of the power may be of God, and not of us"* (2 Corinthians 4:7).

The point of contact is so important. The Lord has told me many times to tell the people to receive the anointing the moment that hands are laid on them. A point of contact can be when my hand touches a person's head, or it could be when I pray on a prayer cloth on behalf of someone wanting a touch from God. When I come to a land or a city to preach, my faith is that when my feet touch the ground in that place, I receive the anointing to minister there. There's nothing holy about the ground or the cloth, but it's a point of contact. It's the place where you release your faith.

You can give some people a cloth and tell them you prayed over it, and they want to come back later to get it recharged—they think the charge ran out like a battery. "Pastor, please pray over this one more time." Sometimes I want to tell them: "Certainly. We have a room in the back where we charge cloths. Bring it back anytime."

Understand there must be faith on both sides of the cloth...the one ministering the anointing and the one receiving the anointing. In 2 Kings 5:1–14, we read the story of Naaman, a leper who went to Elisha, the man of God, seeking healing. When Elisha told him to go wash in the Jordan, he became highly incensed. We don't know what he expected Elisha to do to heal him, but it wasn't a word via a messenger,

"Go dip seven times." But when he listened to his servant girl, humbled himself, and finally obeyed the prophet, he was healed.

If you are told to do something when you receive an anointing from the man of God, don't ignore it. Go do it! Grab hold of these truths, and realize it is not a game when we transfer the anointing to someone as the Lord directs. There are times when my hands feel like hot oil is on them. Other times, it feels like honey flowing, and still others, like electricity. Often, my whole arms will burn—not hurting, but warmth from the presence of God. The anointing really operates by the love of God. God is love! There is no difference between the agape love of God and His anointing—they are the same thing.

When I first met my wife, I would practice transferring the anointing. Adonica would stand on the other side of the room, and I would release the anointing onto her, and she could feel it. I was learning how to flow with the anointing. I knew you could lay hands on the sick and pray for them, but I was still learning about transferring the anointing to someone else. If the anointing is in you, then it can be released through you, by faith. It comes out of your spirit through the Holy Spirit. That is why it's so important to keep your heart pure and your hands clean.

THE ANOINTING IS TANGIBLE

If we could show every preacher and evangelist how to minister with the tangible anointing, it would change their whole ministry. But they must realize that when I put my hands on them, it is not my power—it's His. There is a boldness to my ministry, because I know where the power comes from. The military does not send their soldiers into battle without ammunition, and neither does God. He has all the "rifles and bullets" you need. Do you think He would send you out to destroy the works of the devil and not give you a tangible anointing? Of course not.

Sickness is tangible; pain is tangible; and of course, sin is tangible; so your anointing should be tangible. I'm not talking just about feelings—I'm talking about the power that comes from God. Whether you feel it or not, you still obey God, in faith, and minister to people.

About two weeks after my experience with this tangible anointing and feeling the power flow from my fingers and go into others, it lifted. Then I began to worry. I would pray for people, and they would fall under the power, but I did not feel what I felt before. I thought, *I must have done something to grieve the Holy Spirit, or I must have lost my anointing. "Lord, what have I done? I don't feel the anointing like I did."* I was going by my feelings, but I have learned that we can't always go on what we feel. We need to operate out of our spirit, by faith in His Word.

So, I went to the Lord in prayer and said, "Lord, what do I have to do to get that feeling back? Do You want me to fast for forty days? Tell me, and I'll do it."

The Lord answered me: "There's nothing you can do to get the feeling back. I just gave it to you as a sign and so you can learn, but there's no formula for getting it back. That anointing is for another time in your ministry because you could not handle it now. I gave it to you so that you would be watching out for it. You will have something to point ahead to and to aim for. It will take you through all of the storms—especially in the beginning stages of your ministry when people say you're not called. When you are struggling financially and in other ways, you will know that you are as fully anointed as you will ever be. However, you are not yet ready to handle all I have for you. If you had the release of that anointing your vessel might crack and crumble, because it's an earthen vessel and it still needs some work."

You may be called, but God still needs to do a work in your life. You can try to take shortcuts and try to push the doors open—you could even go on forty-day fasts—but that alone will not develop character, and in the end, it will not produce fruit. You can use your gifts and demonstrations of the Spirit powerfully, but only time and the seasons of life will work to develop character and produce godly fruit. Life is like school—there are tests along the way. You pass the tests and build character by submitting to God and trusting His Word in and through every situation. You have to learn obedience. You have to humble yourself under the mighty hand of God. It is His ministry—not yours. He is the Master; you are His servant.

I gave a word from the Lord to a minister once. The Lord said: "Keep your hands off your ministry!" When I gave it to him, I immediately also received it for myself. Keep your hands off! The ministry belongs to God. We are to treat it with respect—like it belongs to Jesus—not to ourselves.

So, you have to make the decision. Do you just want the power, or do you also want the character and the fruit? You don't have to choose one over the other. Some would say: "I'd rather have the character and the fruit," so they have no power. But I challenge you, in the Name of Jesus, to develop all and receive all God has for you and let the character of Jesus be formed in you. Let the fruit of the Spirit be made manifest in you so that you can run with longevity, and not blow up somewhere along the way and destroy your life and the lives of others round about you.

When you're in a place of hardship and pressure, you may be tempted to run to a place that seems easier, rather than standing and enduring. However, without standing on the Word of God through that hardship, character would not be produced on the inside of you. So unfortunately, when you take shortcuts—when you try to take the easy route—fruit will not be produced and godly character will not be formed in you. Some people never attain what God has for them. They never make it into their promised land because they always duck and run when the pressure comes. Like the faithless Israelites, they end up going around the mountain one more time.

Choose wisely, and the power of God will not only rest upon you for a moment or two but will reside and abide in you through all your days. Some, through their efforts of prayer and fasting, have tapped into the presence of God, yet because they have no godly character, it leaks out as fast as they obtain it. They may go for weeks with no anointing. It is godly character that obtains, and keeps, the anointing on your life.

THE ANOINTING HAS A PURPOSE

The anointing is not a big seesaw where one day you have it and the next day you don't. You don't have to live the life of a monk to be anointed, either. You can be anointed and still be married, have children, and function like a normal person. You can play a round of golf or go fishing, you can go shopping, you can wash the car, and you can take the dog for a walk. If you can't take care of your earthly responsibilities, and still be fully committed to God and walk in the anointing, your relationship with Him must be very shallow.

To be anointed, you don't have to be a super-spiritual flake, with your nose in the air, who can't get along with others. The anointing on your life does not entitle you to lord it over others, either. That type of attitude and behavior only gives the anointing a bad name. You can (and should) be able to carry the anointing and still humble yourself to serve others. Romans 12:16 (AMPC) says:

> Live in harmony with one another; do not be haughty (snobbish, high-minded, exclusive), but readily adjust yourself to [people, things] and give yourselves to humble tasks. Never overestimate yourself or be wise in your own conceits.

I have often wished there was a way we could connect people with the anointing just by laying hands on them and shocking them with the presence of God, getting them touched whether they like it or not. But we can't, because it's a heart thing. For the Lord to do His work, you need to let Him have His way in you. You need to be "receivers," not "resisters." Your heart needs to be open to receive from the Lord. You can't just "do something" in order for the power of God to come on you. It's not a works program. You have to surrender to Him. You need to allow Him to have His way. Your prayer should be: "Lord, You know what I need more than I do. Come and have Your will, have Your way. Touch my heart. Change me. Do whatever You want to do."

When I call people out in a meeting, it's because I can see He is working in their hearts and they are ready to receive from Him. Not everyone in the service is ready to receive. If I laid hands on certain people, it would be like walking up to the flowers on the platform and saying: "Receive, right now!" Nothing would happen. There is no faith in those flowers. And some people have no faith or expectation either.

That same day that the Lord spoke to me about the tangible anointing, He told me to continue to be faithful. He is the source—I am only the vessel. If He had given me a formula I might use it and think it was all me. Don't ever forget that when He anoints you for service, it's not through a formula. It's through a relationship with Him. I've had people come up to me and say: "Now, Brother Rodney, always remember that this is God." I just look at them and think, "Oh, if you only knew how much it was God, you wouldn't even say that." I don't ever think it's all me. I know it's not by what I do or how I do it. It's all in submission and obedience to Him.

The bottom line is that the anointing has a purpose. In our meetings, we could get people under the anointing and laid out, stacked up all over the place, because the power of God is so strong in there. Sometimes it feels like a Holy Ghost bowling ball thrown at a bunch of pins. People are filled with joy, and they leave feeling great, on a high. But the anointing is not there merely so we can feel good or have an experience. Yes, the power of God may be powerfully present in the place, but He is there for a reason and a purpose. The purpose of the anointing is for your life to change, for you to be empowered to win souls, cast out devils, and see people saved, healed, set free and delivered.

Sometimes, when people have not received instruction in the Word of God, they come looking for the wrong thing. They look for a feeling, or a manifestation, rather than a touch and a transformation. If the anointing is not used for its purpose (Acts 1:8), then the people are coming around you just to be touched for no reason. They are no different than addicts. There are a lot of charismatic "junkies" in the Body of Christ who run from meeting to meeting for their next "fix," but they never leave satisfied. It is so important that we come open and ready for God to do an inner work in our hearts, rather than seeking a mere outward manifestation.

If all you want is a manifestation, you could probably find someone to oblige you. Sadly, there have been ministers spring up who have no integrity, claiming to carry revival, but who have led people astray. They never preach the Gospel. They do not honor the Word of God. They act like they are being touched, pretend to be under the anointing, but the anointing isn't there. This is strange fire—no salvations—no furtherance of the Kingdom. All they focus on are manifestations or the crazy things people do in the service, instead of focusing on Jesus. This is deception and a distraction from what really matters.

I've got news for you: you don't have to go only to a meeting to receive the anointing. I have laid hands on men on the golf course who fell with their 3-iron still in their hands. I have prayed for someone on a fishing boat in the Florida Keys who landed in the bottom of the boat. I sat there thinking, *I hope he comes around pretty soon, so we can get back to land.*

So, you want an anointing. What do you intend to do with it? If you want more of what you have, do you want it just to roll around on the ground, or fly through the air? If you want to just play around with it and not use it, you really don't want more. The anointing is there for you to shake nations, but when it becomes just a frivolous thing in your life, you are not using it. You are wasting what you have.

IF YOU PROTECT THE ANOINTING, THE ANOINTING WILL PROTECT YOU

It is so important to be respectful of the anointing and the power of God. Jesus spoke of that in Matthew 11:

> "And thou, Capernaum, which art exalted unto Heaven, shalt be brought down to hell: for if the mighty works, which have been done in thee, had been done in Sodom, it would have remained until this day. But I say unto you, That it shall be more tolerable for the land of Sodom in the day of judgment, than for thee" (Matthew 11:23–24).

He was saying that the power displayed in that place was of the magnitude that if Sodom and Gomorrah had seen it they would have repented. That tells me that you'll go into a place where there will be power displayed, but there will be no respect for it and no receptivity to it. That doesn't mean there's no anointing or that God's not moving. It just means people aren't open to receive. Sometimes, having the anointing is just having the ability to know when it's time to leave town. If people won't receive what God has for them, you can't make them.

The anointing—the power and the presence of God—is holy. It's so holy. I have seen the abuse of the anointing and it hurts me, because I know it grieves the Holy Spirit. Even so, and even if you are tempted to, you can't draw back from flowing in the anointing just because other people abuse it. The anointing is not to be used for personal gain—whether it's to gain followers, influence, or money. When I've seen people using the anointing for their own personal gain, I knew that was not what I was looking for. I wanted an anointing that lifts up Jesus and changes lives. The anointing should make us radical for Him and not take the easy way—the path of least resistance.

After a while, some people talk about the anointing as if it has lifted or left, but actually it does not just lift for no reason—sometimes it's because people get tired, and it doesn't flow. No demand is being placed on it, therefore, no one receives anything. It is like water or electricity—you can switch it on and off. The moment there is a demand placed on it, you will see it begin to flow, but when there is no demand, it will stop flowing. But the anointing is constant; the power of God is constant.

Watch what happens in a meeting. When the people are fresh and hungry for God the anointing flows, but when they get tired, they stop placing a demand, and you don't see the flow. Charles Finney, the great revivalist talks about it in his writings on why revival ceases. It's time to let them go home and rest. When they come back, they are fresh and ready to receive. God is always moving, and He's never sleeping. You never come to the Lord only to be told: "I'm not moving today." You never have to worry if He is feeling led to move. We are the ones who don't feel led. He is always willing to move and touch people.

Many in ministry have said that they feel drained after they minister, but I am affected in a totally opposite way—I feel energized. If you feel drained, it's because you are ministering in the flesh. I get recharged by the same anointing that is flowing out of me. I'm receiving even as I'm ministering. Treat the anointing with reverence and respect; don't treat it like a joke or play around with it. **If you protect the anointing, it will protect you.**

One reason the Holy Spirit may leave is because people allow sin in the camp. If you've had the anointing on your life, and you play around with it by allowing sin to continue in your life, the Holy Spirit will give you space to repent, but He will eventually leave because you've made no more room for Him. The more you accommodate sin, the more place you give to the devil. Don't allow sin in attitude, word, or deed. Keep your heart pure. You do not want to lose the anointing. It's hard to get back to where you were when you walk off God's path. Stay on the path! Stay faithful to the Lord, the Word, and to the Spirit of God.

You may leave a meeting after being touched by the Holy Spirit and a revival could break out at the next place you minister. That happened to Evangelist Randy Clark in January 1994. After we'd prayed for him in our campmeeting in Lakeland, Florida, he came and told us that his hands were burning. He told me that he was going to preach in Toronto, Canada the next week, so I told him to lay hands on everything that moved. A short time after that, I heard that a revival had broken out in the church, one which lasted several years.

God wants to use you. It's not about keeping it to yourself. It's about giving it away. If you want more anointing—then give away what you have. However, there is a price to pay to walk in the anointing. You cannot do your own thing and still carry the anointing that you would have if you had only submitted to the Lord in all things.

You may know the story of Kathryn Kuhlman. The Lord used her mightily to win many souls and bring healing and health to many bodies. At one point, she married a man who had divorced his wife to be with her and then she struggled for a number of years because she knew she had made a mistake. So, she left him and decided to remain single. It was at a great price—so much so that it cost her fourteen years in what she called "her wilderness." Then the ministry we know of today was birthed. She said, "I died a thousand deaths." It's not until you die to your own plans that the kind of anointing she received can be possible. You must die to self—to your own plans, your own will and way—and follow His plan. I have had people tell me that they felt like they were dying and, in a sense, they were. They didn't realize there was dying in the plan—dying to self and selfish desires—crucifying the flesh.

Jesus said: *"Verily, verily, I say unto you, Except a corn of wheat fall into the ground and die, it abideth alone: but if it die, it bringeth forth much fruit"* (John 12:24). It's only when a grape is squeezed that you get the juice. If you want olive oil, you have to press the olive. If you study the ingredients for the anointing oil, you will see that it went through a crushing, a grinding, until it was fine and clear.

Everybody wants the finished product, but they don't want the crushing. So many more people could have, or would have, been used by God if they had just allowed Him to clear out all the things they were hanging onto that seemed so important to them at the time. Until everything else in your life becomes secondary to God's will, plan, and purpose for you, you will not see the greatness of His plan in and through you.

I'm not interested in ministers just being anointed to pray for the sick. Everybody should be praying for the sick. I am looking for people who will shake cities and nations. Give us a hundred like John G. Lake, Smith Wigglesworth and Aimee Semple McPherson. These kinds of people do not grow on trees. You cannot have hands laid on you to become like them; you have to personally press in to God. It's not what you do publicly in church; it's what you do privately at home. You have to press in; you have to yield to Him; you have to allow Him to do what He wants to do in you.

The Lord is saying: "Come." There is an open door before you, but you will have to pay the price. That means you're going to have to say goodbye to some of the friends you have, because they will never let you go through that door. It means you're going to have to break off some of the associations that you have.

It's your choice. Do you want to know the joy of having the Holy Ghost move through you to change lives, or do want to lose out on the will of God for your life? Choose wisely!

8

THE GLORY OF GOD
The Goodness of God Revealed

Wherever I go, people ask me about the anointing. Some have even said, "Brother Rodney, I don't understand why you think everything is about the anointing."

Why not? The anointing is God's tangible presence. Who would not want His presence in their life? I repeat what I said earlier: if you only gave me one subject to preach on for the rest of my life to the Church, it would be the subject of the anointing.

Although I have been teaching on this subject for many, many years, I feel that I am just scratching the surface of all that the anointing holds. But, I believe that in these last days, there will come a greater understanding of the glory of God and the anointing—the manifest presence of God. I just don't want to get to Heaven and say: "Oh, no! I was so close to understanding and moving in another realm." I want it all, and I want to teach and share it wherever I go. So, let's look in the Word and see more about the glory of God:

> And it came to pass, when the priests were come out of the holy place: (for all the priests that were present were sanctified, and did not then wait by course: Also the Levites which were the singers, all of them of Asaph, of Heman, of Jeduthun, with their sons and their brethren, being arrayed in white linen, having cymbals and psalteries and harps, stood at the east end of the altar, and with them an hundred and twenty priests sounding with trumpets:) It came even to pass, as the trumpeters and singers were as one, to make one sound to be heard in praising and thanking the Lord; and when they lifted up their voice with the trumpets and cymbals and instruments of musick, and praised the Lord, saying, For he is good; for his mercy endureth for ever: that then the house was filled with a cloud, even the house of the Lord. So that the priests could not stand to minister by reason of the cloud: **for the glory of the Lord had filled the house of God.** (Emphasis added.)
>
> 2 CHRONICLES 5:11–14

As they praised, they magnified God and declared that the Lord is good and His mercy endures forever. They lifted their voices in praise, along with the instruments, just as we do in our meetings. The Bible says that because the glory of God filled the place, the priests could not stand to minister, which means they fell out under the power of God. The Message Bible says: *"The priests couldn't even carry out their duties because of the cloud—**the glory of GOD!—that filled The Temple of God.**"* (Emphasis added.)

We see the same thing happening in 2 Chronicles 7:1: *"Now when Solomon had made an end of praying, the fire came down from Heaven, and consumed the burnt offering and the sacrifices; **and the glory of the Lord filled the house.**"* (Emphasis added.)

Notice that the glory always comes *after* the offering and the sacrifice—your praise and your worship. When you are in a meeting, such as we hold around the world, much of the service is praise and worship. It is the fruit of our lips giving thanks. It is our hands lifted high and our voices in one accord, followed by our offerings to the Lord. I think we should just keep it in that order. Some of the greatest breakthroughs in our meetings have taken place right after praise and worship, and people giving offerings. People are saved and healed. Lives are changed as the glory of God fills the room. Matthew 26 tells the story of an offering that was poured out and went all the way to the cross:

> Now when Jesus was in Bethany, in the house of Simon the leper, There came unto him a woman having an alabaster box of very precious ointment, and poured it on his head, as he sat at meat. But when his disciples saw it, they had indignation, saying, To what purpose is this waste? For this ointment might have been sold for much, and given to the poor. When Jesus understood it, he said unto them, Why trouble ye the woman? for she hath wrought a good work upon me. For ye have the poor always with you; but me ye have not always. For in that she hath poured this ointment on my body, she did it for my burial. Verily I say unto you, Wheresoever this gospel shall be preached in the whole world, there shall also this, that this woman hath done, be told for a memorial of her.
>
> MATTHEW 26:6-13

If you study the passage above, you will see that they were in the house of Simon the leper, and leprosy stinks. Leprosy, in the Word, represents sin. Sin which leads to death. But when the alabaster box was broken, the fragrance filled the room, and overcame the smell of leprosy. Even today the smell of sin and death is driven out by the anointing—by the glory of God.

Notice that Jesus said, *"For in that she hath poured this ointment on my body, she did it for my burial"* (Matthew 26:12). When she poured the oil on Him it stayed on His body all the way to the high priest's temple. When they took the whips and beat Him, the fragrance filled the air. The sweet ointment was still so strong that it was on Him all the way to the cross. The sweet fragrance filled the area as He hung on the cross, because the woman had anointed Him with the oil. Jesus said: "She anointed Me to prepare Me for My burial." That offering still spoke, even from the cross. There was still the aroma of the anointing. The very word "anoint" means to smear—to rub in. I like to say "marinated."

ABIDE IN THE GLORY

There was a fragrance of the Cross as God broke His alabaster box—Jesus—and poured out a perfume on you and me. Where there is no anointing and no glory, leprosy (our sin) will stink. Death will smell. But when the anointing comes and the glory of God accompanies it, the stench of sin and death will be driven out. Our hope is to stay in the anointing—to live and reside, to abide in the Glory. Stay in that realm. Stay in the cloud of God. The enemy will seek to draw you out, back into the natural realm, back into the flesh. But your hope is to run even more—back into the cleft of the rock. Let Him hide you in the secret place.

> He that dwelleth in the secret place of the most High shall abide under the shadow of the Almighty. I will say of the LORD, He is my refuge and my fortress: my God; in him will I trust.
>
> PSALM 91:1-2

When you stay in the cloud, the enemy will not be able to find you. He might hear your voice, but he won't know where you are. Under the old covenant, the glory of God was manifested as a cloud. Remember that the anointing of God—the presence of God—did not live in the hearts of men. You could say He was inaccessible. The only one who could go into the Holy of Holies was the high priest, and he had to wear a special garment. The garment had bells and pomegranates on the bottom hem. The bells signified the gifts of the Spirit and the pomegranates signified the fruit of the Spirit. As Christians today, if we only have the bells (the gifts of the Spirit) without the pomegranates (the fruit of the Spirit), we are just a loud noise—a clanging cymbal. The greatest fruit is love. 1 Corinthians 13:1–3 says:

> Though I speak with the tongues of men and of angels, and have not charity, I am become as sounding brass, or a tinkling cymbal. And though I have the gift of prophecy, and understand all mysteries, and all knowledge; and though I have all faith, so that I could remove mountains, and have not charity, I am nothing. And though I bestow all my goods to feed the poor, and though I give my body to be burned, and have not charity, it profiteth me nothing.

You can't be in the presence of the glory of God and remain the same. When you enter in, and stay in, God's presence, you'll become like Him. Moses went up to meet with God for forty days and came down with the glory of God still shining on his face.

> And it came to pass, when Moses came down from mount Sinai with the two tables of testimony in Moses' hand, when he came down from the mount, that Moses wist not that the skin of his face shone while he talked with him. And the children of Israel saw the face of Moses, that the skin of Moses' face shone: and Moses put the vail upon his face again, until he went in to speak with him.
>
> EXODUS 34:29, 35

Moses's face shown brighter than the noonday sun. It was reflecting the Glory, the brilliance, the light of Heaven. When Jesus cried, "It is finished," the veil of the temple was torn in two and the Holy Spirit came out of that earthly tabernacle. The glory of God came out of the Ark, the box that man had made by God's own design—a replica of the true tabernacle. Came out to go where? Into the hearts of men. *We* are the ark of God. The tabernacle of God is with men (Revelation 21:3).

"But we have this treasure in earthen vessels, that the excellency of the power may be of God, and not of us" (2 Corinthians 4:7).

Under the old covenant you could not serve as a priest if you were depressed. The only way to come into the presence of God is with joy. *"Enter His gates with thanksgiving and His courts with praise"* (Psalm 100:4). *"By him therefore let us offer the sacrifice of praise to God continually, that is, the fruit of our lips giving thanks to his name"* (Hebrews 13:15). Sometimes you may not feel like it, but that's why it's called a "sacrifice of praise." It means you make yourself do what you don't want to do. You may not always feel like doing it, but you're going to do it anyway, because you don't approach God any other way. *"But without faith it is impossible to please Him: for he that cometh to God must believe that He is, and that He is a rewarder of them that diligently seek Him"* (Hebrews 11:6).

You come to God on the basis of Who He is, on the basis of His goodness and His promises, not based on who you are. You do it by faith and in expectation. Everything you do comes by faith, not by feelings. Your faith in God's Word will tell your feelings how to feel. Follow faith and the feelings will follow. Even your feelings can line up with God's Word.

WHAT IS THE GLORY OF GOD?

The glory is simply the intensity of the anointing. A cloud is an accumulation of moisture. There's moisture in the air, even though you might not feel it. Depending on what season of the year it is, and depending on the low-pressure/high-pressure system, as the moisture comes together, clouds will form. You can get rain, sleet, hail, snow, dark clouds or just fluffy white clouds. You're probably not going to get any rain from the fluffy white clouds, but when the clouds come together, and there's lightning and thunder, there may come a deluge.

Moses experienced this when he was on Mount Sinai: *"And it came to pass on the third day in the morning, that there were thunders and lightnings, and a thick cloud upon the mount, and the voice of the trumpet exceeding loud; so that all the people that was in the camp trembled"* (Exodus 19:16).

When God brought His people out of bondage, He brought them out with the pillar of cloud by day and the pillar of fire by night. The cloud was there to lead them, to guide them, to shelter, and protect them. The pillar of fire brought them warmth in the desert night and the cloud brought coolness in the desert day. When the cloud moved, they moved. They followed the cloud. Today, we don't have to go looking for an external cloud, because there's a cloud in our bellies—the glory of God. As it intensifies there will be lightning in your belly, and a rumbling. Glory to God! There will be lightning in your spiritual being. Out of your belly, out of your innermost being, will flow rivers of living water from the lightnings and the thunders of God.

Some have asked me, "Where is the glory?" It's in you! You must be His cloud. You manifest forth the lightnings and thunderings of God. When you go and you boldly preach, the rain will come, the flood shall come, the river shall come, you'll go to dry and thirsty lands and the spiritual and natural famine shall be broken.

It's glory! It's glory! That's what happened on the day of Pentecost—mighty rushing wind, and cloven tongues of fire. It is His glory, not ours. His glory. He wants to show it forth, and He wants to use you.

That's why Smith Wigglesworth said: "If the Spirit doesn't move me, I move the Spirit." In other words, whether he felt anything or not, he obeyed the Word, preached the Gospel, and operated in the anointing on his life. The Apostle Paul told Timothy to "stir up the gift of God, which is in thee by the putting on of my hands…" (2 Timothy 1:6).

Maybe you don't feel anything—and just maybe that's why you are in the condition you are in. Stir it up! Stir it up! Not just in a meeting, but when you go out into the world—when you go to a foreign country, or when you go to a dead church. Whenever you go to a place that needs revival, stir it up. The life in you changes the atmosphere. You can't let their "death" come on you. Life triumphs over death, so show forth His life wherever you go.

When you think about it, sickness and disease are ministers. They will try to minister to you, but they will minister death. When the glory of God comes, sickness and disease won't be able to stand in the glory. When the glory fills the house, poverty and lack won't be able to stand!

When believers put themselves back under the old covenant, they are saying that they don't understand the presence and the glory of God. The New Creation, the Blood and the Cross are still mysteries to them, as are the Resurrection, Pentecost and the mighty rushing wind in Acts 2. They still lack understanding of Jesus's words in John 7:

> In the last day, that great day of the feast, Jesus stood and cried, saying, If any man thirst, let him come unto me, and drink. He that believeth on me, as the scripture hath said, out of his belly shall flow rivers of living water. (But this spake he of the Spirit, which they that believe on him should receive: for the Holy Ghost was not yet given; because that Jesus was not yet glorified.)
>
> JOHN 7:37-39

I hear people say all the time that they used to flow in the gifts of the Spirit, but they don't do it anymore. When you say you have the anointing, we will look to see if there is fruit and if there are bells. I want to hear Heaven's bells ringing. I want to hear the sound of Heaven. When the priest went into the Holy of Holies, the people listened for the sound of the bells. If his offering was not acceptable to God, there would only be silence, which meant the priest was dead. So, they would pull him out of the holy place by the ropes that were on him and bring in another priest. Sin cannot stand in the presence of God. Sin contaminates.

WHEN SIN GETS IN THE ANOINTING, IT MAKES EVERYTHING STINK

"Dead flies cause the ointment of the apothecary to send forth a stinking savour: so doth a little folly him that is in reputation for wisdom and honour" (Ecclesiastes 10:1). If you choose the way of compromise and don't take the way of the anointing, then you open the door for a "fly" to get in

there. Don't allow any flies in the anointing.

Dead stuff stinks. When it's dead, it's dead, so bury it. Don't try to keep alive what God has called dead. Jesus said to let the dead bury the dead. (*See* Matthew 8:22.) You think you can go to a dead church and hang around where there is no anointing and that it won't affect you, but you don't know what negativity you are putting your family under. In some cultures, in the past, if you committed murder, they would tie the dead body onto your body, and before long, you would become sick and die yourself. Don't attach yourself to, or put yourself under the influence of, that which is dead. It will snuff out the life in you.

We received a call one time from friends in the ministry who were a part of our church for a season, whose children had been impacted by the transforming power of God's presence and were on fire for God. They called us in tears to thank us, because revival had saved their children. There was a minister's daughter, the same age, from another ministry who didn't have revival in their lives, and now the young unmarried daughter was pregnant. Our friends were so thankful when they realized that this could have been their daughter had it not been for the revival in their family. The revival had closed the door to demonic influences in their children.

Many people are looking for the Spirit of God in all the wrong places. There are people who are earnestly searching for the Ark of the Covenant, but *if* and *when* they find it, they will be surprised to find it empty. God no longer resides there. He left when Jesus cried: "It is finished!" And the veil of the temple split in two from the top to the bottom. He moved out of the Ark, made by the hands of man, and moved into your heart and my heart. WE are the temple of God.

> What? know ye not that your body is the temple of the Holy Ghost which is in you, which ye have of God, and ye are not your own? For ye are bought with a price: therefore glorify God in your body, and in your spirit, which are God's.
>
> 1 CORINTHIANS 6:19–20

Let's look at another scripture in the Amplified Bible, Classic Edition that emphasizes the fact that because we are His temple, we should have nothing to do with sin:

> What agreement [can there be between] a temple of God and idols? For we are the temple of the living God; even as God said, I will dwell in and with and among them and will walk in and with and among them, and I will be their God, and they shall be My people.
>
> 2 CORINTHIANS 6:16

It amuses me when people go to Jerusalem, stand by the Wailing Wall and say: "The anointing here is so intense." That is the modern-day Charismatic and Pentecostal church. I have stood by the Wailing Wall, and yes, the anointing was intense, because I was standing there and the anointing was in me—His temple.

But they think the anointing's in the Wailing Wall. I can go on a golf course and get anointed. The anointing's wherever you are. You can go to the Wailing Wall. But do you know why they feel the anointing? Because that's their point of contact. "Oh, I just know when I get there I will feel the presence of God." So, they do, but when they come back here they feel nothing. They say: "I have to go back."

God's not living in a box. He's not living in a wall or a building. If He is, then His Word is wrong. My Bible tells me that He came out of there and His anointing is now in you. You are the temple of the living God.

What's a temple? Firstly, it's a house—a container. When people die, they leave their earthly houses—their bodies. Secondly, this word "temple" refers not to the temple as a whole, but rather specifically to the Holy Place and the Holy of Holies. That's why the Apostle Paul wrote: *"Wherefore come out from among them, and be ye separate, saith the Lord, and touch not the unclean thing; and I will receive you, And will be a Father unto you, and ye shall be my sons and daughters, saith the Lord Almighty"* (2 Corinthians 6:17–18).

THERE IS A PRICE TO PAY TO WALK IN THE ANOINTING

He does not want His temple contaminated with the things of the world. He does not want His temple contaminated with idols, nor does He want His temple contaminated with impurities. If you want to be made a vessel unto honor, you have to sanctify yourself—purify yourself. Purge yourself of sin and disobedience and do away with the things of the flesh. Salvation is free, but the anointing is not.

Isaiah 55:1 (AMPC) says: *"Wait and listen, everyone who is thirsty! Come to the waters; and he who has no money, come, buy and eat! Yes, come, buy [priceless, spiritual] wine and milk without money and without price [simply for the **self-surrender** that accepts the blessing]."* (Emphasis added.)

The price to walk in the anointing is self-surrender. You must surrender everything that's in you to the Spirit of God. The anointing will cost you everything you have in your flesh. Your prayer should be: "Father, burn everything out of me that's not of You." The price for you to walk free and to walk in the power and anointing of the Holy Spirit was paid on Calvary.

When we first came to America as missionaries in December of 1987, the state of the church was, in some ways, very similar to what it is now. People were, and are, apathetic. If people are not bored and distracted, then they are trying to be "cool" and popular with the world—trying to avoid persecution or criticism. They are more interested in what *people* think, instead of what *God* thinks. They have never seen a move of God and they don't expect to, either.

The move of God is boring to some and controversial to others. The move of God has ebbs and flows—not because God stops moving, but because people back off of the power of God. They either pull back or they try to take it in a direction that He isn't moving.

We have come full circle, in part because people treat the move of God like it is the latest fad instead of the eternal plan of God. They say: "That's old now, we've seen that already, so let's have something new." As if the move of God is a circus act or some kind of entertainment. They always want to hear what "new" things the Lord is doing. There are people who always want something weirder than normal, as if it is not enough to just walk in the anointing normally. They want to do and see something newer and more exciting. "Well, we're walking upside down on the ceiling, you know. Sometimes we just float around the building."

Now that is a joke, but I'm always amazed at the crazy things people manage to make up. Most of that stuff is just a distraction, causing people to take their eyes off of God and His Word and put them on people and on manifestations. They don't realize the Lord is moving just like He did in Bible days and that is more than exciting!

Part of the problem is that the preachers get bored. Do you know why? They don't have fire from God. When you have the real fire, you won't be bored. I get tired physically, and that's because I don't have a glorified body yet, but I have never been bored! One day, we all will have one, but for now, our bodies need rest.

The Lord had to tell me to pull back, to pace this physical body because it is limited. If I could, I would preach three meetings a day and then be translated to preach in another place. My dream is to preach in three time zones on the same day, on different continents. I am still going to do that one of these days. I'll book a meeting in the United Arab Emirates in the morning, preach a meeting in London at lunch time, and finish up in New England with an evening meeting. I'll do it just for fun. Hallelujah! Wouldn't it be fun to preach on Sunday a.m. and p.m. in New Zealand, jump on a plane and preach the same Sunday a.m. and p.m. service in Hawaii? A friend of mine did that for two years.

You can't be respectful of the anointing of God and get bored. When people say, "I heard that before," then you know that they may have *heard* it, but they don't *know* it. They don't understand it. They are not doers of it, they are hearers only, and what they have is mere religion.

The devil has lied to some people. They are bored with God's Word and looking for something more exciting. If the devil can't trap people in religion, fighting the move of God, then he'll get them looking for sensational manifestations. People are hungry for the supernatural and if they seek manifestations instead of Jesus, they open themselves up to be deceived by the devil.

STRANGE FIRE

Some people don't want to pay the price to have God's presence; they want it their way; they want to find a shortcut. Instead of yielding to the Holy Spirit and only doing and saying what He wants, they want it their way. Some people want to direct and control the anointing. When you try to move in the Spirit with wrong motives, or when you make things up, you are dabbling in "strange fire"—not the fire that originates in the mountain of God.

Look back and find out about the days when the lamp of God went out in the house of God.

> And the child Samuel ministered unto the Lord before Eli. And the word of the Lord was precious in those days; there was no open vision. And it came to pass at that time, when Eli was laid down in his place, and his eyes began to wax dim, that he could not see; And ere the lamp of God went out in the temple of the Lord, where the ark of God was, and Samuel was laid down to sleep; That the Lord called Samuel: and he answered, Here am I. And he ran unto Eli, and said, Here am I; for thou calledst me. And he said, I called not; lie down again. And he went and lay down. And the Lord called yet again, Samuel. And Samuel arose and went to Eli, and said, Here am I; for thou didst call me. And he answered, I called not, my son; lie down again. Now Samuel did not yet know the Lord, neither was the word of the Lord yet revealed unto him. And the Lord called Samuel again the third time. And he arose and went to Eli, and said, Here am I; for thou didst call me. And Eli perceived that the Lord had called the child. Therefore Eli said unto Samuel, Go, lie down: and it shall be, if he call thee, that thou shalt say, Speak, Lord; for thy servant heareth. So Samuel went and lay down in his place. And the Lord came, and stood, and called as at other times, Samuel, Samuel. Then Samuel answered, Speak; for thy servant heareth. And the Lord said to Samuel, Behold, I will do a thing in Israel, at which both the ears of every one that heareth it shall tingle. In that day I will perform against Eli all things which I have spoken concerning his house: when I begin, I will also

make an end. For I have told him that I will judge his house for ever for the iniquity which he knoweth; because his sons made themselves vile, and he restrained them not. And therefore I have sworn unto the house of Eli, that the iniquity of Eli's house shall not be purged with sacrifice nor offering for ever. And Samuel lay until the morning, and opened the doors of the house of the Lord. And Samuel feared to shew Eli the vision. Then Eli called Samuel, and said, Samuel, my son. And he answered, Here am I. And he said, What is the thing that the Lord hath said unto thee? I pray thee hide it not from me: God do so to thee, and more also, if thou hide any thing from me of all the things that he said unto thee. And Samuel told him every whit, and hid nothing from him. And he said, It is the Lord: let him do what seemeth him good. And Samuel grew, and the Lord was with him, and did let none of his words fall to the ground. And all Israel from Dan even to Beersheba knew that Samuel was established to be a prophet of the Lord. And the Lord appeared again in Shiloh: for the Lord revealed himself to Samuel in Shiloh by the word of the Lord.

1 SAMUEL 3

What happened to those who played with strange fire? They were trying to imitate the anointing, but you *can't* imitate the anointing, the manifest presence of God—and God judged them and destroyed them.

That's why you had better not be trying to conjure up something, running around looking for angels and feathers and gold dust and all kinds of things. Watch out! It's not a game.

Somebody asked me: "Then what can I believe God for?" You can believe for whatever's in the Word—Matthew, Mark, Luke, John, and the Book of Acts. If it's not in the Bible, then stay away from it. It really grieves me when I see some of the crazy stuff people are doing. There isn't any anointing there; there is no glory there; it's just a mess and it will come to naught.

UPSTATE NEW YORK 1989

I believe the reason we have been able to maintain the anointing, even with all we have been through, is because we always reverenced the things of God and never treated them lightly or frivolously. There are many who have walked with us through the years, and they know we have all been able to maintain a reverent level of the anointing the whole time.

So, when we came to America and saw the state of the churches in upheaval, we cried out for revival. We cried out for God to move—not just through us, but through anyone who had a heart for revival. Then came that Tuesday morning meeting in April 1989 in upstate New York, when the glory of God rolled in like a wave of the sea, and the very atmosphere of the room changed.

I was doing what I had always done, but something was different that day. When the cloud of God rolled in, I never saw it, but I felt it. People started falling out of their seats. Some were weeping, some were laughing, and others were shaking. The sound was so great, I had to preach above the noise of the crowd.

There was a lady sitting three rows back, looking up at the ceiling, blinking rapidly like a bullfrog in a hail storm. I thought there was something wrong with her. I looked at her and said: "Lady, what's wrong with you?" She told me nothing was wrong with her, but she said: "While you have been preaching, a thick fog—a thick cloud has been coming into the room. I can't see the roof or the ceiling, and the lights are gone." I looked up and saw the lights, I saw the roof, and I didn't see any cloud. She saw the cloud of the glory of God. I didn't see it, but I could feel it. It was as if somebody slipped up behind me and wrapped me in a heavy blanket.

Sometimes, when the glory of God comes down on me, it feels like a coat or a heavy garment. Just because you can't physically see it, doesn't mean it's not there. The Lord asks us to trust Him and walk by faith. Some people see all sorts of things, apparently. They see angels. They see demons. They see Jesus. They see everything. They ask me: "Did you see that?" And I say, "No, I didn't see anything." I have never seen a demon; I've never seen an angel. The only angel I've ever seen is my wife or maybe my children—when they're sleeping—and my grandchildren when they're awake!

John 20:29b says: *"Blessed are they that have not seen, and yet have believed."* So, you may not have seen Jesus, but if you believe, you are blessed because of your faith.

Stephen saw the glory of God when he was being stoned. (*See* Acts 7:55.) Sometimes you have to get stoned to see the glory. No, I'm not talking about drugs…I'm talking about being martyred for the sake of the cross, when they stone you—with real stones. It was as if Stephen was already in the presence of God and didn't feel the rocks hitting his body.

When Moses was in the glory, he didn't eat or drink for forty days. That is supernatural. He was so filled with the glory of God, that his face shined so brightly, the people couldn't even look at him. Even into old age, he didn't seem to age. At 120 years old, his eye was not dim, and his natural force wasn't abated (Deuteronomy 34:7).

STAY IN THE GLORY OF GOD

I ask the congregation—the believers—at The River Church not to come to church dirty—carrying their dirt into the church. If you come in smelling of leprosy (sin) you will be the dead fly in the ointment—contaminating that which was pure. Now, if a person is unsaved, we want them to come as they are, and Jesus will save and deliver them. If you are a believer, you need to act like a believer and walk like a believer! The Holy Spirit empowers you to walk free from sin. Stop making excuses for your disobedience.

Pastors, tell your people that they need to come to church prayed up, full of the glory. They need to be sure whatever junk they are carrying doesn't come in the door with them, the stuff some people get up to during the week! It's no wonder we have to worship so long, trying to get a smile on their faces, or get them to raise their hands. Don't be a "corpse" who won't raise your hands in worship. We can have joy every time we come to church if we live in the glory—if we serve God fully, daily—and come into church full of His presence.

Do you treasure the "true treasure"? When the glory of God comes on you, you can do supernatural things like Elijah did:

> And it came to pass in the meanwhile, that the Heaven was black with clouds and wind, and there was a great rain. And Ahab rode, and went to Jezreel. And the hand of the LORD was on Elijah; and he girded up his loins, and ran before Ahab to the entrance of Jezreel.
>
> 1 KINGS 18:45-46

Elijah did something that was impossible in the natural—he outran a chariot of horses. Judges 15:4 says: *"And Samson went and caught three hundred foxes, and took firebrands, and turned tail to tail, and put a firebrand in the midst between two tails."* You can't even catch one little fox now, but with the glory of God on you, you could do what Samson did.

You are called to demonstrate the glory of the Lord. Now, that doesn't mean that you should walk through supermarkets laying hands on people, sending them flying all over the place. You wouldn't be able to hold a job if every time your boss looked for you, he found you on the floor in the hallway.

That's not what it's all about. You couldn't live a normal life, or even be married. Every time your husband or wife looked for you, you would be lying out under the power. The dishes would pile up in the sink. None of the clothes would get washed. No one would be there to pick the children up from school. The bills wouldn't be paid. No one would get any dinner because you're out, under the anointing. No, no! This is just a touch to empower us, just like on the day of Pentecost when they were in the upper room. They were all filled with the Holy Ghost and went out to spread the good news. Look at how God can use you when you walk in His anointing—the glory of God.

> Then Peter said unto them, Repent, and be baptized every one of you in the name of Jesus Christ for the remission of sins, and ye shall receive the gift of the Holy Ghost. For the promise is unto you, and

to your children, and to all that are afar off, even as many as the Lord our God shall call. And with many other words did he testify and exhort, saying, Save yourselves from this untoward generation. Then they that gladly received his word were baptized: and the same day there were added unto them about three thousand souls.

ACTS 2:38-41

The glory of God will make you the best wife and mom, or the best husband and father you could be. You can be the best boss or worker in your business. The glory will make you excel as an engineer, or be the best doctor or scientist in your field. Many people don't know how to relate to what happens in the anointing, so they go out to buy a loaf of bread, and act so weird they look like something's wrong with them. The move of God gets a bad name because people don't understand your "Christianese." You don't win people when you speak in your "preacher voice." You just confuse them.

Don't be like the man who pulls up to the drive-thru window at Wendy's and says in a religious preacher's voice: "Praise God, Amen. Give me two cheeseburgers, Amen, and I'll take some of them golden fries, Hallelujah. Chocolate milkshake-ah, Hallelujah. I want a happy meal-ah, with a little toy, Praise God!"

You're not always going to have a wind blowing around you and a flame on your head, but the fire will be burning on the inside of you. Just because you feel something, doesn't mean you have to act weird. Jesus is your example. Look at what the disciples did. They received the fire of God, then they went out to preach and minister.

We have two extremes—some people want nothing to do with the supernatural, and some people think that every goofy thing is the supernatural. Neither one of those is correct. God's supernatural power is still at work in the earth, but it's not something we can force, or control, or make up. God's power is REAL! When we submit to Him—spirit, soul, and body—He will show up and move. Some people have no fear of God and no respect for His Holy Spirit. His presence is always going to be holy. His presence will convict of sin. We need to respect and reverence Him. Don't make things up. Don't pretend. Don't fake anything. Sincerely press in to God and open your heart to be touched by Him.

When you've pressed in to God and when He's touched your life, what you should do is let the living water flow. Then, as you water others, you'll get watered yourself. When the anointing flows out of you, that's your life you're pouring out. That's living water from your belly. You have to keep it flowing. People may want you to stop because they are offended, but don't let them "put a lid on it." As for me, I have to burn brighter for Jesus, even if it means death. Even if everyone leaves, I will not stop burning. Understand that you're somebody's beacon—somebody's lighthouse—and if the fire goes out in you, they will lose their way. He sends you forth as lights into the world. The Word of God declares that He's made His ministers flames of fire. People will want to put your fire out, but don't let them. Don't let them. Glory to God!

Romans 12:2 says: *"And be not conformed to this world: but be ye transformed by the renewing of your mind, that ye may prove what is that good, and acceptable, and perfect, will of God."* If your mind's not renewed, then your mind will convince you to do what other people say. But inside of you the lightnings and the thunderings of God are telling you that the cloud of God is moving. Keep following the cloud.

I love Him so much, and I want to see His face. But we can't focus so much on Heaven that we neglect our assignment here on earth. We must look at the work that is ahead of us, for the time is short. But we can still sing it and let the world know how much we long to see His face. We used to sing an old song that says it well: *"Oh, I Want to See Him."*

The chorus says:

> *Oh, I want to see Him, look upon His face,*
>
> *There to sing forever of His saving grace;*
>
> *On the streets of glory let me lift my voice,*
>
> *Cares all past, home at last, ever to rejoice.*

There are times in the meetings when the glory of God comes in so strong it would be easy to just step right over and leave this world, but you know that you can't. It feels almost as though there's a stairway leading up toward Heaven. You could just run into His arms and never come back.

How about you? If you could, would you want to go? Leave right now? The only reason we stay is so that, in the time left to us, we could accomplish His eternal purpose for us. So, we pick up our crosses and we endure; we stand; we prevail; we march on to the finishing line. Coronation day shall come—for some of us sooner than others—but in the meantime, we occupy till He comes!

When we are in a meeting where there's no anointing, an hour-long service will feel like ten. If the anointing's there, ten hours will feel like an hour. I remember when I went to Brother Kenneth Hagin's funeral. It lasted seven hours, but it felt like only two. When a saint goes home you rejoice in the Spirit. As they played clips of his revivals, with him prophesying, I was so full of the glory of God, I walked out of there stone drunk. From a funeral! There are not many funerals you can attend and leave drunk—caught away in the glory.

9
IMPARTATION OF THE ANOINTING
Pouring out the Anointing on Others

I believe the moment the Lord touches you, then you have an obligation to touch the lives of others. There are lots of people who want more anointing, but it would really be a waste, because they wouldn't use it. It would be like living in a house with plenty of voltage coming in, but where no one ever switches on the light, yet they still want more electricity brought into the house. Well, why would you need it if you're not going to use it?

The power is there so that you can use it, but that does not mean you use full power all the time. You may have a fast race car with a 565-horsepower engine, but if you have any wisdom, any intelligence, you won't use all that power going through a school zone.

RELEASE THE ANOINTING

So, the power has been made available. I felt the Lord tell me that all the anointings that are needed have been released for the end-time move. It's now up to the people to release the anointing. He pours out His Spirit, but He uses you as the vessel.

The problem is not with God pouring out His Spirit. The problem is that when the Spirit pours the anointing into the vessel, it does not always get poured back out of the vessel. You are the living vessel, anointed by God, and you must pour out the anointing—you must pour out your life.

He pours it out into you—then you pour it out to others. I get so tired of hearing people say: "Lord, pour out Your Spirit; pour out Your Spirit." Then they go to another meeting and say: "Pour out Your Spirit; Lord; pour out Your Spirit" all over again. Why do they keep asking? They're not doing anything with it. The Lord may pour out His Spirit on them, but it just sits in them and they never use it. They have all this oil in their vessel, and they don't know how to let it go. They don't know how to release it, or even why it was given to them.

Remember what Jesus told His disciples: *"Heal the sick, cleanse the lepers, raise the dead, cast out devils: freely ye have received, freely give"* (Matthew 10:8). The Apostle Paul said: *"For I have received of the Lord that which also I delivered unto you"* (1 Corinthians 11:23). But you can't give what you don't have. So, in order to get it you have to go to the source. You have to "get under the spout, where the glory comes out," and let the Lord touch you and anoint you.

When He touches you and anoints you, then you have a responsibility and an obligation to take that anointing outside the four walls of the church. You have a responsibility to use that anointing to go out and set the captives free. The anointing is not just there to make you feel good or to make you feel comfortable.

That's the problem with the Charismatic world today. People are running around, looking for a service where they can get an anointing that will make them feel good. They are no different than the crack cocaine addict who's going around looking for his next high. He wants to forget his problems and feel good, so he is looking for another hit. Some Christians have no intention of pouring the anointing out on someone else. They want it for their own personal gratification, while people are going to Hell all around them. They are not thinking about the lost who are dying in their sins without the Lord. God wants to touch you, but He anoints you so He can use you—not just so you can feel a feeling.

FINANCE FOR KINGDOM PURPOSES

It's the same situation in the business world. People say they going to fund the Gospel, but when God brings them millions of dollars in their business, they buy a mansion and drive expensive cars and, God gets nothing. The Lord is pouring His anointing out, blessing their businesses and their lives but their finances are not flowing in the right direction. They promised to help fund the Gospel, but they have forgotten, so their finances are not being used in the right places. Then you see them five years later and they've lost everything because of their greed, but they don't know that the problem was that they didn't understand that the purpose of the provision was to fund the end-time harvest.

If you have the funding without a purpose, it is redundant, and if you have the anointing without a purpose, it's just as redundant.

There are many ministers who are fully anointed of God, but if they let the anointing flow out of them it would cause too many problems, and they'd be kicked out of their denominations. They would be thrown out of their churches with a whole army of people arrayed against them. They fear criticism and don't want to be blacklisted, so they take the path of least resistance. They don't open their mouths and they don't let the river flow out of their bellies. Instead, their rivers are flowing out of their heads, so they only speak based on intellectual reasoning.

But are they changing people lives? Absolutely not! They are nothing more than success motivators going around motivating people to succeed while they go to Hell. I don't want people to succeed to go to Hell. I'd rather you have nothing and go to Heaven than to succeed and go to Hell. Jesus asked the question: *"What shall it profit a man if he gain the whole world and lose his own soul?"* (Mark 8:36).

So, you must have two important elements working together. There must be God's eternal purpose, which is the reaping of the nations and the harvest of souls, and then you must have the finances—the anointing in the natural realm to get the job done.

You have the anointing in the Spirit, and you have the anointing in the natural. But both have to flow by impartation. The man who is anointed financially must be imparting the finances to where they need to go. The problem is that the more people make, the less they want to give to God.

Why is that? I think it's because the amounts they can give seem too large suddenly. They say, "It was fine when we were giving a hundred-thousand dollars, but we can't dump that million dollars now. It's too much money."

Well, then let it become moth-eaten. Let it get rusted. Let it be cankered. James 5:1 says: "Go to now, ye rich men, weep and howl for your miseries that shall come upon you." There is nothing wrong with riches, but they must be used for God's eternal purpose. Otherwise, they are dung; they are just an attraction for flies.

So, the anointing is there for a purpose, just as finances are there for a purpose. And if God anoints you, then you have an obligation to take that anointing to a lost and dying world. You have no excuses, because there *are* no excuses. You can wait for all the conditions to be favorable, but there will never be a favorable moment. You are going to have to give it away, no matter what circumstance you find yourself in: abundance or lack, comfort or discomfort. You have to give it away, because the way it flows is by impartation. If you want more, then give away what you have.

POURING OUT THE ANOINTING

Do you want more of the anointing? Then give away what you've been given. Empty yourself of yourself—empty yourself of everything He's poured into you, and then the Lord will give you more. Hold on to what you have and He can't give you any more, because you're already full. Spend your days emptying yourself by pouring out your life and He will fill you up with more. The oil will never run dry. We find a good example of that in 2 Kings 4:1–7:

> Now there cried a certain woman of the wives of the sons of the prophets unto Elisha, saying, Thy servant my husband is dead; and thou knowest that thy servant did fear the LORD: and the creditor is come to take unto him my two sons to be bondmen. And Elisha said unto her, What shall I do for thee? tell me, what hast thou in the house? And she said, Thine handmaid hath not any thing in the house, save a pot of oil. Then he said, Go, borrow thee vessels abroad of all thy neighbours, even empty vessels; borrow not a few. And when thou art come in, thou shalt shut the door upon thee and upon thy sons, and shalt pour out into all those vessels, and thou shalt set aside that which is full. So she went from him, and shut the door upon her and upon her sons, who brought the vessels to her; and she poured out. And it came to pass, when the vessels were full, that she said unto her son, Bring me yet a vessel. And he said unto her, There is not a vessel more. And the oil stayed. Then she came and told the man of God. And he said, Go, sell the oil, and pay thy debt, and live thou and thy children of the rest.
>
> II KINGS 4:1-7

Remember, the oil flowed as long as there was a pot for them to pour the oil into, but when they ran out of pots, the oil was stayed. Keep looking for pots, because as you find a pot to pour into then the oil will keep on pouring, and God will continue to fill your own pot.

I have heard people say they think that God has stopped moving like

He used to do. No, God hasn't stopped moving. He's always moving. You just stopped pouring it out. I laugh at all the people who say that the revival has stopped. They are just telling me they have stopped pouring. Revival has never stopped. It's as hot today as it was. It was great in 1993 and 1994, but it's still great today. Even if we had great meetings in the past, we don't live in the past. We keep pressing in, today. We keep preaching, praying, and prophesying, today. We keep doing the works of our Father, today.

Many churches, and people, who used to flow in the move of God, are not flowing any more. It has nothing to do with God stopping the flow. People have stopped the flow by not pouring out what God is pouring into them. We have to make the decision every day that we will pour the oil out into others. We will have opportunities every day to impart into others what He is pouring into us, but understand: the enemy will come against you, trying to get you to stop pouring. He'll intimidate you, he will use people to lie about you, and he will stir up others against you so you feel like giving up. "What's the use?" you will say. And eventually, if you listen to him, you will stop pouring. You will stop imparting the anointing God has given you.

There were several times I nearly stopped pouring out. I thought, *What's the use of giving it away if I am only going to abused by people?* The worst offenders were other ministers. They came to the meetings and got what they wanted, but then they turned around and abused our ministry. I even thought of walking away from the ministry. I got upset about it for a while, but the Lord rescued me. He released me from the bad attitude I had. Thank God He brought me back, because *my* life is in the pouring out of the oil He has poured into me. *Your* life is in the pouring forth of your oil…in the breaking of your alabaster box. The moment you stop breaking your alabaster box, your life of pouring out will stop. Keep breaking it and He will keep replacing it—with something higher than what you had before. Let your fragrance keep on filling the room, as in Matthew 26:6, when the woman took what was precious to her.

RIVERS OF LIVING WATER

Allow His presence to flow out of you. Remember the words of Jesus: "Out of your belly shall flow rivers of living water" (John 7:38). Some people will want to dam up your flow. Are you hearing me? They will want to block your well and divert your river. So, what do you do then? Flood your banks! We're not talking about a man-made river here. We are talking about the mighty river of God. The decision is yours as to whether to flow ankle deep, knee deep, waist deep or just get in over your head. You must make the decision. (*See* Ezekial 47:1-5)

If you are a minister, don't let some board make a decision on how deep you're going to go. I've had people tell me over the years: "You can't go out to those international crusades. You don't have the finances necessary to sustain the ministry." Do you know what I did? I booked more crusades. I determined to do what God had called me to do and depend on Him to supply what the ministry needed. If it went bankrupt, I would shut it down myself, but I knew God had called me to pour out the oil of anointing on a hungry and thirsty world. I refused to go places simply because it was beneficial to me in some way. I refused to hold back from going to particular places, just because it wouldn't be beneficial to me.

That's why many ministries fail. They ask: "Will this be good for me?" Maybe not, but it will be beneficial for the people that you go there for, because they need what you have.

So many ministries are stuck in the same circuit, the same old rut they have been in for so long. They go where they are comfortable. They are getting fat when there are starving people out there, waiting for them to come with the only thing that can fill them. We can't camp out at the oasis that's already there. God is calling us to the dry places—we bring the oasis with us. If you want to be fulfilled you have to know, deep in your heart, you are actually pouring out oil into hungry, thirsty people.

The hungry people, the desperate people are not always going to be in the crowd. They may be up a tree, hanging from a branch, trying to see what is going on just like Zacchaeus in Luke 19:4. The desperate person may not be in the house, but on the roof like the man brought to Jesus by his friends, in Mark 2:4. Are you seeing this? It's about pouring out your life, wherever you may be, and giving out what God has put in you.

Most evangelists will not go to the frozen North in the winter months because it is not beneficial to them, but that is where we have had some of our greatest revivals. We have gone to Alaska, Minnesota, North Dakota, and New England during the winter months of November, December, and January, where it is cold and often depressing. In some places, people have nothing to do because they only have three or four hours of daylight. In other places it is totally dark most of the time, but we have gone in and had crusades. They can't fish or hunt. So, the buildings were usually packed to capacity for both morning and evening meetings.

I have never gone up to Alaska on a fishing trip, but I know many preachers who schedule meetings around their fishing trips instead of the other way around. They're supposed to be there to preach, but they are actually going so they can go fishing.

I have nothing against fishing, but it's very important that you know what your motive is and what brought you there. So, when people ask me to come up in the summer to preach and fish I say, "No, I'll just come some other time and fish." Am I going to preach or am I going to fish? One person told me, "We are going to do a little bit of both." Now, I'm sure you can do that, but the purpose is diluted. You need to check your heart. Are you there because there is something in it for you? Or are you there because you are giving and sowing into the lives of the people you are ministering to?

I think many ministers are either bored or lazy. Their meetings start at seven and finish at eight-thirty, and they are out of there. Many are catering to the lukewarm and to those with itching ears. They are growing a bunch of people that want everything instantly.

They are growing a bunch of people who want everything instantly. The things of God are not instant. You have to come and press into God and put your flesh under the leading of the Holy Spirit. Our meetings are not for carnal or fleshly people. They will come to the meetings, but find an excuse to leave, because their "blessed assurance" will get uncomfortable after a short time.

DISCIPLINE THE FLESH

The army of God needs to discipline its flesh. We need to train up people with spiritual stamina who can run and stay the test of time. If not, we are creating a bunch of weak believers with very short, spiritual attention spans.

I have been to some places where people are moving around all the time. They are up and down, they are distracted and restless. Sometimes, I have to say: "Sit down!"

"Well I need—"

"No, you don't. Sit down!"

"Well, I need to go to the restroom."

"You were just there!"

They don't teach you these principles in church growth seminars, but we are not here to just grow a church. Some people want to see growth for their own personal gratification and importance. I'm not interested in that. Why would anyone want a 10,000-member church if 9,800 of them were spiritually dead? What will those pastors do when they get to Heaven and realize that 9,800 of their members went to Hell? They will have to stand before God and give an account, because they produced no actual fruit.

Here's the problem. Pastors have said: "Well, my people can't handle meetings that long." It's amazing what they handle in the world. They can watch movies for hours. They can watch football or baseball for hours. But they can't sit and focus in church. People will do what's expected of them. They will do what they are trained to do. They are adults, not kindergarteners. If the Spirit of God is moving, time flies by anyway. Before Jesus, they could spend days being bombed out of their mind on drugs and alcohol. But now they want us to give them the anointing in little doses, because "we don't want to overdo it." They overdid it in sin, but now they want us to "under-do" it when it comes to righteousness.

The Lord taught us as many years ago that who you cater for is who you are going to have. If you cater to religious people, you will have religious people. If you cater to lukewarm people, you will have lukewarm people. You need to be willing to teach the Word and bring correction where it is needed. As you go out and preach you will have to deal with people's flesh. They act like little children when you try to sit them down and teach them something. They don't want to listen. They want to play. It's time we tell them that we are through playing, because there is a time for play, but now it's time for the Word of God.

It's one thing to be in a conference where we have set aside time to come and worship, receive from the Lord, and be filled with the oil of His anointing. But what about Sunday mornings? It is important for us to gather together, as the Body of Christ, on a regular basis. Going to church every Sunday morning is a good habit to be in. It is a good habit to teach your children. Some people think it is religious to attend church on Sunday mornings. Some people treat it like an ordinary day. But Paul tells us that it is important for us to watch out for each other and, *"Not forsaking or neglecting to assemble together [as believers], as is the habit of some people, but admonishing (warning, urging, and encouraging) one another, and all the more faithfully as you see the day approaching."* (Hebrews 10:25 AMPC). The fact of the matter is that we need to set aside a time that we all come together to worship God—and Sunday mornings are that time! Dedicate that time to the Lord, and let's come to worship Him.

Let's look at it this way. Suppose I took you to meet my best friend in the whole wide world and told you how wonderful he is and how much you can learn from him. I explain that he will change your life, that it will never be the same if you will listen to what he has to say. He will share his wisdom with you and impart unbelievable things to you that will totally revolutionize your life.

Then, you sit down and listen to him for a few minutes, perhaps even fifteen minutes or so, and then get up and leave. I would be really insulted, because you really didn't believe that my friend was all that I had said he was. And yet, people do that to Jesus all the time.

I love to have family and friends over for a meal and fellowship. What if I invite you to my house, have a chef prepare a special meal I think you would enjoy? He really goes all out to prepare the food and spends six hours in the kitchen getting everything ready. He doesn't just cook the food—he serves it straight from the oven to your plate. The table is decorated to perfection. We have music playing, candles burning—the place is "decked out" just for you. Then you arrive and are seated. You pick at your salad for about two minutes, jump up and declare: "I need to go."

I would be totally insulted. We had gone to such great lengths to prepare a meal for you, and you were too busy to receive what we had for you.

Do you see the spiritual connection? The Lord Jesus has prepared a table for us, and nothing of this world should be of more importance to us than His table and the invitation to sit at His feet and join Him in the eating of the heavenly bread and the drinking of the living water and the new wine. If you can't sit still and enjoy fellowshipping with Him now, what are you going to do when you get to Heaven? Will you jump up and say, "Excuse me, Lord, I need to go?"

Your flesh will always tell you there's something better somewhere else. Most people would rather eat their dessert than their vegetables, but if that's all they ate, they'd be really unhealthy. Your spirit longs for more of God, but your unrenewed mind will pull towards worldly entertainment if you allow it.

TEACH, TRAIN AND LEAD YOUR FAMILY

That's why it is so important to keep your children in church where they will hear the Word and learn to sit under the anointing. They need this anointing as much as you do.

When I was a child we sat! My mother made us sit. I hear mothers say their children won't sit. What are you talking about? We were made to sit, and if we didn't, it didn't go well for us. On several occasions, my dad walked off the platform, took my brother and me outside, gave us a spanking, and brought us back in and sat us down. So, what do you mean "they won't sit?" If they don't learn to sit now, they won't sit as adults, but train them to sit now and, as adults, they will sit and listen.

We have children in our church who are part of our congregation—they are in every service. They sit there as long as the service lasts, no matter how long it goes. Their faces shine like the sun, because they have hearts for God. We are grateful for the dads and moms who give their children that heritage. The hand of the Lord is on our children, and God will use them in a mighty way. We have some of the great men and women of the future in our church, because you can't sit under the anointing for hours and hours and remain the same. You can't go out into the world and be just a mediocre Christian; the Word of God is burned in your spirit and you will see nations shaken.

The Apostle Paul wrote to Timothy, his beloved son in the ministry, and reminded him where his faith had come from. Look at 2 Timothy 1:5 (AMPC): *"I am calling up memories of your sincere and unqualified faith (the leaning of your entire personality on God in Christ in absolute trust and confidence in His power, wisdom, and goodness), [a faith] that first lived permanently in [the heart of] your grandmother Lois and your mother Eunice and now, I am [fully] persuaded, [dwells] in you also."* Thank the Lord for godly grandmothers!

So what do Paul's words tell you? Faith flows down through the family, but the impartation must start with the head of the home, from the father and mother down to the children and grandchildren. They **must** see your commitment, your boldness, your anointing, your prayer life, your faith, your walk with God, and your talk in front of them. To be honest with you, I have the total confidence to turn our children loose under interrogation, from Kirsten, my oldest, to Kelly when she was here with us, or my son, Kenneth. You can ask them any question you would like. I wouldn't have to say: "I hope they don't say this or that. I hope they don't tell the real truth." I know that if you question our children, you will come away with much more than you expected, because they've seen the hand of God move—on the platform and behind the scenes.

Someone once sent us a video done by a ministry that was attacking me. They had taken excerpts from our ministry and put them all together on a video, totally out of context, trying to embarrass me and hurt our ministry. When our children saw it, they rolled on the floor laughing, like it was a comedy. They thought it was hilarious, because they knew the truth and they knew the ridiculousness of the accusations and the things that were being made up about our ministry.

THE FRAGRANCE OF HEAVEN

The impartation that you get depends on what and who you "hang around." If you associate with people with no anointing, that is what will rub off on you. If you hang around a stench, you will come away stinking. When you are around the fragrance of Heaven, it is going to rub off on you, so that you will smell like the Rose of Sharon—the Lily of the Valley.

In the book of Acts, we can see how the people saw Peter and John. *"Now when they saw the boldness of Peter and John, and perceived that they were unlearned and ignorant men, they marvelled; and they took knowledge of them, that they had been with Jesus"* (Acts 4:13). Whether they were learned or ignorant really had nothing to do with it, because the people could see they had been with Jesus. His fragrance had "rubbed off" on them.

When our first granddaughter, Tayla, was a toddler, we gave her plenty of hugs and kisses. One morning, after my shower and shave, I picked her up and hugged her. She hugged me and put her little face against my face before I put her down. A little later, Grandma came and picked her up. She laughed and said, "I can see you rubbed your face against Grandpa's face, because you smell like his cologne."

The thought came to me that I want to rub my face against His face and smell His cologne. When He puts me down, I want people who come around me to say, "Oh, you have been with Jesus. You have been close to His face." That's what anointing is, because the word *chrio* in Greek means "to smear or to rub." If we love to pick up our children, kiss them and hug them, then don't you think the Lord loves to pick us up, kiss us, and hug us? He wants to show us love, just as we do with our children. But, some children don't want to be picked up.

IT WAS FOR YOU AND ME

It was not an easy road to Calvary. There was nothing comfortable about God's impartation to us. John 3:16 says, *"For God so loved the world, that he gave his only begotten Son, that whosoever believeth in him should not perish, but have everlasting life."* God loved the world so much He gave His only begotten son. He imparted the best that He had—for us.

When Adonica and I, along with Eric and Jennifer Gonyon, saw the movie *The Passion of the Christ* at a pre-screening in Atlanta, we began to weep in the opening scenes in the Garden of Gethsemane. The anguish of the prayer Jesus prayed was heart-rending. Then we saw the disciples sleeping…because they were not going to drink the cup that He was about to drink.

It was so realistic, watching as Judas betrayed Him, and then went out and hanged himself. My heart broke for Judas, because he was one of the twelve, and yet he had betrayed Jesus for only thirty pieces of silver. Jesus was arrested because of him, but, of course, no one would have been able to touch or harm Jesus unless He had laid His life down first. It was all in God's plan. I wept again when Peter denied Him over and over, because I could see in myself all the times I had failed Him.

The movie was rated "R" because of the beating Jesus endured, and even so, Mel Gibson had to play the scene down, because the real beating was so terrible. There were chunks of flesh flying off of His body, and so much so, that in the film the Roman soldiers had pieces of His flesh on their faces. The film portrayed the beating so intensely, going on and on for so long, that some people had to run out to the restrooms to throw up. They attributed it to the intense violence of the beating, but some of it was probably because demons were manifesting in people who couldn't handle what really took place.

The sobbing of the people in the audience was overwhelming. As we sat in that movie theater, they cried and wept for two hours. It was the most graphic beating I have ever seen on film. It was painful to watch as they placed the crown of thorns on His head, shocking as they hammered the nails into His hands and His feet and then pierced His side. As He hung there on that Cross, there came the overwhelming reminder that He had given His all—poured it out for our sins.

As the movie ended, I shouted out loud in the theatre: "It was for me." All I could think of was that it was my sin that drove the nails in His hands and His feet. It was my sin that tore open His back. My sin put the crown of thorns on His head. He had carried the cross for me. And for me, He bled and died.

If He did all that for me, there is nothing I could ever have to endure on this earth, be it persecution or even death, which I would not willingly give for the cause of the Gospel of the Lord Jesus Christ. I am prophesying right now that there's about to come a whole new wave of martyrs in the end-time church. It happened in the early church and it will be the same in the latter church. The Lord told me that this joy in the anointing will be the voice of the end-time martyrs.

RISE UP IN BOLDNESS

What we must understand today is the rising tide of Islam in the world. It is rising at an alarming rate. They are pumping billions of dollars into funding their message—a message of martyrdom and death. They will stop at nothing to achieve their goal. Right now, they are working on taking over the United Kingdom, Europe, Scandinavia, and Africa. They have set their sights on taking over every western nation and even our nation of the United States of America.

It's time for the Church to rise up in boldness and move aggressively in evangelism, even if it costs us our lives for the sake of the Gospel. They are taking our children—children from all over the world to promote their cause. They are being trained in the ways of Islam—barbaric acts of terrorism and death. We, the Church, must wake up and stop playing games—or this country as we know it, along with our freedom, will be lost.

The day is coming when we will be arrested and thrown into prison for preaching the Gospel. Already we can see it moving in that direction. They pass ungodly laws like abortion and homosexual marriage and penalize the Church when we won't put our money into it or participate in it. We see, even today, people turning on each other because they are not ready for the changes, and what is happening in the world. They are either totally unaware of what's coming, or they are in denial. Saddest of all, the Church in America is not ready for what's ahead—even though God has warned us in His Word, and we should be able to see the signs of the end-times. We need a move of God and a revival in our land. Money is not the answer to your search for security. They will take your home, freeze your accounts, and your money will be gone. You need to make Jesus Christ the Lord of your life and be ready for what is ahead.

Jesus spent seventy percent of His life and ministry healing the sick and casting out devils. That tells me if He spent that much time doing something, then we should pay attention to it. We must set the captives free. The impartation is not just by the laying on of hands, but by the word of your mouth, and impartation by association.

IMPARTATION BY ASSOCIATION

As I travel around the world holding meetings I meet many pastors. Usually, when you meet their associate pastors they are very similar to the pastor. They walk like him, their methods are like his, and they even think like him. Why? Because it rubs off on them. If the pastor loves souls and the harvest, his people will also love souls and the harvest. If the pastor loves to give, his people will love to give. The same is true concerning the Word. People will learn to love the Word if they have a pastor who teaches the Word constantly and imparts his love of the Word to them.

Over the years, because of the nature of our ministry and the Lord's instruction to give away what I have been given, I've endeavored to lay hands on as many people as I could. For a long time, we kept a count of all the people I had prayed for, but finally had to stop. In the meetings I counted, we had a cumulative attendance of about 1.2 million people, and laid hands on about 400,000 people. I think the most people I ever laid hands on in one service was about 9,000 people, which took about five hours. Someone was following me with a clicker, tracking the number of people as I laid hands on them. I was so drunk in the Spirit afterwards I couldn't even function. I had to drink a big pot of coffee and eat a whole plate of jalapeño poppers, trying to sober up for the night service. I was trying to bring myself back into the natural, because I wanted to be able to preach. I was so far gone that I couldn't speak in English; only tongues were coming out of my mouth. I thought, *I can't get up there and just talk in tongues tonight.* Thankfully, I managed to pull myself together to minister.

In the days when I preached two meetings a day, six days a week, and forty-six weeks of the year, I nearly killed myself, physically. I had been doing that year after year. While I was under the anointing, I felt energized. Outside of the meetings, I felt how tired I actually was. There were times when Adonica woke up in the morning and was still tired, but I was always refreshed. We finally realized that I was drawing strength from her. She told me that she could feel me pulling strength from her as I held her at night. We need each other. We draw strength from each other.

I am so glad that we made the choice to travel with our children. It was refreshing for me to be able to just hug our children when I came in from the meetings. Even after laying hands on thousands of people, I could hug our children and feel recharged.

That's why the Lord tells us to assemble ourselves together, because we draw strength from one another. That's what impartation is. We need each other. We need people of faith. We need to surround ourselves with people of faith and draw strength from one another. Just a touch, a smiling face, a hug, a pat on the back, or an encouraging word will bring strength so you can make it through the day. It's all impartation. The anointing can be released as you speak the words of the Lord.

IMPARTATION BY THE WORD

As I mentioned earlier, when T.L. Osborne was at our church, he said something that hit me like a sledge hammer. Here was a man eighty years of age at the time, who had gone to the nations of the world, and is still considered the father of mass crusade evangelism. He said, "I knew that wherever my voice went, if they could hear me speak they would never be the same." The Lord had released His anointing on T.L. so that he did not have to lay hands on everyone, because it is impossible to lay hands on 200,000 people in a meeting. You can't even step off the platform, because you could be crushed by the crowd as they rushed forward for prayer.

I remember then how the Lord had started me in ministry by the laying on of hands and impartation. I thought, *that's amazing, because I've always said the same thing.* I knew if I could, first of all, put the Word in them, get them under the anointing, then lay my hands on them, they would never be the same again. Even if hands are not laid on you, you can receive from the anointing in the presence of God. Isn't it amazing how the Lord has many ways of imparting to His people? Then I thought back to my growing up years in Southern Africa, where we didn't have the privilege of sitting under so many ministers and having them touch you and lay hands on you. I used to sit, as a little boy, and listen to reel-to-reel tapes, or long-playing records, and when I closed my eyes it was as if I had stepped inside a great tent crusade and received by impartation.

I learned how to receive from a cassette tape even better than in a live service, because there were no distractions. If there was any anointing on the tape, I was like a vacuum cleaner, sucking the anointing right off the tape. There are still certain tapes dating years back that I can listen to for three minutes and I'll be gone under the anointing. We are so privileged to live in this hour when we can capture the anointing on CDs and on DVDs, or smartphones, and take it home with us.

We have had pastors come to our meetings and buy every recorded message we had for sale. They'd go home, lock themselves in a room for days, and listen to one after another. One Baptist pastor, now full of the Holy Ghost, said he was just saturated and "smeared" with the truth. We need to be smeared with the truth so it will rub off on others we rub shoulders with.

But be sure what you are imparting to others is uplifting, not full of fear and doubt. Don't let fearful people pull you down. Lift them up to your level. That means imparting the things of God to them, lifting them higher.

Let me repeat what I asked earlier: "Do you want more of the anointing?" Then give away what you've got through impartation to others. The more you give away, the more comes back to you in greater measure.

10

THE MINISTRY OF LAYING ON OF HANDS

Imparting Blessings and Life to Others

In the last chapter, we talked about impartation, and now I want to go a little further along those lines. The Word commands us to lay hands on people for healing and to receive the Holy Spirit. Jesus laid hands on people. The disciples laid hands on certain people to impart the gifts of the Spirit and to anoint them for a specific ministry calling.

Even though believers are commissioned to lay hands on people, you don't want just anyone laying hands on you. The Bible tells us that we must know those who labor among us (*See* 1 Thessalonians 5:12), so you need to know that the person ministering to you is doing it under the anointing, and not in the flesh, or in some other kind of spirit. If a person is filled with the Holy Spirit and ministering from a pure heart, they will impart the Spirit of God to others. If a person has an unclean spirit on themselves, they will impart that spirit upon others. When you follow Bible principles, you get Bible results. Look with me in Acts 3:1–10 for an example of Biblical principles:

> Now Peter and John went up together into the temple at the hour of prayer, being the ninth hour. And a certain man lame from his mother's womb was carried, whom they laid daily at the gate of the temple which is called Beautiful, to ask alms of them that entered into the temple; Who seeing Peter and John about to go into the temple asked an alms. And Peter, fastening his eyes upon him with John, said, Look on us. And he gave heed unto them, expecting to receive something of them. Then Peter said, Silver and gold have I none; but such as I have give I thee: In the name of Jesus Christ of Nazareth rise up and walk. And he took him by the right hand, and lifted him up: and immediately his feet and ankle bones received strength. And he leaping up stood, and walked, and entered with them into the temple, walking, and leaping, and praising God. And all the people saw him walking and praising God: And they knew that it was he which sat for alms at the Beautiful gate of the temple: and they were filled with wonder and amazement at that which had happened unto him.

People often ask why we make an announcement in our meetings: "Please don't lay hands on anyone unless you are asked to do so." First of all, when the revival broke out in April of 1989, the Lord spoke to me about certain things concerning the anointing and the transference of the anointing in the context of the meetings. He said that some things would be acceptable, and some things would *not* be acceptable. I believe that it is my responsibility to protect the people who are coming to our meetings—hungry for the things of God—from someone else coming in and interfering.

So, I began to preach on the laying on of hands. You know, if Peter and John made a habit of going by lame people, commanding them to rise and walk, but nobody walked, after a while nobody would even pay attention. If they said, "Look on us," nobody would even look at them. When people come for the laying on of hands and don't get anything time after time, why would they waste their time going back?

It's not a game. If it was just about falling down, we could just walk in and say, "One, two, three, we all fall down," and we could go home. This is not spiritual "tenpin bowling." The purpose of the laying on of hands is to get people under the anointing, but there must *be* an anointing there to get them under. Otherwise, you're laying empty hands on empty heads. The hands of the preacher are empty and the heads of the people coming for prayer are empty.

THE TRANSFERENCE OF THE ANOINTING

There is a tangibility to the anointing. The anointing is tangible; the anointing is transferrable. Now, you can lay hands on someone in faith; there's nothing wrong with that. The Bible says to lay hands on the sick and they shall recover. There's nothing wrong with just doing what the Word says to do. But there is that which is known as the *ministry* of laying on of hands. There is an actual transference that takes place, and the person who is laying hands on others must know what they're doing. They must not treat it flippantly but must reverence and respect the Holy Spirit.

Sometimes, we have laid hands on people and they were out on the floor under the anointing, being mightily touched, and others came, uninvited, and laid hands on them. I'm not sure if they wanted to take the credit for their touch or if they were just full of unbelief. It was as if nothing could happen unless *they* did the praying. Or perhaps they have a controlling spirit. They can't trust the Holy Spirit to do His work, unaided.

When God is working on someone, leave them alone! If they are crying, don't try to comfort them. Let the Lord do what He needs to do in them, especially if it's your child or spouse!

I have been in meetings where people in the audience began to interfere by touching other people—playing around. Touch. Touch. Touch. That grieves the Holy Ghost. They think they are being funny, or think they are flowing in the anointing, but they are only playing. They are not serious about the anointing. Many places where the anointing once flowed are now like muddy swamps. They wonder why God stopped moving. God never stops moving, but He will not anoint the flesh. The anointing is a holy thing. Salvation is free, but the anointing is not. There is a price to pay to walk in the anointing.

I have heard it said that anybody can lay hands on people. Yes, that's true, but unless the person carries the anointing of God, you will either get nothing, or you might get something you don't want. We don't allow people we don't know to lay hands on anyone, because we don't always know where those hands have been. You can't allow just anyone who wants to lay hands on people to do it. You have no way to know who will be showing up.

I remember when the revival hit Central Florida. We were in a huge auditorium in Lakeland when the ushers called me to say there were people on the floor out under the power. Some witches had come into the meeting and were laying hands on kids. We had to gather up all those kids and lay hands on them to get them free. The witches had come to put devils on the kids. I made a rule right then that nobody was to lay hands on anyone unless they were authorized to do so. I had to do that for the protection of the people so they could feel safe. No one wants to go to a meeting and get a devil.

While we were still in South Africa in the 1980s, our pastor invited an American minister to preach at the church. He brought a few people with him. One of the men he brought laid hands on people during the course of the meetings and, unfortunately, they immediately began to have demonic manifestations. We had to do two things: forbid him to pray for anyone else and get all those Christians delivered.

These things ought not to be. I don't know where this man came from, but he was definitely not operating under the anointing. You cannot allow a person like that to pray for anyone.

Over the years, I have seen all forms of abuse concerning laying on of hands. One preacher was so "touched" by revival he began giving mouth to mouth resuscitation to another preacher. He said it was prophetic.

No, it wasn't, it was pathetic. I have also seen people come to a meeting in flippers and snorkels, wearing frog suits, because they are "getting in the river." The stories go on and on. One church even painted what looked like an underwater sea around the church, so when people came they could see they were underwater in the river. I think their favorite chorus was, "Under the sea, under the sea."

THE REAL VERSUS THE FAKE

And then people wonder why the anointing of God is not made manifest. When the anointing is not there, people will look for everything else to try to replace it. But why settle for the fake when you can have the real?

You run a big risk when you try to conjure something up and say that it's the anointing. Every time you do that it's going to be more ludicrous than it was the last time. "Last night an angel appeared above the baptismal font." "Tonight the baptismal font split in two." "People were floating above the pews." What's next? Meanwhile, nobody gets saved, and nobody gets healed or delivered. There's just all this spiritual "mumbo jumbo" going on.

This type of thing has always been around. So, why do I make mention of it? Because we need to teach the Word of God. We hold our meetings around the world to get the Word of God out, so that those who grab hold of it with a pure heart can run with revival and the move of God, and still be running with it ten, twenty or even fifty years from now. If Jesus tarries, you'll still be running with the anointing of God when He comes. You won't be running with a counterfeit, and you won't be running with the flesh.

Sometimes you think people want to come out with some new thing, so they can be the pioneer of it. "I'm the pioneer of the new move of the frog suit people." You think I'm making this up? Brother Kenneth Hagin, author of the book *The Laying On of Hands*, tells a story of a woman who came to one of his meetings. She sat in the service and rocked the whole time. She just rocked backwards and forwards. He didn't know what was wrong with her, so he sent an usher over to check on her. She told the usher she had gone to a meeting where a prophet laid hands on her and prophesied that she had the gift of rocking, and anytime the anointing was present she would rock. Brother Hagin said, "I must have really been anointed, because she rocked all evening."

He had also heard of one man who had hands laid on him by a person who prophesied that he had the gift of casting permanent waves out of people's hair. If he had gotten the gift of putting them in, he would have had it made!

The move of God has taken on many forms, but when the flesh takes over then the glory of God will not be present. Remember the story of the golden calf that came forth when Moses was on the mountain with God? (*See* Exodus 32.) The people grew impatient, while waiting for Moses to return from the mountain with the Word of God, and they turned the gold that God had given them into a calf to worship. When people want to worship what they can see and feel rather than the God they cannot see, they end up with a golden calf. People wonder why the anointing of God lifts. It is because He is not going to anoint the flesh. He won't anoint carnality.

HUNGER AND THIRST

One of the things the Lord told me to do early in my ministry was to pray for the fire of God to fall first. Then call out only those I could see the anointing had fallen on. I didn't always lay hands on the rest of them. When they got hungry enough, you could see the fire fall on them. Too often, we just stand there and wait for something to happen, when what we should do is pray for them to get hungry. The number one ingredient for receiving the anointing is to be hungry. You must cultivate that hunger, and constantly stay hungry. The moment you feel like you have "arrived" and you have it all is when God can't touch you anymore. The second requirement is that you must be thirsty. Being thirsty for the anointing is just as important as being hungry. Those two ingredients—hunger and thirst—are crucial. When you are so hungry and thirsty you can't stand it, the anointing will flow every time.

You may have been touched by the anointing in days gone by, but now you are beginning to get hungry again. Start developing that hunger by making a decision to open up your heart. Say it out loud: "I am getting hungry and I am going to get really hungry, so I can grab hold of what the Lord has for me." Do you realize you could get so hungry for God that this could be the day when God touches you like He has never touched you before? You need to press into God, believing that He is faithful and will show up and meet you where you are as you diligently seek Him. The writer of Hebrews says: *"But without faith it is impossible to please him: for he that cometh to God must believe that he is, and that he is a rewarder of them that diligently seek him"* (Hebrews 11:6).

IT'S NOT A FREE FOR ALL

As time went on, we began holding more revivals and extended meetings. I would have different people lay hands on the folk who came for a touch from God—when you see the anointing on people you can turn them loose to lay hands on others. But, at times, we would be in churches that had prayer *teams*. Now, I don't have a problem with prayer teams. But I do have a problem with un-anointed people laying their hands on people in our meetings. Some of them would pray for the people, go out and light up a cigarette, then come right back in and lay hands on people.

That's not what this is all about. When you allow people to pray and lay hands on others in your meeting, you want hands that are set apart for God. We do turn certain people loose to preach and minister, but we usually know who they are and where they've been.

Along the way, some people were offended because we didn't allow just anyone to lay hands on people. The problem is that many well-known revivals from the past were neutralized and stopped because of that very thing. It became a free for all and the Holy Spirit was elbowed out.

God always uses a man or woman to lead as the Spirit leads them. It's not a democracy. We don't lead from the pew. There are no "backseat drivers" in the Kingdom of God. Sure, God can raise up a nobody and make them a somebody, but they have to earn the right to stand in the pulpit and to lead God's people. Every believer is an ambassador for Christ and can and should share the Gospel and lead people to Jesus, but not everybody is called to a pulpit ministry.

If you have the faith, you can lay hands on people and see them healed and delivered. But, in the context of a meeting, no one should do anything uninvited.

Some people think this is legalistic, but it isn't. As I've said before: "Go ahead and do it your way and see how long it lasts." The Holy Ghost is "out of there" when good things are being abused. He withdraws, because He can't be a part of it.

BEING A GIVER NOT A TAKER

And, you shouldn't lay hands on people for financial gain.

We had a special meeting at The River and someone called the office and said: "I'll give a large sum of money to the church if I can have a front row seat." We sent word back to tell them to sit at the back. We don't sell seats.

I was asked to fly to another city and, for a large sum of money, to pray for a millionaire. I refused out of principle. If they'd just asked me to come, I might have done it, but when you put money into the equation, you pollute the water. We cannot do anything for a money motive. God will meet your needs, but don't minister for the money. Do it for the love of God and people!

The laying on of hands is also not to display your spirituality or how anointed you are. The laying on of hands is *to minister to others*. The laying on of hands is to impart life and to bless people. You know, the world will also lay hands on you—it also might minister with the "five-fold" ministry (of fists). But the laying on of the world's hands is not to impart blessing. It's to knock your lights out.

THE MINISTRY OF LAYING ON OF HANDS

Our ministry is to impart blessing and bring the Light in. We see in the Word of God that Jesus laid hands on people. Look with me at Matthew 19:

> Then were there brought unto him little children, that he should put his hands on them, and pray: and the disciples rebuked them. But Jesus said, Suffer little children, and forbid them not, to come unto me: for of such is the kingdom of Heaven. And he laid his hands on them, and departed thence.
>
> MATTHEW 19:13-15

The Bible says that He laid His hands on them and blessed them. So, we know the laying on of hands is to bestow and impart blessings. Jesus blessed them. He laid hands on them. Jesus spent many hours and days praying in private, but when He ministered to people, He didn't do it with long prayers. He laid hands on them and they were healed. He commanded sickness and demons to leave and they left. He spoke the Word and they were healed. He commanded them to be raised from the dead and they were. He touched them, and they touched Him. When the anointing is on you, the laying on of hands is so powerful for impartation and blessing that you don't necessarily even need to say a word.

Now, there would be no time to pray for everyone you need to pray for if they all want you to say a long prayer. I was in a meeting one time, praying for a number of people one by one, when I went by a lady and said: "Now! Filled!"

She grabbed my hand and said: "Come back here and pray some more." She was not happy. She thought I should have stayed longer and prayed more words over her, because she didn't understand about impartation, and she didn't understand about receiving. The length of time or the number of words prayed have nothing to do with the power of a prayer.

I will never forget when we were in Auckland, New Zealand, with about 3,000 people in the auditorium on the show grounds. We had a special laying on of hands service and I was going down the line praying for the people. I had to pray for three thousand people, so I was just passing by them saying: "Filled! Filled! Now! Filled! Fire!" A pastor brought his wife in a wheelchair. This lady was paralyzed and needed prayer for her healing.

I went by, laid hands on her and said, "Filled!" She got so mad because I didn't stop to pray a long prayer over her that she started cussing! A pastor's wife! She was cussing so hard it would have made a sailor blush. Her poor husband was so embarrassed that he must have thought: "I had better get her out of here before she causes a bigger scene." So, off he went outside, pushing his paralyzed wife in her wheelchair, and loaded her into the car.

He put her in the passenger seat and she was still fuming and cussing. She had come there expecting some long, special prayer, and all I did was lay hands on her, say, "Filled," and went on to the next person. She was still angry, and it was getting hot in the car (they don't have air conditioners in the buildings or cars in some of the milder climates), so she reached out and began to roll the window down. It was only then that she realized: "I can't do that. I'm paralyzed."

God had healed that preacher's cussing wife. Her total miracle was not instantaneous, but every day she got better and better until she came right out of that wheelchair—totally healed!

Now the Lord uses her in a wonderful way and she's totally fine—no trace of any paralysis. But initially she was furious because she thought the Lord hadn't touched her, because all I said was, "Filled!" I didn't come to pray this long prayer, or whatever it was that she was expecting, yet God still gave her a miracle.

We've already seen that the laying on of hands is a point of contact for you to release your faith. But faith must be released on both sides—on the side of the person coming to receive and on the side of the person praying and releasing their faith for the miracle. When the two come together, there's a powerful connection that takes place.

Some think that because the tangible healing didn't happen

instantaneously, they think nothing happened at all. I'm reminded of another incident that took place in a meeting in Louisville, Kentucky in February 1991.

We were in an extended meeting, and a man walked in and sat down with his wife at the back of the church. They were in every one of the services, and there were seats up front, but he always chose the back row. He sat down there watching all the services, and just stared ahead. It didn't seem like he was against what was going on, but it didn't seem like he was for it, either.

This went on for days. My curiosity began to grow concerning who this man was, and what his problem was. But, I didn't interfere with him; I felt led to just leave him alone. Then on Thursday night, the Spirit of the Lord fell and God spoke to me "Lay hands on people, because there's a special anointing here tonight."

So, I called people out and began to lay hands on them. As I walked down the row, the power of God began to hit people. I went all the way down the line and when I got to this man to lay my hands on him, he just stood there. He did not even close his eyes; he just looked at me. As I put my hands on him I thought, *Oh, Lord.* I thought nothing was happening to him, and he probably thought: "Nothing is happening to me." I kept my hands there as long as I could, because if the Lord leads me to pray for you I'm going to lay my hands on you, and keep them on you, until I'm conscious of the anointing going into you.

Then I felt it. There was a divine flow going right into him. The anointing was flowing out of me into him.

Outwardly, it looked like nothing had happened, but when I arrived at the church Friday morning, I could tell something *had* happened. The man's face was shining, his eyes were bright, and as I looked at him, I said: "Wow, something has happened to this guy." He was now on the front row.

I thought: *"Anything that moves a guy from the back row to the front row, I want to hear about."* So, I went straight to him and asked him to tell me what had happened to him. He said: "Man, let me tell you my story. I'm a preacher that was ready to quit the ministry. I heard about these revival meetings, so I came just to check them out. I'm not against what God's doing. I believe in it. But I have been so hurt in the ministry—so abused—that I just sat here wanting the Lord to touch me. But, I didn't even know how to get touched. When you came and laid hands on me, I didn't feel anything in particular." I told him I didn't think he had.

He continued on: "But something had happened. I got home last night, and I went to bed, and then, at three o'clock this morning, the whole bed began to shake violently. I woke my wife up and told her to stop shaking the bed.

"'I'm not shaking the bed,' she said. 'You are.'

"And she was right. I looked down at my hands and my legs. My whole body was shaking uncontrollably. My wife even told me I would have to go to the other room if I was going to keep shaking, because she had to go to work the next morning.

"So, I got up and went to the other room, and the Lord shook me throughout the night until early morning. I never slept at all. I just shook under the power of God." He continued. "I'll tell you right now, I was on the brink of quitting the ministry, but now I'm going back. The Lord has set me free; He's touched me...and delivered me."

THE ANOINTING IS MORE THAN A FEELING

You see, people make a mistake when they come in the line to receive an anointing and leave disappointed because they didn't feel what they thought they needed to feel or what they heard somebody else felt. They didn't see stars, do backward somersaults, or fly through the air, so they think they didn't get anything. You have to understand that even if you only left hungrier for God than you were before, you *did* get something! As long as your heart is open to God, whether you felt something or not, you will receive. It may take sitting under the anointing a little longer, pressing in a little deeper, but the Lord will do His work in you. We don't always see immediate results, but in the days to come we will see the evidence of God's touch in and on our lives. Don't dig up the seeds that were sown through doubt and unbelief. Trust God that whatever He begins in you, He will bring to completion.

It is often true, too, that whether they are in one meeting or many, people do not realize exactly how much the Lord has actually done in them. Perhaps several weeks go by and they find themselves in a situation where they need the Lord's help. Suddenly, the Lord gives them wisdom and strength, and He empowers them to come through it. They realize then that more was accomplished in them than they realized.

I believe that's because some people don't realize that the anointing was put on them for a purpose. There are different manifestations of the anointing. So, they think they didn't get anything, because it wasn't like what somebody else got.

I've had ministers get in the line and hands were laid on them, but they went away seemingly the same way they came. Then they would call me back a week later. "You're not going to believe this, but I went to my church on Sunday morning and while I was preaching I raised my hands, and the whole place fell out under the power of God. Wow! I think something's happened to me." They didn't realize what God had done in them through the laying on of hands until they began to minister and the Spirit of God flowed through them to touch others.

EXPECT GOD TO MOVE

When you receive that anointing, you are to lay hands on those that you minister to. Expect God to move on your behalf. Lay hands on them in the services, lay hands upon them when you meet them in the house. Lay hands upon them in the restaurant. Just put your hands on them, in faith and expectation, allowing the anointing to flow through you, and the Lord will confirm His Word. The extraordinary things He will do in and through your hands will shock and astound you.

The Body of Christ needs to bring back the emphasis on the laying on of hands. The treasure we have in our earthen vessels must be released by the Word. Speak the Word and lay hands on them, touch them with the touch of faith.

The ANOINTING

My wife and I were married in October of 1981, and immediately started traveling and preaching wherever the Lord opened the door. Then in December of 1982, we were invited to minister in this little town on the Northeast Cape of Southern Africa. It was not a church—they didn't have a Holy Ghost church in that town—it was a home fellowship. They would meet in the living room of a farm house. The dates were set for May of 1983. They had been preparing for us to come for several months.

We arrived at the little farm house and there were eleven people there waiting on us. We had conducted a very good meeting in Cape Town, where hundreds of people were coming, and the power of God was touching them. We had driven many hours all the way to this farm house to only eleven people, so I felt let down. They had months to prepare for this meeting and the best they could do was eleven people. Jesus help us, I thought. They could at least have brought in a few cows to add to the crowd.

I had just preached twenty-three powerful meetings in twenty-one days, and so I preached that night as if there was another big, hungry crowd. I remember, I was preaching on the integrity of the Word of God. I thought to myself: *Well, nothing's going to happen here tonight with just these eleven people in this farm house.* What a mistake! I gave an altar call and two people came up: a brother and a sister. So, I stepped around this little wooden thing they had as a podium and just missed my guitar, which was leaning against the wall. As I raised my hand, the power of God smacked that brother in the head so hard it looked like a baseball bat had hit him. They both went flying through the air, clear across the whole room. It felt like the air had been sucked out of the room. The people were saying: "Uhhhh!" But I was more surprised than they were, because I never felt a thing.

The next night, thirty people showed up. The third night, sixty people jammed the farm house, and we had revival. It caused quite a stir in the town. They wanted to run us out of town. The preacher at the leading (religious) church in town, the Dutch Reformed church, was so totally bent out of shape that he denounced us right from the pulpit, from then through the next few years, because he was so offended at the power of God and so afraid his people would come on over and be forever changed.

It was a small town in the middle of a farming community and only had about 910 residents in the town itself. Everyone there knew each other. It was a "one-horse town," and that one horse had died a long time before. There was one traffic light and if you drove through town and blinked your eyes you would already be on the other side.

The Lord spoke to us to start a church in this town, and we held our first official service there in June, in the town hall. The first Sunday, which was my 22nd birthday, 186 people showed up for the first morning service. Many of them were curious townspeople.

About four months after we started the church, I received a call from someone who said that a family member had had a car wreck. So, I went over to the hospital and, when I walked in, I saw the man lying there. He had injured his back, so he couldn't move. He had a brace on his neck and was in excruciating pain. As I laid my hands on him, I felt the divine flow. I asked him what had happened, and he said: "The pain is gone."

"Well, what are you going to do about it?" I asked. He took the neck brace off and jumped out of bed.

After that, there were other people in the ward who asked if I would pray for them. I prayed, and we emptied three wards in the hospital that night. I went back to the church for the evening service, and a man came to church in his pajamas and sat on the front row. Straight out of the hospital and still in his pajamas! These signs shall follow them that believe. (*See* Mark 16:17.)

Remember the passage of scripture we read about Peter and John going up to the temple at the hour of prayer where they saw a lame man? He looked at them, begging for help and expecting to receive something. *"Then Peter said: 'Silver and gold have I none; but such as I have give I thee: In the name of Jesus Christ of Nazareth rise up and walk'"* (Acts 3:6).

Such as I have...such as I have. God is looking for preachers with boldness, who will go forth and give "such as I have." What do you have? *This treasure in earthen vessels.* It's worth more than all the treasures of the earth! Your job is not to store it up, with a padlock to protect it. Your job is to open up the treasure and give it out to a lost and dying world. Put your hands on them. Believe the Word of God and let the impartation flow.

11

THE PRICE OF THE ANOINTING

It May Cost You Everything

I was born-again when I was five years old, and one night, when I was thirteen years of age, I had a dream that is as clear today as it was that night. In my dream I saw Jesus, and I saw the Cross. Off to one side of the Cross there was a road going up, and I could see the lights of Heaven. I saw people on the road, making their way up to the lights. But on the other side of the cross was a mass of humanity, on a wide road, laden down with sin. It seemed as if they were smiling and unconcerned, even while carrying heavy loads on their backs. Each of them was merely following the one in front of them. It seemed that they were oblivious to what was ahead of them on the road—a large cliff. As the crowd continued to follow and walk on, I watched as they went off the cliff, one after another, into huge flames that were coming up from below.

The dream was so vivid, and it so moved me, that I began to weep uncontrollably. As I looked up at Jesus, I saw that He was just standing there. I looked at Him and asked: "What are you going to do about these people?" He did something I will never forget. He smiled at me. I wondered how He could smile at a time like this. I didn't know at the time I was being set up.

The Lord looked at me with so much love. I could see He was totally peaceful, not concerned about anything. He answered my question: "I have done everything I'm going to do about these people. I went to the Cross."

"But who is going to tell them what you did?" I asked.

"You must tell them. You must tell them."

I remember weeping as I told Him: "Lord, I will tell them. I will tell them!" I cried so hard that when I woke up my pillow was soaking wet. I had what I now call a "New Birth experience" that night. When I got out of bed that morning everything seemed new. The sky was bluer, the grass was greener—I was seeing the world through new eyes.

THE LORD'S KEEPING POWER

You know, when you get saved at the age of five, you don't really know what it's like to be lost. Sitting in church for as long as I could remember, I had heard testimonies in church from people who had spent years in the penitentiary for murdering people or robbing banks, and the end of the story was always: "And then I got saved."

Everybody loves to hear that, sitting on the edge of their chair, listening to every word. I remember sitting there as a little boy, thinking that I knew God had called me into the ministry, but what testimony was I going to tell? I had hit my brother over the head. One time I stole a cookie. And I had kicked the dog once or twice. I didn't have a dramatic testimony. I thought that maybe I'd need to go into the world and do some crazy stuff, then come back to the Lord so I had a testimony to tell.

After the dream, I told the Lord I would tell the world, but I didn't have a testimony to tell. He told me: "Yes, you do have a testimony. You have a testimony of My saving grace and My keeping power. I am not only able to save you, but I'm able to keep you." The dream was so overwhelming and so fresh in my mind that I went on a quest, and in the next three months I led more than thirty of my friends to the Lord. And I have never looked back!

GOOD NEWS NEW YORK

Now let's fast-forward to February of 1998. We were staying in a Holiday Inn in Ozark, Alabama. After dinner, we went to bed for the night and I had another dream. In the dream I was standing in New York City. I looked up and standing alongside me was Billy Graham. (Billy Graham held a crusade in New York City, at Madison Square Garden, back in 1957, where 57,000 people had been saved.) I knew the circumstances because I had watched his films.

The Lord will sometimes speak to people in dreams. It happened to Joseph, the husband of Mary—an angel warned him in a dream to escape from Herod to Egypt with Mary and Jesus. The wise men were also warned in a dream to go home via another way to avoid King Herod. God will, at times, speak in an audible voice. He may send an angel to you to convey His message to you, and He also speaks in dreams. More often, He speaks to me—and you—through His Word, and through the inward witness.

The Lord has not often spoken to me through powerful, spiritual dreams like this one, so I know I should pay attention when He does. In the dream, as Billy Graham was talking about the crusade in 1957, I started weeping uncontrollably. My whole body was shaking so hard I thought I was going to die. I knew that it was real, because when I woke up in the morning my pillow was again soaking wet with my tears. My thoughts immediately went back to when I was thirteen and what I had promised the Lord in my dream. I told Him that I would go and tell the people—I would tell them what Jesus did on the cross.

The moment my feet touched the floor I heard this in my heart: "Go to New York City and launch one of the biggest soul-winning crusades since the fifties."

In the natural, this was not feasible. It would take a massive amount of money and resources to do—more than we had available, anyway. So, I argued with the Lord. I said: "Lord, who am I? I don't have a big organization, or a big television ministry, or thousands of partners."

Some people think our ministry was larger than what it was. At that time, we were not on radio and television. There were many organizations that were much larger than us. To be able to do something like that requires hundreds of staff members and a huge amount of financial support.

As ministries go, we were relatively small, with few staff members, even though the Lord had used us to go around the world. The impact has been great but let me add this: our impact has always had less to do with us and more to do with Him. We came as missionaries from Africa in December of 1987 with three children and $300 cash in our pocket. God has done it all. All we did was obey Him and go when and where He directed.

But I was still sure there were other people who were better qualified and equipped to go to New York City. Finally, I reminded the Lord there was a stigma attached to me—the ministry of joy He gave us.

THE JOY OF THE LORD

When the revival broke out in 1989 and the joy first started happening in the service, I thought everybody would love it. I expected everybody to want joy in their lives. I really did not think we would have so many problems over joy. Remember, Nehemiah 8:10 tells us that the joy of the Lord is your strength. After all, I would think you would get into trouble if you went around and everywhere you ministered, people got depressed. (I can tell you honestly, before the Lord, I never for one moment considered that joy would be so controversial.)

When we started our ministry, we preached the Word, went after the harvest of souls, and then we prayed for the sick. Through the years, there has been controversy surrounding some high-profile healing ministries and people who came under attack because of it. Not necessarily because they did anything wrong, but because the devil always finds someone to stir up opposition to the supernatural ministry of the Holy Spirit. I was thankful that we had not been attacked in that way, and I would have preferred not to be.

That's when the Lord added joy to the meetings, and I was attacked worse than any of the healing ministers. I wondered at the time if I should have just stayed with a healing ministry! Seriously though, the joy is not something we do. It is something HE does.

The Lord told me: "You don't make them laugh. I do. And if you are ashamed of this ministry, I can take it away and give it to someone else!"

I realized then that people wouldn't understand and people would probably criticize, but I was not going to disobey God, nor pull back just because of some pressure from the enemy or because of the opinions of man. Joy is the fruit of the Spirit, not of the flesh. The fruit of the joy in the meetings—in people's lives—is people saved, healed, delivered, bondages broken, marriages and relationships restored, addictions broken, people set on fire and called to serve God, people called to ministry, and every possible need met. You'd think everyone would be thrilled about the joy!

As you may recall, when we came to America in 1987, the Church was in an upheaval. Ministries had fallen, people were depressed at the state of moral decline in the Church, and the saddest place to be on a Sunday morning was in church. There was such apathy, it was hard to have an extended meeting anywhere.

I talked to the pastor of the church where I was going to hold a meeting, and he told me that I could have services on Sunday morning and Sunday night, and on Tuesday and Wednesday nights. He said that we couldn't hold a meeting on Monday night because no one would come. I didn't know at the time, having come from Africa, that pastors did not want us to have meetings on Monday night because of Monday

Night Football. I didn't know anything about that, because we didn't play or watch American football in Africa.

Week after week, we went from church to church ministering the Word, but I began to think I must have gone wrong somewhere, because just about every Sunday it was the same—dry and stiff. There were days where we thought we were at another funeral. All that was missing was the coffin.

Usually when a preacher sees someone looking at their watch he knows they are anxious to go home. But now it was me, looking to see how much longer I had to go. Don't get me wrong—we had some great meetings and people were ministered to, but I felt like we weren't seeing a lasting result, a lasting change. People were ministered to but went right back to "business as usual" when the meetings were over.

The Lord began to stir something in us. As Wigglesworth said, "I'm only satisfied when I'm dissatisfied." In other words, we should not allow complacency. We should be hungry, we should be pressing in for more all the time. We knew there was more. We were hungry for more. So, we began to cry out to the Lord. We prayed: "Lord, please show up in our meetings. Please touch these people. We don't care if they don't remember our name, as long as they remember Your Name and that they leave knowing they received a touch from You!"

If you have studied the Revivals and the Great Awakenings of the past, you are probably familiar with the names of John Wesley, Jonathan Edwards, Peter Cartwright, and Charles Finney. If not, I would urge you to get the unedited, unabridged versions of their writings, so that you can read the accurate accounts of the amazing things that happened in their meetings. Since I had read many books about these men and their revivals, I knew that when God moved, He moved in a way that man could not claim to control. They made Him welcome, and He showed Himself to the people and His works were made manifest. In a true move of God, He alone gets the glory.

THE GOSPEL IS GOOD NEWS

The New Testament is full of stories that show the miraculous workings of the Lord, and those He trained to do the same works after He went away. We looked at one such miracle in Acts 3:1–11 where Peter and John, in the Name of Jesus, healed the man at the gate of the temple. *"And he leaping up stood, and walked, and entered with them into the temple, walking, and leaping, and praising God"* (Acts 3:8).

The Gospel is about Good News to those who will repent, but terrible news of divine judgment to those who will not. In John 3:18, Jesus said: *"He that believeth on him is not condemned: but he that believeth not is condemned already, because he hath not believed in the name of the only begotten Son of God."* It was Good News to Jairus, a leader in the synagogue who came and fell down on the dusty road at Jesus's feet because his daughter was dying. (*See* Mark 5:35–43.) It was Good News to blind Bartimaeus, crying out: "Jesus, thy son of David, have mercy on me." (Read his story in Mark 10:46–52.)

It was Good News to the four men who ripped up the roof on the house where Jesus was and let their friend down through the roof. (*See* Mark 2:3–12.) It was Good News to the woman with the issue of blood who reached out and touched the hem of His garment. (*See* Mark 5:25–34.) It was Good News to Zacchaeus, who climbed up a tree and got out on a limb to see Jesus. (*See* Luke 19:1–10.) The Gospel is simply summed up in the message that the angels gave to the shepherds on the night Jesus was born. *"Fear not: for, behold, I bring you good tidings of great joy, which shall be to all people. For unto you is born this day in the city of David a Saviour, which is Christ the Lord"* (Luke 2:10–11). It is Good News anytime Jesus walks into the room and says, "Your sins are forgiven you," or "Take up your bed and walk." (*See* Mark 2:9.) Only Good News will cause people to go "walking and leaping and praising God" as we saw in Acts 3.

So, we began to cry out to the Lord. Now, if you are wanting to carry the message of the Gospel and can't live with the persecution or stigma attached to you, then you would be better off just working for

McDonald's, flipping burgers. Jesus said in Luke 21:17 that we would be hated for His sake and the Gospel. When you are hanging around Jesus, you will be persecuted. They will make up all kinds of stories about you. They did it to Him—they accused Him of casting out devils by the devil. (*See* Matthew 12:24.) We are to be willing to bear the reproach for the Cross of Jesus Christ.

AMERICA NEEDS A GREAT SPIRITUAL AWAKENING

For those of us in America, bearing the reproach may not mean the same as it does for those in foreign fields, because right now there are people giving their life's blood. They are being executed and martyred for the cause of the Cross of Jesus Christ. In America, it could mean your name will be slandered. But if we don't have an awakening in America, it will come to bloodshed, and people will die for their faith. You can mark that down. If you don't believe it, then your head is in the sand, or you're smoking some "very bad weed."

We must have a move of God in this country. I don't care what denomination you are from or what your beliefs are: Evangelical, Charismatic or Pentecostal. If you can't come around the Cross and the Blood of Jesus—if that isn't your center focus—then you're nothing more than a cult. When we stand in Heaven there will not be a section for Methodists or Baptists and a private section for those who are Charismatic and Pentecostal. The only thing that will get you in there is the Blood. Are you washed in the Blood of Jesus?

The Body of Christ has a problem because we have not learned to put aside our differences and stop letting them separate us. We must unite, despite our differences, so we can come together to bring in the great end-time harvest of souls. Remember, 1 John 4:20–21 says: *"If a man say, I love God, and hateth his brother, he is a liar: for he that loveth not his brother whom he hath seen, how can he love God whom he hath not seen? And this Commandment have we from him, That he who loveth God love his brother also."*

You may not agree with me, but it is really not going to make any difference to me. I am going to love you and pray for you. I am not going to argue with you or fight with you. Because I am on a mission.

When you hold your eighteen-year-old daughter in your arms as I did, in the early hours of Christmas morning, it will change your life. When she died that morning at 4:37 a.m. after an eighteen-year struggle with Cystic Fibrosis, I vowed that the devil would pay for what he did—with the souls of men. I vowed to go after one-hundred-million souls. Now as far as I'm concerned, people are either going to get in the flow or we are just going on without them. I'm not stopping to argue. I have a mission. I have a passion for souls. We must see a great harvest.

FOCUS ON THE HARVEST

One of the things we are excited about is the fact that many of the churches in our area work with us. Our teams have gone out, shown them how to win souls, and helped them bring people into their churches, which astounded some of the pastors. They couldn't understand why we would do so much to help them. That's easy to answer.

I want everybody to go to somebody's church. We are here to flood the Kingdom, not just one local church. The problem with a lot of ministers is that they ask: "Well, how is this going to benefit me?" That's not the right question. They should ask: "How is this going to benefit eternity; how will this benefit the Kingdom?"

It's time we changed our focus. It doesn't matter if they come to our church or go to yours. What matters is that we see them in Heaven. One church can't hold the whole harvest, anyway. We need every church in town on board.

So, let's focus on the harvest. Let's not get side-tracked by the equipment or the plow. It doesn't matter who is on the combine. The issue is not who is driving the tractor or the harvester—the issue is the harvest. Let's reap the harvest!

The harvest was so heavy on the heart of Jesus. *"Say not ye, There are yet four months, and then cometh harvest? behold, I say unto you, Lift up your eyes, and look on the fields; for they are white already to harvest"*

(John 4:35). If it is important to Jesus, then it should be important to us. We must get busy, because Jesus is waiting for the harvest.

The harvest of souls is a costly business. It costs a lot of money. Through the years, there have been some months when our balance sheet looked like we were just days away from bankruptcy, because we pushed ourselves to such extremes for the harvest.

It would be very easy to just pull back and stay within the confines of what we can afford, but we can't do that. If it means giving everything, then we give everything. We thank God, who is still the God of Elijah and Elisha. He still causes the axe head to swim. When the axe head comes off the handle and there's no way you're going to come through the battle, and all is lost; He is still God. Let's look at 2 Kings 6:1–7 for the story of the axe head that swam:

> And the sons of the prophets said unto Elisha, Behold now, the place where we dwell with thee is too strait for us. Let us go, we pray thee, unto Jordan, and take thence every man a beam, and let us make us a place there, where we may dwell. And he answered, Go ye. And one said, Be content, I pray thee, and go with thy servants. And he answered, I will go. So he went with them. And when they came to Jordan, they cut down wood. But as one was felling a beam, the axe head fell into the water: and he cried, and said, Alas, master! for it was borrowed. And the man of God said, Where fell it? And he shewed him the place. And he cut down a stick, and cast it in thither; and the iron did swim. Therefore said he, Take it up to thee. And he put out his hand, and took it.

When it looks impossible, God comes through, makes a way, and saves the day. The key is to do what He tells you to do.

When everybody says you're going too far, you're going to bring a reproach, but then the Master reaches in and the axe head swims, you know that somehow God has brought you out supernaturally. Stretch yourself when necessary. Jesus walked on water—He calls us to "walk on water," stepping out in faith to do the impossible. Jesus gave everything, so don't you be afraid to give everything, and watch what He'll do. Don't compromise or draw back.

It's all fine when the media is not coming after you, but when they are, then you have to make a decision. Do you compromise your message, or change what God has given you to say? Do you ask them what they want you to do, and then do that? You can't change what you believe just because the media is coming after you. I'm not going to change my message. I believe the Word of God, and that is my message. Everyone must bow their knee to Jesus—even the media. God's Word is eternal—it doesn't change depending on what year we are living in.

Several years ago, we went back to South Africa, our home country, where I ministered in two of the largest churches in the nation. I called them and told them I was going to be in the country, and I didn't want anything. I just wanted to come help.

Each Sunday, God gave us a thousand people who came to give their lives to the Lord. The altars were flooded with people. So, on the plane flying home, I was talking to the Lord, and I said: "Lord, You know I went to help these people." Really, I was complaining. Have you ever complained to the Lord about something? I'm sure you have at one time, or another. I was complaining, and I said: "Lord, nobody ever comes to help me."

I shouldn't have said that. Two days later, I got a call from Joyce Meyer. The Lord uses her in a mighty way. She said: "Rodney, this is Joyce." You know how she is: very straight and to the point. She said: "I was praying for you and Adonica, and the Lord told me to come help you."

I nearly drove off the road, because I thought, *No, she couldn't have heard what I said on the airplane,* but she used the exact same words.

"Well, what does that mean, Joyce?" I asked. "What does 'help me' mean?"

"I am coming to be here with you a whole Sunday at the church," she said. "I'll be at the eight o'clock service, the eleven o'clock service and the seven o'clock service."

And so, she came. That Sunday, we were packed out at all three services. We received a love offering for her, but at the end of the night when I handed her the check she turned around and gave it all back to me.

"No, I didn't come for this," she said. "I came to help you."

What we didn't know was that the St. Louis newspaper had followed her down here. They were doing a major article and investigation on Joyce Meyer Ministries.

About two or three weeks later the St. Louis paper did a major five-day exposé on Joyce's ministry. They went through everything. They got pictures of her house—I mean everything. Each day, they focused on a different aspect of her ministry.

THERE IS A PRICE TO PAY

Up to that time, she had never had that kind of barrage or attack against her ministry. For most of the time, she has had pretty easy sailing—just preaching and running her ministry. On the other hand, it felt like all we had ever known was persecution and criticism, from multiple directions. I felt like we must have had a bullseye on us. I thought sometimes maybe somebody else should step up and take some of it instead of us all the time. We were not on television and we felt that our ministry and our budget was small, compared to these larger, more visible ministries, but it seemed like we were still being hassled about everything.

When I heard about the attack on Joyce, I pulled up the story, and there I was! I thought, *How did I get in the story?* I felt a lot like Peter when he denied Jesus. "Get away from me. I don't even know this woman."

I have found in the ministry that when someone comes under attack, everyone around them comes under the same attack. Then friends of your ministry begin to back off, because they can't handle it. The Body of Christ needs to get their differences settled and stand together to put out the correct information. If the media wants to publish it, we expect that they should at least get their facts right. But it is usually twisted and exaggerated, because they have an agenda.

The news media had listed what they called "The Eight Top Prosperity Preachers," and Adonica and I were listed as one of the ministries. That may be funny to you, but not when it's your name being written up in the newspaper.

So, I called Joyce to encourage her. I said: "Joyce, Adonica and I just called to say that we count it such an honor to be so counted amongst your number that we would be persecuted alongside with you. What a privilege it is, and we thank you for allowing us to even be associated with your name."

The reporter from St. Louis was here to investigate Joyce and decided to add me to his list. He reported that we broadcast to a worldwide audience via the Internet and preached in a sixteen-million-dollar church. As if there is anything wrong with that!

It *was* built for sixteen million. But the Lord gave us the property—eighty-three acres with the building—for eight-million dollars. The whole thing was a miracle. The Lord gave us this property and we are not going to apologize for the blessing of God!

Then the reporter started on our home, which was an average priced home, suitable for a family with three children, but he made it sound extravagant for a preacher to own. It wasn't, but it wouldn't have mattered. If we had lived in a mobile home, he would have found something to make it sound wrong.

When do you back down? What level do you go to that will make people happy? Do you change your message?

No, I believe the Lord wants to bless His children. If we put God first, He will take care of the rest. In Matthew 6:25–34, Jesus gives us a clear explanation of His provision for us. Look at verse 33: *"But seek ye first the kingdom of God, and his righteousness; and all these things shall be added unto you."* You focus on being a blessing, and the Lord will take care of your blessing!

Jesus promised He'd bless us, but He didn't promise that we would be persecution-free. *"And Jesus answered and said: Verily I say unto you, There is no man that hath left house, or brethren, or sisters, or father, or mother, or wife, or children, or lands, for my sake, and the Gospel's, But he shall receive an hundredfold now in this time, houses, and brethren, and sisters, and mothers, and children, and lands, with persecutions; and in the world to come eternal life"* (Mark 10:29-30).

Everybody wants the hundred-fold, but they don't want the persecution. Well, it feels like I've had a thousand-fold persecution. If you don't believe me, just go on the Internet, type in my name and see what you'll pull up—some of the craziest "science-fiction" stuff I have ever heard in my life. People who don't know me and who have never been in any of my services just outright lie and make things up.

The people who hated Jesus made up lies about Him, too. The bottom line is that you're going to be criticized, and if you can't handle that, maybe you are not ready for ministry. **In reality, God can only use you to the level of criticism you can handle.**

Have you ever been criticized for something? I'm not referring to sins you have committed or deeds you knew were wrong. I mean for those things you are doing for the Lord that others may have wrongly judged you for doing. It is not a pleasant thing to be attacked and lied about, but it will happen. You had better have the joy of the Lord in your life when that happens. And it will, because there is a stigma attached to those who trust in the Cross.

Even Billy Graham was attacked by people who have done nothing themselves. Ministers are criticized for believing in the New Birth or for baptizing believers or for speaking in tongues. I am criticized for the joy, and for preaching on the blessing, provision and promises of God. I have got news for you—I'm not backing down from the Word of God, no matter what people have to say about it. They call me: "That Joy Preacher." Yes, I am; thank you! Joy is a fruit of the Spirit. I'll take all I can get of Him!

I am criticized for preaching prosperity. Yes, I do preach it, because God's Word is true! There were years and years we struggled in Africa, having to believe God for enough money to put gas in the car to get us to the next meeting. There was even a time the fuel gauge said it was empty, when we were an hour or so from our destination, but God was faithful, and the car kept running until we arrived. Now we are able to fund the harvest and pay for crusades to tell a lost and dying world about this glorious Gospel. God is faithful to His Word and to those who believe and trust in Him.

Criticism? Oh, yes, it comes. But I am ready to die for what I believe, and I will neither back down nor compromise my message. I will never change the truth of the Gospel to make it acceptable. The day you change it, you will lose the flow of your anointing, because you are not trustworthy anymore. It may cost you everything to stay faithful to the Gospel, but, if you want to be like Jesus, then it is worth it a thousand times over.

12

SPECIAL ANOINTINGS
Not Your Ordinary Assignment

Although we often hear remarks about someone having an anointing to preach great sermons or sing uplifting songs, many of the other attributes of the anointing have been largely ignored by the Church. When many people are healed in a meeting, we know the pastor or evangelist must have a strong anointing on his or her life for healing. But there are other special anointings that are available to the Church. Let's look at Acts 19:11–12 for one of them.

> And God did unusual and extraordinary miracles by the hands of Paul, So that handkerchiefs or towels or aprons which had touched his skin were carried away and put upon the sick, and their diseases left them and the evil spirits came out of them (AMPC).

Paul had a special anointing for miracles that were unusual and extraordinary. He didn't even have to lay his hands on the people for them to receive. The anointing that was on him went into cloths and napkins, which were placed on people and they were healed and delivered.

I count it such a high honor, and a privilege, that all these years, I have been able to carry the message of the anointing, which has the power to save, heal, and deliver. When you preach on the anointing, then people can begin to receive the anointing. When the Body of Christ does not understand the power found in the anointing—they miss out on all that God has for them. Every believer is empowered by the Holy Spirit to do the works of Jesus, if they believe! The anointing is the manifest presence—the presence and power—of God, so if you have His Spirit, you have the anointing.

BAPTISM IN THE HOLY SPIRIT

When we are born-again, the Spirit of God comes into our hearts to live. The Apostle Paul bore witness to that when he wrote in Romans 8:9: *"But ye are not in the flesh, but in the Spirit, if so be that the Spirit of God dwell in you. Now if any man have not the Spirit of Christ, he is none of his."* That means that, if you are born-again, you have the Spirit of God living in you. But God has more for you—He wants you to be baptized in the Holy Spirit.

When you get baptized in the Holy Ghost you're going to receive power! Acts 1:8 says: *"But ye shall receive power, after that the Holy Ghost is come upon you: and ye shall be witnesses unto me both in Jerusalem, and in all Judaea, and in Samaria, and unto the uttermost part of the earth."* So, when we are baptized with the Holy Spirit, we receive power: dunamis—strength, power and ability. Power to preach, power to perform miracles, power to do the works of Jesus. We receive the boldness to be a witness—to preach and to demonstrate the Kingdom of God.

We realize, also, that God pours out special anointings. This has to do with the call of God on an individual's life and it also has to do with the degree that they have yielded to the will of God in their life. We see men and women around the world being used by God in a greater, or more unique, way than others. It is evident that they have a special anointing.

Now, you might think: "Well, where does that leave me? Am I chopped liver? Has God left me on the back burner?"

PRESS THROUGH THE CROWD

No, He hasn't forgotten you. But I want to emphasize that *you* need to press in—and it's not *with* the crowd—I mean you have to press *through* the crowd.

The crowd will be there, but they will not press in. They will not be pressing through to get to Jesus. They'll just be there. Jesus said: *"For ye have the poor always with you."* (See Matthew 26:11.) So it is with the crowd. You'll have them with you, but they aren't pressing in; they're just following. You have to get through the crowd of those who are just following. You often have to go through the masses to get to Jesus. The woman with the issue of blood experienced that. Many other people touched Jesus that day, but her touch was different—she was desperate and she was expectant.

It takes faith to get that special touch. It only comes by your faith, by your desperation, by your expectation, and by your heart's cry. You must press in and come in out of the ordinary to see the unusual. If you had the option of getting something that's common, or a limited edition, which would you want? You know you would try to get something that's special. When someone gives you a gift that is common or average, you would make the effort to thank them, even you are not that excited about the gift. But when it turns out to be something special, that you have always wanted, you would be excited and have no trouble showing your gratefulness.

Well, the Lord has something special for you. God is not a respecter of persons, but He is a respecter of faith. Down through the years, there have been people God used mightily, like those we mentioned earlier: Maria Woodworth-Etter, John G. Lake, Aimee Semple McPherson, Smith Wigglesworth, and Kathryn Kuhlman. Why were they used so greatly

SPECIAL ANOINTINGS

in the early revivals? Because they pressed in—they didn't let criticism or pressure from the crowd stop them from reaching out to touch Jesus.

We can still find people today whom God is using, but I usually mention those who are dead, because they have run their race and kept the faith. We always need to be giving God the glory for all He does or is doing. In many cases, though, it seems that it is only after you are dead that the value of your ministry is known or acknowledged.

We see that in the world all the time. An artist's paintings are never fully appreciated until he is dead, and then everyone wants one of them. Many of the great masters died penniless, yet their creations sell for millions today. Some of the favorite musicians of our time gained wealth and fame while they were alive, but their music sold considerably more after their deaths, because then everybody wanted it.

It is the same thing with a special anointing. You must die to get it. No, I don't mean you physically die, but you must die to self before God will use you to the fullest in your gift.

I know that this is not preached in many sermons, because pastors are not teaching that we must die to the flesh. People would rather say, "I am alive in Christ." Yes, you are, but you also must be dead to the world.

Those who don't believe in dying to the flesh will often find that their flesh reigns supreme. Be careful that what you believe—and teach—does not accommodate the flesh, otherwise you will never see the glory and the supernatural in your life. And don't expect to be used by God in an unusual way. I don't know about you, but I made up my mind a long time ago—I want everything that Jesus purchased for me. Titus 2:14 says: *"Who gave himself for us, that he might redeem us from all iniquity, and purify unto himself a peculiar people, zealous of good works."*

Christians are a peculiar people, because we are set apart and marked with His grace. Look around you in the Body of Christ. There are many special ministries, with special anointings and giftings placed on them by the head of the Church, the Lord Jesus Christ. The Lord uses them in a unique and unusual way, to accomplish His plan and purpose. Take, for example, the story in Acts 5:14–16:

And believers were the more added to the Lord, multitudes both of men and women. Insomuch that they brought forth the sick into the streets, and laid them on beds and couches, that at the least the shadow of Peter passing by might overshadow some of them. There came also a multitude out of the cities round about unto Jerusalem, bringing sick folks, and them which were vexed with unclean spirits: and they were healed every one.

The anointing was so strong on Peter, that people were healed when his shadow fell on them. I believe there will come an increase of special anointings in these last days. There are anointings waiting for you that will enable you to carry His special grace to the world. But remember, with those special anointings come requirements and responsibilities. The people God uses are those who have a relationship with Him, and who have died to themselves and their own interests. They must be trustworthy; they must have a love for the lost and dying.

When we first came to America in December 1987, Adonica and I saw the great need in the Church. It seemed as if a great depression had come on it. Everything felt dead in the Church. Many times, I walked out of a church thinking, *Can these bones live again?*

It felt like we put a great effort in, for few results. And I would ask God, "Lord, if it be possible, let this cup pass from me." But He always brought to mind the words of Jesus, "Not my will, but thine be done." So, I began to pray.

I shared earlier that when we started out, our main focus was on the healing ministry. Our first emphasis was on salvation, but then we also prayed for the sick. When we first started praying for the sick, especially the terminal cases, not all of them were healed. Some of them died. It can be discouraging, but we had to keep praying for people, because God's Word commands us to.

Actually, we did have miracles, but we didn't always hear about them, because the preachers never called us to tell us about the healings. We only heard about the casualties. The phone would ring:

"Brother Rodney. Remember the lady that came to the meeting who had twelve hours to live? She died a few days after you prayed for her." Or: "Remember the man that came with terminal cancer and had six months to live? He died three weeks after you prayed." I had begun to feel like I was the one killing people who would have possibly lived another six months.

I finally had to go to the Lord and pray about what was happening, and He really comforted me. When those people came to me for prayer, I was their last resort. It's one thing if somebody is diagnosed and immediately comes for prayer. But these people had been to doctor after doctor; they had gone through chemo and all kinds of therapy, so by the time they got to me, they were almost ready for life support. That's why I had to learn to just follow the Holy Spirit. You can't be moved by what you see or hear.

The Lord told me to just keep praying for the sick, and soon we started seeing God do many miracles. In the early days of my ministry, I would go into the African bush for a meeting in a mud hut and call out all the deaf people. I prayed for the first person and nothing happened. I prayed for the second person and still nothing happened. I prayed for the third person and their ears popped open. Then the fourth, the fifth, and so on down the line. All the deaf in the building were healed. The next night, we prayed for the blind and the night after that we prayed for people with tumors and cancer.

You may say, "I have never seen a deaf ear open." Well, how many deaf ears have you prayed for? None? Well, that figures. You actually have to put yourself out on a limb. You have to be in a situation where if God doesn't come to your rescue, you're finished. If God's Word says: "Lay hands on the sick," then lay hands on the sick and trust Him to heal them. You can't heal them, but you can lay your hands on them in faith and obedience!

SPECIAL GIFTS, SPECIAL GRACES, AND SPECIAL ANOINTINGS

At that time, I had no idea what the Lord was going to do with us. I didn't know that He was going to release a special anointing on and through our ministry. So, in April of 1989, after we had been crying out for months for God to come and touch His people, I was preaching in a meeting in upstate New York. On Tuesday morning, the glory of God rolled in like the wave of the sea and different people just started shaking, weeping, sliding off their chairs onto the floor, speaking in tongues, and laughing. I knew this was not normal, and I knew that what was happening had nothing to do with me. I said: "Lord, You're ruining my meeting." We had always stood on God's Word and preached His uncompromising Word to the best of our ability. We made it a point to teach His Word, line upon line and precept upon precept (Isaiah 28:10). We were not flaky, weird, anything-goes preachers.

But, as I said before, when the joy broke out, I asked: "Lord, why are you doing this?" He said, "My people need joy." I said: "But Lord, it is causing trouble." The Lord said to me, "If you're afraid or ashamed of this I'll take it away from you and give it to another." I said: "No, Lord, it is okay. Leave it here." It's much more important to please God than man! So many times, people pray for revival and for God to show up, but when He does, they resist Him and reject the move of the Holy Spirit. Usually, because they are too concerned about their reputation, or what other people think of them. The move of God is too precious. Don't allow anyone, or anything, to stop you from receiving all that the Lord has for you.

God gives special gifts, special grace, and special anointings. There are those who have stepped over into special anointings where the gifts of the Spirit are concerned. The word of knowledge, the word of wisdom, and the discerning of spirits. The utterance gifts: diverse kinds of tongues, interpretation of tongues and prophecy. The gift of faith, working of miracles and the gifts of healings.

If you go to church and there are no gifts of the Spirit evident, then you are probably sitting under the ministry of a dead minister. Because, like the priests we spoke of earlier with bells and pomegranates on the hems of their garments, if he has only bells and no fruit, then he is just a loud, clanging cymbal. There must be the combination of the fruit and the gifts. If the bells have stopped ringing, then that means he's probably dead. Pull him out and get another priest. (*See* Exodus 28:34–35.)

Jesus had the Spirit without measure. He operated in every one of the five-fold ministries. He was the apostle, the prophet, the evangelist, the pastor, and the teacher. You can break those down however you want to—man has many different definitions for them—but Jesus was the perfect example of every one of those five ministries. I know some people might wonder how He could really have been a pastor, because he traveled most of the time. In their minds, a pastor doesn't travel. We must realize a pastor is a shepherd, and Jesus was (and is) THE great Shepherd.

Every ministry is different. People have a concept of what defines the different ministries, but we need to stick with the scriptural definition. We do know that not every believer is called to the five-fold ministry. The thing we look for is the anointing, the supernatural touch of God, that propels the ministry and sets it apart. Those who are called to the five-fold ministry have an anointing available to them by and from the Holy Spirit in order to get the job done.

Then, just because you are called, it doesn't mean you will automatically walk in that anointing. There is a price to pay for the anointing. It all depends on how far you want to go with God. We will get into that more a little later.

I believe with all my heart that you CAN have the anointing and the touch of God to do whatever it is that God has called you to do. I repeat what I said earlier: "God does not send you out without the equipment to do the job." It is simply a matter of how much you desire to be used of God.

> But unto every one of us is given grace according to the measure of the gift of Christ. Wherefore he saith, When he ascended up on high, he led captivity captive, and gave gifts unto men. (Now that he ascended, what is it but that he also descended first into the lower parts of the earth? He that descended is the same also that ascended up far above all heavens, that he might fill all things.) And he gave some, apostles; and some, prophets; and some, evangelists; and some,

pastors and teachers; For the perfecting of the saints, for the work of the ministry, for the edifying of the body of Christ: Till we all come in the unity of the faith, and of the knowledge of the Son of God, unto a perfect man, unto the measure of the stature of the fulness of Christ: That we henceforth be no more children, tossed to and fro, and carried about with every wind of doctrine, by the sleight of men, and cunning craftiness, whereby they lie in wait to deceive

EPHESIANS 4:7-14

THE FIVE-FOLD MINISTRY

The purpose of the five-fold ministry is to bring believers to a place of maturity, so they are not tossed to and fro by every wind of doctrine. God intends for us to come to a place where we are no longer babies in our walk with the Lord, but mature, full-grown men and women in the Gospel whom God can use in an awesome way.

Ask yourself this question: "Have I really matured since I became a child of God?" You are the one who controls the rate of your growth. There is a saying, pertaining to natural things, that says, "You are what you eat." As long as you stay open and hungry for God's Word, you will continue to grow and mature. Sometimes people grow to a certain place, but then they get set in their ways—they don't want to change or mature any further, so they stay the way they are, and their growth is stunted.

1 John 3:2 says: *"Beloved, now are we the sons of God, and it doth not yet appear what we shall be: but we know that, when he shall appear, we shall be like him; for we shall see him as he is."* When we see Him, we will be like Him. Until then, we are a work in progress. As long as we live, we need to be growing in Him. You will never grow past the place of your last touch—of your last change—without the work of the Holy Ghost in your life. He is the One who brings about our growth, as we receive His work and His touch, as He changes us from glory unto glory unto glory (2 Corinthians 3:18).

I know I am not the same as I was a year ago, and I will not be the same a year from now, or two years from now. I am being changed from glory to glory, into the image of Jesus Christ (2 Corinthians 3:18).

You may say: "Well, I am not called to the five-fold ministry."

What does that have to do with it? There's still an anointing for service available for you—and how do you know what God's called you to do or not to do? God calls people at different times in their lives. Some people are called before they are born, and others are called as little children, but many are called in their teens and later. Smith Wigglesworth accepted his call at the age of fifty-six. He was a plumber and got so busy preaching that he couldn't "plumb" anymore.

God may have called you to do a special work for Him, but it may take quite a number of years for you to recognize the call, because rather than obey God, you keep "going around the mountain one more time" trying to decide what you want to do. Eventually, you realize that nothing you have tried has worked and that you need to just "get with the program" and obey the Lord.

There are those who will step over into special gifts of healings. There are those who will step over with unusual faith. There are those who will step over into realms of revelation in an unusual way. Get ready in these last days for a release and an increase of special anointings to the Body of Christ. Why? The Lord wants to bless the Church and win the lost.

13

DO YOU HAVE FRESH OIL OR STALE OIL?

Fill Up with the Oil of Joy

God often uses situations in my life as object lessons, which end up becoming messages years later. One such lesson happened early in my ministry.

In Africa, when I was growing up, we did not have air conditioning. Where I lived, we had a mild or temperate climate, but during the summer months it could get very hot. Right at the start of my ministry, I was at an African church in the hills of the Transkei on the southeastern coast of South Africa, to hold a meeting. The pastor where I was speaking asked me if I would anoint some people with oil.

James 5:14 says: *"Is any sick among you? Let him call for the elders of the church; and let them pray over him, anointing him with oil in the name of the Lord."*

I told him I believed in anointing with oil, so I would do it. He went behind the podium and came out with a bottle of oil. I'll tell you—that oil had gone bad because there was no air conditioning and the temperature was so hot. There's no telling how long that oil had been there. Some of it had dripped onto the outside of the container and was rancid, so I could smell it coming. And when I opened it—it was so stinky, it was terrible.

I asked him: "You want me to anoint them with *that?*"

He answered: "Yes."

I told him I didn't even want that on my hands, and I knew those people didn't want it on their heads. Imagine going to church to get blessed and leaving with a foul-smelling head! I told him to send one of the ushers down the street to buy some oil—even cooking oil if that's all he could find—just as long as it was fresh. The lesson of the stale oil has stayed with me, and years later the Lord gave me this message.

DO YOU HAVE FRESH OIL OR DO YOU HAVE STALE OIL?

You should be prepared all the time with your vessel full of fresh oil. I believe that if you are reading this book, hopefully you've already had an "oil change." But, if by chance you haven't, then this is your day. This is your hour. It's time for you to get a "Holy Ghost lube job."

Motor oil is the substance we put in the engines of our cars. The main function of motor oil is to reduce wear on moving parts; it also cleans, inhibits corrosion, improves sealing, and cools the engine by carrying heat away from moving parts. The oil needs to have a specific viscosity—not too thick and not too thin. Temperature also affects viscosity, which is why specific engines require specific grades of oil. Over time, the oil begins to break down, and loses its effectiveness.

Now they have all sorts of additives, so you don't have to change your oil as often, but nonetheless, the oil must be there to protect the engine, because without oil in your engine it will seize up.

Have you ever had your engine overheat and seize up? I was riding with someone in a car when the engine seized, and it is not an experience you want to have. The car wouldn't move, and we were stuck where we were. Usually, the damage done to the engine is catastrophic, rendering it unable to be repaired, requiring a new engine.

Your automobile needs an oil change every 3,000 to 5,000 miles, and if you let it get too low on oil, you may have to push it. Most of the time engines seize up because they didn't have an oil change…because nobody checked or replaced their oil.

We can recognize Christians who are not on fire for God anymore because they are stuck right where they are. Some people are like a car that you have to push to get them started. Push them into the church, push them into their seats, push them to raise their hands in worship, and push them to open their wallets. They have "seized up" from lack of fresh oil.

When I was a little kid, I used to watch my father change the oil in his car. He would always take a pan and put it right under the car. He would loosen the nut so the oil would drain out. The oil that came out was always thick and dirty, but then my dad would tighten the nut and put in fresh, golden oil. As a five-year-old boy, I tried to work it out in my mind how it went in such a pretty golden color but came out so dirty. He explained to me that it was the working of the engine and its heat that made the oil dirty.

KEEP YOUR TANK FULL

The same thing happens in our Christian lives. Some people think that when God anoints you with fresh oil that it is sufficient for the rest of your life. But the Bible says in Ephesians 5:18 (AMPC): *"And do not get drunk with wine, for that is debauchery; but ever be filled and stimulated with the [Holy] Spirit."* The Greek text says: *"Be ye being filled."* That means we should be continually filled with the Spirit. Just because we are full today doesn't mean we will be full tomorrow. Some people are full today but will leak out by tomorrow morning. We need to stay filled!

How do you check the oil in a car? You take hold of the dipstick and pull it out, then you wipe it off and stick it back in to check the level of oil. Isn't that right? That's how you check the oil in your car, but what about your life? Have you checked the oil in your vessel? We need to check people's oil from time to time, to see if they have fresh oil from Heaven.

Somebody said: "Oh, I got fresh oil a couple of years ago." Yes, but you have been through quite a bit of heat since then. You've got to check your oil again and again.

Acts 3:19 (AMPC) says: *"So repent (change your mind and purpose); turn around and return [to God], that your sins may be erased (blotted out, wiped clean), that times of refreshing (of recovering from the effects of heat, of reviving with fresh air) may come from the presence of the Lord."* You know that after being out in the sun all day in the smoldering heat, when you get home you walk in all haggard and looking like you need to be revived. You sit down in the air conditioning or with your electric fan with some ice-cold iced tea or ice water—the colder, the better—to refresh yourself.

Too many of God's people are being burned and scorched by the heat of life, and they look tired and haggard. The bags under their eyes are so heavy that you want to ask them who carries them. They carry those bags of worry and concern all by themselves, when there is oil available for every person. Listen now: this is important. *There's enough oil for every person. The oil will never run dry.* Let's look again at Luke 4:17–20 where Jesus returned to Nazareth, and as was His custom, He went into the synagogue on the Sabbath.

> And there was delivered unto him the book of the prophet Esaias. And when he had opened the book, he found the place where it was written, The Spirit of the Lord is upon me, because he hath anointed me to preach the Gospel to the poor; he hath sent me to heal the brokenhearted, to preach deliverance to the captives, and recovering of sight to the blind, to set at liberty them that are bruised, To preach the acceptable year of the Lord. And he closed the book, and he gave it again to the minister, and sat down. And the eyes of all them that were in the synagogue were fastened on him.
>
> LUKE 4:17–20

The ANOINTING

Jesus read to them the words of Isaiah, as he prophesied of the Messiah to come in Isaiah 61. Let's look at the entire passage:

> The Spirit of the Lord God is upon me; because the LORD hath anointed me to preach good tidings unto the meek; he hath sent me to bind up the brokenhearted, to proclaim liberty to the captives, and the opening of the prison to them that are bound; To proclaim the acceptable year of the LORD, and the day of vengeance of our God; to comfort all that mourn; To appoint unto them that mourn in Zion, **to give unto them beauty for ashes, the oil of joy for mourning, the garment of praise for the spirit of heaviness;** that they might be called trees of righteousness, the planting of the LORD, that he might be glorified. (Emphasis added.)
>
> ISAIAH 61:1–3

THE OIL OF JOY

What is that sound I hear? It's the sound of people having an oil change. The Bible calls it the oil of joy. It's the OIL of JOY. He'll give you beauty for ashes. The oil of joy for mourning. Do you think for one moment that when you get to Heaven there will be a moment of depression? No! Gone are the wrinkles and gone are the frowns. Gone are the sad faces. In our meetings, we see His oil being poured out on the people. Fresh oil! You can be anointed with fresh oil! Fresh oil!

This fresh oil is for everyone. Some of the people, who are powerfully touched in the meetings, are the quietest introverts, and some are the saddest people you ever want to meet, but when God touches them, they are full of joy—crying with joy, overflowing with joy. I'm telling you, it has nothing to do with your personality or your situation. It has to do with your hunger for the Holy Spirit and His anointing on your life. I cannot even begin to imagine life without the Holy Spirit, the giver of the oil of joy.

We have heard for years about the expected "oil shortage." Things are critical in the world today. Many countries are trying to control the world's supply of oil. But, in the Church today there is an oil shortage just as critical, affecting the lives of people. The church I pastor, The River at Tampa Bay, is a "refinery" where people come in to "load up" and go back home. But, we are also teaching people how to drill their own wells and become "refineries" for themselves. We are teaching them how to become suppliers of oil for other people. This is not a game—it is crucial—and desperately needed in this time in which we live.

I was in a meeting in El Paso, Texas when a woman stood up and asked me: "Why are you people in here laughing when people are out there dying?" I told her: "Lady, you have missed the point. It's because we are getting the oil of joy in *here* that we are able to have the energy to go *out* and minister to the lost and dying people out there. She looked at me and said: "You don't know who I am, do you?"

THE OIL BLOCKER

I told her I didn't know, and it really didn't matter. I was just giving her the truth. As it turned out, she was the daughter of a well-known preacher who had been attacking my ministry, especially when I went to New York. She had the same spirit manifested in her that was in her father. She was an "oil blocker," someone who puts out an embargo against the oil of joy. She was from a group who thinks we must all come to church to weep and mourn, as if that will change the situation out in the world. God's Word tells us, *"Thou wilt shew me the path of life: in thy presence is fulness of joy; at thy right hand there are pleasures for evermore"* (Psalm 16:11) and *"You have made known to me the ways of life; You will enrapture me [diffusing my soul with joy] with and in Your presence"* (Acts 2:28 AMPC). We come into a meeting to rejoice in the presence of God, and then go out and bring others into His presence.

I want to stress why this is so important. We are living in a world today that is much like the days of Noah. Let's read from Matthew 24:37–51:

But as the days of Noah were, so shall also the coming of the Son of man be. For as in the days that were before the flood they were eating and drinking, marrying and giving in marriage, until the day that Noe entered into the ark, And knew not until the flood came, and took them all away; **so shall also the coming of the Son of man be.** Then shall two be in the field; the one shall be taken, and the other left. Two women shall be grinding at the mill; the one shall be taken, and the other left. **Watch therefore: for ye know not what hour your Lord doth come.** But know this, that if the goodman of the house had known in what watch the thief would come, he would have watched, and would not have suffered his house to be broken up. **Therefore be ye also ready: for in such an hour as ye think not the Son of man cometh.** Who then is a faithful and wise servant, whom his lord hath made ruler over his household, to give them meat in due season? Blessed is that servant, whom his lord when he cometh shall find so doing. Verily I say unto you, That he shall make him ruler over all his goods. But and if that evil servant shall say in his heart, My lord delayeth his coming; And shall begin to smite his fellowservants, and to eat and drink with the drunken; The lord of that servant shall come in a day when he looketh not for him, and in an hour that he is not aware of, And shall cut him asunder, and appoint him his portion with the hypocrites: there shall be weeping and gnashing of teeth. (Emphasis added.)

MATTHEW 24:37–51

Does that remind you of our world, our surroundings today? The way even some Christians are behaving? As if Jesus is not coming back. As if they won't have to give an account to the Master. I believe this is speaking about the Church in the last days, just prior to the coming of the Lord Jesus Christ. We need to live ready to meet Him today!

Look at the next chapter, Matthew 25:1: *"Then shall the kingdom of Heaven be likened unto ten virgins, which took their lamps, and went forth to meet the bridegroom."* They were all virgins, so this is talking about born-again brides-to-be, who took their lamps (they each had a lamp, but only half of them were full of oil) and went forth to meet the bridegroom. The virgins—all ten of them—were waiting for the bridegroom to come.

THE BRIDE OF CHRIST

We are the Bride of Christ, and like the ten virgins, we are waiting for our bridegroom. Usually, when a bride is waiting for the bridegroom to come, she is not sorrowful, sad, depressed, forlorn, or dejected. The closer to the time of the wedding day, the more excited she gets. She is in a time of preparation, getting herself ready for the bridegroom. She is excited and full of joy.

Jesus is coming back for a church that is full of joy—a joyful church. Joyful, because we are looking forward to the Marriage Supper of the Lamb. We will all sit at His table, we will eat with Him, and we will sup together with Him. I believe the tables are set and all the place cards are ready, *with our names on them*. Hallelujah! I believe that the angels are getting the dishes ready and straightening everything, waiting for that moment. It won't be long now, and the Father will say to the angel Gabriel: "Blow the trumpet to bring My children home."

> "For the Lord himself shall descend from Heaven with a shout, with the voice of the archangel, and with the trump of God: and the dead in Christ shall rise first: Then we which are alive and remain shall be caught up together with them in the clouds, to meet the Lord in the air: and so shall we ever be with the Lord" (1 Thessalonians 4:16–17).

But, obviously some are not going to make the marriage supper, because they are not ready—they didn't keep their lamps full. If it says that five were wise and five were foolish, that means that fifty percent of the church is not going to be ready for the coming of the Lord Jesus Christ. Now, that's a sobering thought. But the time of the bridegroom's coming is supposed to be a joyful time, not a sad time.

EXPERIENCE HIS JOY

Don't be like some people, who are running around criticizing the joy of the Lord that is in our meetings. Why would people be upset with joy and the oil of the anointing? Joy is a fruit of the Spirit—it is something we should all want for ourselves. Nehemiah 8:10 says: *"the joy of the Lord is your strength..."*

The joy of the Lord is given to us to carry us through the tough things we go through in this life. We should stay full of the fresh oil of the Holy Spirit. Like Jesus, we should stay full of the oil of gladness (Psalm 45:7 and Hebrews 1:9). We should stay full of the oil of joy.

What are some people going to do when they find themselves left behind—because they are not ready? They are so busy with their own things and their own lives, they have taken their eyes off of God and His Word. When people stop trusting in God, they start behaving like other worldly, ungodly people. These people eat and drink with drunkards (act like unredeemed people) and smite their fellow servants (abuse their brothers and sisters). They are not paying attention to the oil in their own vessels, and because of that, they neglect to keep it full. They lose their peace and their joy.

Because there is **fullness of joy** in God's presence, if He is present with us, we should be **experiencing His joy**—in our own lives, in our church services, wherever two or three are gathered in His Name! It's amazing to me that some people think church should be somber and sour and that we should not show any emotions. It didn't bother the disciples when people showed emotions.

In Acts 3:8, we see the man who was healed: *"And he leaping up stood, and walked, and entered with them into the temple, walking, and leaping, and praising God."* He wasn't leaping for sadness. He was leaping for joy!

> And my language and my message were not set forth in persuasive (enticing and plausible) words of wisdom, but they were in demonstration of the [Holy] Spirit and power a proof by the Spirit and power of God, operating on me and stirring in the minds of my hearers the

most holy emotions and thus persuading them], So that your faith might not rest in the wisdom of men (human philosophy), but in the power of God.

1 CORINTHIANS 2:4-5 AMPC

There is such a thing as "holy emotions" and it is perfectly acceptable to respond to the Word of God, or the power of God, in an emotional way—with weeping or with joy. This is not merely a "feeling" that comes and then leaves, but it is a stirring in your heart that brings conviction and moves you into a deeper relationship with God. When I was just a young boy we used to sing an old song in church about joy.

When your cup runneth over with joy,

When your cup runneth over with joy,

You'll find it easy to pray and sing all the way,

When your cup runneth over with joy.

You hear people say things like: "Well, Pastor, I didn't come to church Sunday, because I just didn't feel like it." "I tell you, I had a hard week." "I would have come to the healing service, but I was sick." "Pastor, I'm sorry I didn't make it to the revival meeting, but I was just too depressed." One that never fails to amaze me is when they tell me they couldn't come to the marriage seminar because they were getting a divorce. Or the couple who didn't have time to come to the meeting on how to prosper, because their house was being repossessed. You can drive by the hospital or the clinics and see the consulting rooms full of sick people. They found time to go there. They go in sick and come out sick and give more offering than they would have in church, but at least, if they had come to church, they could have gone home healed.

Jesus is the source of all good things in our lives: salvation; healing; deliverance; restoration; peace; joy. So why would people be upset with the oil of joy? The whole world is looking for joy, but in the wrong places. You go down to any club or bar; watch the laughing and partying going on. That's what they are looking for. JOY! And yet many people don't want to see the joy in church.

There's no true joy in the bars and clubs...the true joy is found only in Jesus! There should be joy in the church. If we have Jesus, joy is available to us. You need the oil of joy—as much as you can get. You not only need to fill your vessel, but it needs to have a reserve tank with oil to spare.

If it had not been for the oil of joy—the joy of the Lord—we would not be sharing this message around the world. My wife, my family, and I are a testimony to the blessing of the oil of joy. When our daughter Kelly went home to be with the Lord, we were back in the pulpit the next Sunday. The following week we were ministering, and in the subsequent weeks we were holding crusades as usual. Some people would have needed a sabbatical of several months or maybe even wanted to quit. That is a testimony of the grace of the Lord and the power in the oil of joy.

I don't know what we would have done without the joy of the Lord. Yes, we had our moments, and I won't say we didn't have a hard time over losing her, but had it not been for the joy of the Lord—which is our strength—we could not be ministering life and freedom still today.

So, the wise took oil in their vessels, and while the bridegroom tarried, they all slumbered and slept. And at midnight there was a cry: *"Behold, the bridegroom cometh; go ye out to meet him. Then all those virgins arose, and trimmed their lamps, but the foolish said unto the wise, give us of your oil; for our lamps are gone out."* In other words, their lamps had been burning, but they went out because the oil ran out. When they looked at their supply they had none. They said, *"Give us of your oil; for our lamps are gone out. And the wise answered, saying, Not so; lest there be not enough for us and you: but go ye rather to them that sell, and buy for yourselves"* (Matthew 25:8-9). The wise just filled their lamps up with the supply that they had in their vessels. So, they were ready at midnight hour. They were ready for the coming of the bridegroom. We must be ready for the soon return of our bridegroom, the Lord Jesus Christ.

NOW IS THE TIME

The day will come when people will run to try to get in one of our meetings or other meetings, but there will not be a meeting to attend, because we won't be here. They will say: "Get me one of those tapes. Somebody get me a video of one of those anointed meetings. I need to get under that anointing." They will be told: "Too late, too late." Now is the time to get the oil. Now is the time to be sure your vessel is filled up with oil before it's too late.

The Bible says that while they went to buy, the bridegroom came, and they that were ready went in with him. Those that were ready went into the marriage and the door was shut. *"Afterward came also the other virgins, saying, Lord, Lord, open to us. But he answered and said, Verily I say unto you, I know you not"* (Matthew 25:11-12). He was saying, "I never had an intimate relationship with you."

Today, He would say, "You just came to church on Sunday mornings; that was the extent of your commitment to Me. You did your 'religious thing,' but you didn't live for Me. You lived for yourself. Your Mondays, Tuesdays, Wednesdays, Thursdays, Fridays, and Saturdays were consumed with yourself, not with Me."

In the religious world, people think if you just show up at church on Sunday morning, then you are fine. It's not just about going to church; you *are* the Church, so it's whether the Church is *you*. When people meet you, do they feel like they are meeting with the Lord? They should, because He lives in you. Or when people meet you do they feel like they just met with Hell? What, or whom, do you carry?

"Watch therefore, for ye know neither the day nor the hour wherein the Son of man cometh." (Matthew 25:13). We need to be ready for anything. We need to be ready to preach, pray or die at the drop of a hat. We need to make ready for the bridegroom.

Jesus is not coming back for a depressed Church. He's coming back for a glorious Church. People have conferences called Solemn Assemblies where everybody is sad. They don't know the word "solemn" as used in the Bible: "solemn assembly" or "solemn feast" doesn't mean "to be sad." It has to do with God's people getting together for the serious purpose of worshipping and celebrating the Lord and His goodness. It means "joyful"; it means "celebration." The *Strong's Concordance* defines "solemn feast" as: to move in a circle, i.e., (specifically) to march in a sacred procession, to observe a festival; by implication, to be giddy; celebrate, dance, (keep, hold) a (solemn) feast (holiday), reel to and fro.

Have you ever thrown a party at your house? Isn't it great when everybody comes in happy, they are joyful and ready to have fun? Who wants to have a sad party? If I told you that on Tuesday night, over at our place, we were throwing the saddest party you have ever seen, would you come? You may laugh about that, but I tell you the truth: the world doesn't want to come to your sad party.

Here's where the problem comes: people try to live with one foot in the Kingdom and one foot in the world. You can't have the oil of joy and the slop of tradition, religion, and sin. You can't have both. You can't put the two together. No matter how many times you come to a service; no matter how many times the oil is poured out and you get touched, if you go right back to the "hog slop," I'm telling you right now that you're going to stink like a hog. Then when you come back to the service, we have to "hose you down again." There are lots of people that we just need to hose down over and over.

It's like those old cowboy movies where the cowboy comes in after he's been out on the range for three weeks. He hasn't had a bath since he left, so he smells like an old buzzard. He walks up to the bar and stands there waiting on his drink. The bartender motions toward the corner and three guys will come and pick him up, take him to the horse trough and dip him in it.

That's what I feel like I have to do every service. You think I'm kidding you, but I'm serious. Sometimes when I'm ministering, I look out there and see somebody walk in and my first thought is: "Man, they've been riding the range for three weeks." Then I have to get three ushers to bring him to the front quickly. After all, I am a "Holy Ghost bartender," so people come here to drink of the new wine. But I can't serve "Stinky" at the bar, so we have to take him and wash him first!

Fresh oil from Heaven! Let me tell you how strong this oil really is. This oil is so strong that even in the years when I was having two meetings a day, six days a week, forty-six weeks a year and my body was almost finished, the oil was the only thing sustaining me. People often ask, "How did you go so long, pushing yourself as hard as you did? I will tell you: "It was only because of the oil. If it hadn't been for the anointing, I would have 'fried out' in five years." We ran like that for fourteen years!

TAKE CARE OF YOUR BODY

I'm going to say this again regarding the natural side—I realized this back then—and I know it even more now. You must rest your body. You must protect your body, because your body is the temple of the living God. You can't starve your body; you have to eat food; you have to drink water; you have to look out for your body. That's the only thing that's keeping you here on the earth. Take care of your body; it's the only one you have. You can't wear this one out and then just go pick a new one.

The anointing can take you further than you can take yourself, but don't abuse His grace on your life. You may be cranky simply because you're tired. You haven't slept in days. You don't eat the right foods and you don't rest your body. You can have hands laid on you until the "moon turns green and monkeys chew tobacco," but it isn't going to help because there are certain natural laws that you cannot disobey.

GET YOUR HEART READY

By the same token, you can't be involved in sin and expect to have fresh oil. The moment the fresh oil touches the sin, the oil gets rancid. You can't expect to have fresh oil when you are contaminated by all your "stuff." That's why you have to empty out…purge the old sin. Let the Lord help you; get rid of all that's unclean in you and make room for new, fresh oil.

Perhaps you are angry with somebody, bitter over something, then you try to put fresh oil on top of that bitterness? It doesn't work that way.

You may walk in unforgiveness, possibly hating the brother standing next to you in a service. You are singing, "I love you, Lord" with your mouth, yet all the while you are looking at that brother thinking, "I'll get you after the service!"

You think that doesn't happen? You're enjoying the service until you spot somebody you don't like and your attitude changes for the worse. Maybe a husband and wife have had a big fight on the way to the church and are still angry at each other, but now they're standing in the service together. The pastor says, "Who wants fresh oil?" They are the first to say: "Me, me, I want fresh oil." What good is it going to be if the moment it hits you it's going to be contaminated again?

Matthew 15:8 says: *"This people draweth nigh unto me with their mouth, and honoureth me with their lips; but their heart is far from me."* Have you noticed that when you go to church with an attitude you don't get anything? We need to clean up our heart attitude and draw closer to God in order to receive what He has for us. Prepare your heart; get your heart ready. Judge yourself and get your heart right with God. Clean out anything the Holy Spirit convicts you of. Keep your heart tender and soft. Then there will be room for the oil and it will stay fresh and pure.

YOU SHALL BE FULL

Let me close this chapter by sharing with you some of the benefits of being anointed with fresh oil, looking first in the King James Version.

> When the wicked spring as the grass, and when all the workers of iniquity do flourish; it is that they shall be destroyed forever: But thou, LORD, art most high for evermore. For, lo, thine enemies, O LORD, for, lo, thine enemies shall perish; all the workers of iniquity shall be scattered. But my horn shalt thou exalt like the horn of an unicorn: I shall be anointed with fresh oil.
>
> PSALM 92:7–10

The Amplified Bible, Classic Edition expresses this passage in a little different light. Let's compare the two versions for a deeper look into David's words.

> That though the wicked spring up like grass and all evildoers flourish, they are doomed to be destroyed forever. But You, Lord, are on high forever. For behold, Your adversaries, O Lord, for behold, Your enemies shall perish; all the evildoers shall be scattered. But my horn (emblem of excessive strength and stately grace) You have exalted like that of a wild ox; I am anointed with fresh oil.
>
> PSALM 92:7-10

Continue on with verse 11-15 (AMPC) to see many benefits of being anointed in oil.

> My eye looks upon those who lie in wait for me; my ears hear the evildoers that rise up against me. The [uncompromisingly] righteous shall flourish like the palm tree [be long-lived, stately, upright, useful, and fruitful]; they shall grow like a cedar in Lebanon [majestic, stable, durable, and incorruptible]. Planted in the house of the Lord, they shall flourish in the courts of our God. [Growing in grace] they shall still bring forth fruit in old age; they shall be full of sap [of spiritual vitality] and [rich in the] verdure [of trust, love, and contentment]. They are living memorials] to show that the Lord is upright and faithful to His promises; He is my Rock, and there is no unrighteousness in Him

I love verse 14: *"They shall be full of sap!"* The dictionary says that sap is the juice or vital circulating fluid of a plant; energy; vitality. Do you know what that means? They will be full of juice—energy and vitality. They shall still bring forth fruit in old age. They shall be fat (rich; fertile; vigorous) and flourishing (fresh; green; luxuriant; prosperous). Don't tell me that you're too old to serve the Lord. He knows how old you are. When He anoints you for a special assignment then get up and get started!

Every single morning when I wake up, I know I am going to have an opportunity during that day to choose certain things. One of the first things I can choose is to walk in the Spirit or I can choose to walk in the natural. During the course of the day, I'm going to have many things come against me—situations and circumstances. They are specifically designed by the enemy to take me out. But the Lord has not left us destitute or without answers. He has given us the oil of joy. We must purpose in our heart that we will be anointed with fresh oil each and every day.

Jesus taught us to pray: "Give us this day our daily bread" (Matthew 6:11). We must have the daily bread and the living water. We need to fill up with the Word of God every day. We need to drink of His Spirit every day. Every morning as I am getting in the shower, I ask Him for fresh oil. I don't want to live on yesterday's oil.

Some people ask, "But, Brother Rodney, what if I don't feel like it today?" Think about all the times the enemy has come against you and what he has told you he will do to you. Put your hand on your belly and just laugh at him. Get the oil flowing—pump oil! It doesn't matter how you feel; do it in faith. The Lord has not left you on the earth to run your earthly race without the necessary equipment. He has given you fresh oil for your journey. Step out in faith! The oil will never run dry. Whatever you have to do, keep the oil flowing. Fill yourself up with the joy, and the presence, of the Lord.

14

THE POWERS OF THE WORLD TO COME

Tasting of the Heavenly Gift

There is very little understanding, even among some Christians, of the powers of the world to come, but I believe the Lord will give us revelation on the subject, more and more, as we approach the time of the coming of the Lord. Many claim to know the Lord and will say they are going to Heaven, but many don't even have the basics down, never mind understanding the deeper things of God. What do we really know about what the Word says concerning the matter? Let's look into this a little deeper in Hebrews 6:

> Therefore leaving the principles of the doctrine of Christ, let us go on unto perfection; not laying again the foundation of repentance from dead works, and of faith toward God, Of the doctrine of baptisms, and of laying on of hands, and of resurrection of the dead, and of eternal judgment. And this will we do, if God permit.
>
> HEBREWS 6:1–3

THERE IS A PROGRESSION IN OUR WALK WITH GOD

Jesus is the foundation upon which we build. We need to receive and know Him as our personal Lord and Savior. We can't build on any other foundation.

Then there are some basic principles we all need to know in order to walk in God's plan for us and to walk victoriously in our Christian walk. When verse one talks about "leaving the principles," it doesn't mean to forsake them. It just means that we should study them, receive them, understand them, walk in them and then continue to grow in God's Word. We shouldn't need to keep being reminded of the basics, like children. At some point, we should be "grown up" and solid in our faith.

Of course, as long as we live, we will never be able to plumb the depths of all the revelation there is available in the Word of God, but we should keep on pressing in to learn and grow in Him.

> For it is impossible for those who were once enlightened, and have tasted of the heavenly gift, and were made partakers of the Holy Ghost, And have tasted the good word of God, and the powers of the world to come, If they shall fall away, to renew them again unto repentance; seeing they crucify to themselves the Son of God afresh, and put him to an open shame.
>
> HEBREWS 6:4–6

I want you to see the progression in this passage. Enlightened. Tasted. Partakers. What does "once enlightened" mean? This is not a person who was born-again yesterday—it is a person who is born-again and who has a revelation of the foundational doctrines of Christ. He goes on in Hebrews 6:4 to say, *"and have tasted of the heavenly gift..."* So, there are those who have gone a step further: they have tasted of the heavenly gift. They have experienced the presence and power of God. But that's as far as they have gone. Others, who have been made partakers of the Holy Ghost, have gone another step further in their walk with the Lord. It has to do with a dispensation, not a location. We must know that in our spiritual growth and maturity there's another level: *"and have tasted the good word of God, and the powers of the world to come..."* (v.5). A better way to translate this is to say, "the powers of the *age* to come." Even though we are still living on earth, in earthly bodies—by the Spirit of God, we can taste a little bit of Heaven!

GOING DEEPER

The way we come in to the deeper things of God is through the Word of God. There are people who have never really come into an understanding of the Word of God, nor are they ready to dig deep into His Word to get everything they can get from it. Others have gone into that realm, but they've stopped short of the powers of the world to come.

You can't understand the things of God with your natural mind; they are spiritually discerned (1 Corinthians 2:14). There are many who will die and go to Heaven and will be in a state of shock when they arrive. If God doesn't supernaturally catch them up to speed, they will walk around Heaven for a thousand years with their mouths hanging open, because there is such a difference between here and there. When the catching away of the church takes place, some people will enter into Heaven shouting at the top of their voice, because of their shock at the quickening of the Holy Ghost.

If you've ever climbed on one of those amusement rides like the one they have in Orlando, Florida, called the Tower of Terror, where you get dropped ten floors, you know what I mean. I remember the first time I rode one of those things was out in Texas with some friends. It was called the Texas Cliff Hanger. I told them I wanted to ride it because nobody on it was screaming, so it couldn't be too bad. I realized why when I was riding it. It was a straight drop down from a dizzying height. You don't have time to scream. All you could do was hold your breath. It was so extreme, that when we stopped, I was laughing hysterically. Some people are going to be in shock when they finally experience the mighty power of God.

We talk about the natural realm and the supernatural realm; we read about tasting of the good Word of God and the powers of the world to come. That tells me that there is a progression in our walk with God. You cannot enter into that realm and taste of the powers of the world to come and still be ignorant of spiritual things.

Why? Because God will open up a whole new dimension to your understanding. Many, who had no concept of Heaven, will be shocked when they begin to grasp the reality of the glory of God, the river of living water, the throne of God and the angels of God. They will be like the Apostle Paul on the road to Damascus; they will experience the heavenly vision and their lives will never be the same.

When the glory of God comes down in our meetings, time seems to stand still, and we get caught up in the heavenly realm where God reveals Himself to us as we have never seen Him before. He gives us an understanding about things we have never known, a little glimpse of Heaven, and we leave with a new revelation of who He is.

I'll never forget when I was preaching in a Hispanic church of about 1,000 people in Chicago, Illinois, back in 1991. Although I think Spanish is a beautiful language, I speak only a few words, so I always speak through an interpreter. After I preached, I was walking around, praying in the Holy Ghost as I ministered to the people. I was laying hands on some of them when someone stopped me and said: "You are speaking perfect Spanish as you are praying for the people."

I asked what I had said and the person told me I was saying: "Come to the paradise; come to the paradise of God." Then it hit me that I was inviting them to come into the presence of the Lord in a language I didn't know.

All I knew is that I was speaking in tongues, laying hands on the people and seeing them fall under the power of God, totally drunk on the new wine. I left the meeting that night thinking about what had happened. The Lord had allowed us to catch a glimpse of eternity. He had allowed us to come and dip our feet in the River of Life. So, when people criticize and mock us for what they think is excessive or "overboard," they just don't understand that we are tasting the powers of the world to come.

When Kelly went home to be with the Lord, my wife had a vision of her walking the streets of gold. A preacher in another state called us and told us of the identical vision that he had had. Adonica saw Kelly walking in Heaven, wondering at all she saw, and saying, "My daddy told me about this! It's just like my daddy told me. It's just like he said it would be."

See, I had told her: "Baby, when you get there, it will be so wonderful you won't want to come back." Why would you want to come back from Heaven? There is nothing on earth to compare with the glory of Heaven. Come to the paradise; come to the paradise of God. Now, step out of the natural realm and into the realm of the supernatural.

CAUGHT UP

But understand, you cannot plug into that realm of the supernatural with your head. You connect with your spirit man. Remember Enoch. He walked with God and was not, for God took him. (*See* Genesis 5:24.) Enoch had walked so deeply with God for most of his life, and he pleased God, so God took him. He had stepped so far over into the heavenly realm that God just took him on home.

We read the words of the Apostle Paul in 2 Corinthians 12:1–4, for another example of being "caught up:"

> It is not expedient for me doubtless to glory. I will come to visions and revelations of the Lord. I knew a man in Christ above fourteen years ago, (whether in the body, I cannot tell; or whether out of the body, I cannot tell: God knoweth;) such an one caught up to the third Heaven.

And I knew such a man, (whether in the body, or out of the body, I cannot tell: God knoweth;) How that he was **caught up** into paradise, and heard unspeakable words, which it is not lawful for a man to utter.

Caught up into paradise, tasting of the powers of the world to come. Revelation 1:10 says, *"I was in the Spirit on the Lord's day..."* Let's look at John's entire experience.

I was in the Spirit on the Lord's day, and heard behind me a great voice, as of a trumpet, Saying, I am Alpha and Omega, the first and the last: and, What thou seest, write in a book, and send it unto the seven churches which are in Asia; unto Ephesus, and unto Smyrna, and unto Pergamos, and unto Thyatira, and unto Sardis, and unto Philadelphia, and unto Laodicea. And I turned to see the voice that spake with me. And being turned, I saw seven golden candlesticks; And in the midst of the seven candlesticks one like unto the Son of man, clothed with a garment down to the foot, and girt about the paps with a golden girdle. His head and his hairs were white like wool, as white as snow; and his eyes were as a flame of fire; And his feet like unto fine brass, as if they burned in a furnace; and his voice as the sound of many waters. And he had in his right hand seven stars: and out of his mouth went a sharp twoedged sword: and his countenance was as the sun shineth in his strength. And when I saw him, I fell at his feet as dead. And he laid his right hand upon me, saying unto me, Fear not; I am the first and the last: I am he that liveth, and was dead; and, behold, I am alive for evermore, Amen; and have the keys of hell and of death.

REVELATION 1:10–18

The Word of God is full of these occurrences. We can see throughout the Old Testament mention of the prophets who stepped over into glory realms. Then, in the New Testament, we see Peter, James, and John in a supernatural realm as they saw the transfiguration of Jesus on the mountain.

And after six days Jesus taketh Peter, James, and John his brother, and bringeth them up into an high mountain apart, And was transfigured before them: and his face did shine as the sun, and his raiment was white as the light. And, behold, there appeared unto them Moses and Elias talking with him. Then answered Peter, and said unto Jesus, Lord, it is good for us to be here: if thou wilt, let us make here three tabernacles; one for thee, and one for Moses, and one for Elias. While he yet spake, behold, a bright cloud overshadowed them: and behold a voice out of the cloud, which said, This is my beloved Son, in whom I am well pleased; hear ye him. And when the disciples heard it, they fell on their face, and were sore afraid. And Jesus came and touched them, and said, Arise, and be not afraid. And when they had lifted up their eyes, they saw no man, save Jesus only.

MATTHEW 17:1–8

Notice Peter's comment: *"It is good for us to be here."* When you have a glorious experience like they had, the first thing you will say is, "It is good to be here!" Then, as usual, Peter spoke out when he should rather have kept quiet: *"If thou wilt, let us make here three tabernacles; one for thee, and one for Moses, and one for Elias."* Isn't that just like many people today? They get an anointing, and immediately they want to build a new denomination. They have a move of God, and they want to build a building. They make an idol out of the location, thinking that it's the only place will God move.

DON'T FEAR THE ANOINTING

"While he yet spake, behold, a bright cloud overshadowed them: and behold a voice out of the cloud, which said, this is my beloved Son, in whom I am well pleased; hear ye him. And when the disciples heard it, they fell on their face, and were sore afraid." That's why people draw back from the anointing. They are afraid. They draw back because of fear of the heavenly realm, the supernatural realm. They are frightened of the unknown, and their

flesh will want to pull back. No matter how much they want to step over, their natural man is afraid.

I first learned about this from my dad. He used to tell the stories about what God did in all the prayer meetings at our home and at the church.

This one actually took place at church. A group of people were standing in the back of the church, in what they called the Minor Hall. My dad said that as they were praying he got lost in the Spirit, and his spirit stepped outside of his body. He saw his body standing there and suddenly it went, "Boom!" and fell to the floor. He remembered thinking: "Hmm, just like a sack of potatoes."

The experience was so overwhelming at the time (he had just recently been baptized in the Holy Ghost), he said: "Oh, no, Lord, no!" The next thing he knew, he was back in his body. He really believed the Lord was going to take him and show him something supernatural, but because of fear, he pulled back. He always regretted that he missed out on what God wanted to do with him.

When my father told me the story, I realized there is a realm you can go into with God that the flesh would be too frightened to go.

When the Apostle Paul had a particular supernatural encounter with God, he didn't know if he was in his body or out of it, but he knew he was caught up to the Third Heaven. When you have an experience in the Spirit like that, you are tasting of the powers of the world to come. My dad said when he was baptized in the Holy Ghost, he, my brother Gilroy, and my mom were all sitting in the living room. He said that it looked like the ceiling had disappeared, because he could see the stars. He saw three balls of fire coming at him, they kept getting bigger and bigger until they were bigger than the sun, and then the first one hit him. Boom! The second one hit him. Boom! When the third one hit him, he began speaking in tongues. Later on, I told him: "Dad, I'm sure that was the Father, Son and Holy Ghost."

My mother also began to speak in tongues, and my brother counted thirteen different languages that she spoke, one right after the other. That all happened in our living room. My parents were people of faith and prayer. In the years after that, when I was a young boy, the power of God was so strong in our home that people would come to the house and ask if they could just sit in our living room for a while—not to visit—just to sit in the anointing, the presence of God. I will tell you right now, if it wasn't for their commitment and their walk with God, I probably wouldn't be in the ministry today.

GOD HAS A HIGHER REALM AVAILABLE FOR YOU

There's a supernatural realm that's available for the Body of Christ. You can get saved, live your life saved, but never progress beyond a certain point. You can sit under the teaching of the Word, yet never mature as a Christian. There's a progression for the believer, all the way to tasting of the powers of the world to come. God has a higher realm available for you, but the choice is yours. You can choose religion and you can choose tradition. Or you can choose life and power. You can be a "Sunday morning" Christian, or you can be a 24/7 Christian.

One meeting we held was in Pittsburgh, Pennsylvania, in January of 1990, and the glory of the Lord was in the place. The presence of God came in like a cloud, and most of the people were not in their seats. They were lying on the floor under the power of God. People were filled with joy, bubbling out of their bellies. People were totally drunk in the Holy Ghost. The anointing of God was so strong there was Holy Ghost ecstasy in the place. People were beside themselves. The Lord spoke to me and said: "You are tasting of the powers of the world to come. You are tasting a little bit of Heaven." We had a glimpse of Heaven, a glimpse of glory and, by the grace of God, we have seen it many times since then.

There have been times in the services when the glory came down so strong that people didn't know what to do with it in their physical bodies. People told me they felt like: "If the power of the Lord gets any stronger, I'm going to die."

When that happens to me, I'm not worried about dying, because I'm going home—I'm going to see Him. I'm stepping out of this realm; I'm stepping into that realm of Heaven. You may look at somebody under the anointing and think they are just extroverts making a noise, but it has nothing to do with the personality of the person concerned. You don't see that Heaven just came down and kissed them. You don't see that the glory of God came down and touched them, because you're looking at the outward signs. You're not seeing what is really happening. If you could see with the eye of the Spirit, you would see the angels of God standing above people, pouring oil on them.

The fact of the matter is that angels, with blessings, have walked by some people in church this week. Perhaps they were coming to you, but your attitude was wrong, so they went on past you. What you see might not make sense to you, but that doesn't mean anything. People come to our meetings all the time, trying to analyze with their natural minds what's going on in the services, and they don't know any more after they leave than when they came. They are like a Canadian goose lost in a thunderstorm.

They don't know because it is a "heavenly thing" and they are trying to understand it in a natural way. I can only tell you that it feels just like Heaven and bears the fruit of Heaven.

RAISED FROM THE DEAD

Pastor Daniel Ekechukwu, who lives in Nigeria, was shocked when we first met, because of my questions or lack thereof. He has an amazing story that people who meet him want to hear all about.

He was in a terrible, fatal car wreck years ago. His body was taken to the local mortuary where they embalmed it and prepared it for his funeral. For three days, his body lay waiting to be buried.

God supernaturally spoke to his wife, and she insisted that God was going to resurrect him so he could get back to what God had called him to do...preach the Gospel. His family did not believe her, so she hired some men to help her take him in his casket to a Reinhard Bonnke meeting, which was being held some distance away. When she arrived, they wouldn't let her take the casket into the meeting but allowed her to take his body down to the basement of the church, where they laid it on a table.

THE POWERS OF THE WORLD TO COME

As the pastors gathered around him, to everyone's amazement, Daniel's chest began to move, as if he was breathing, but he was still dead. They tried to move his arms and legs, but they were still stiff. Suddenly, he sneezed, and his body began to move by itself. He rose up, alive and healed by the power of God.

When I met him I asked him how he was doing, how his wife was, and how his children were. He said: "Brother Rodney, you are the first preacher that has met me and never asked me a word about what happened to me. I'm shocked. You didn't ask me about Hell; you didn't ask me about Heaven; and you never asked me about Jesus. You only asked me, 'Daniel, how are you? How's your wife? How are your children?'"

He then asked me: "Why did you not ask me about Heaven?"

I answered: "Because I care more about you personally, than your story. Besides that, I've already been there, Daniel. I've been there in the Holy Ghost."

There have been times in the meetings when it feels like the Lord opens up a window and lets you see into the supernatural realm, but only a glimpse. I will tell you that if a stairway suddenly opened up that led up there I would probably sprint. I would run. And I would never come back again. The Lord mustn't give me even a little slot, because I'll take it.

NOTHING COMPARES TO THE GLORY OF GOD

When you have tasted the powers of the world to come, there's nothing else that can compare. Nothing else on the face of the earth can compare with the glory of God and the presence of God. Nothing! Not all the money in the world, not all the fame in the world, not all the success in the world. Nothing! Everything else is all but dung!

The Apostle Paul said in Philippians 3:8: *"Yea doubtless, and I count all things but loss for the excellency of the knowledge of Christ Jesus my Lord: for whom I have suffered the loss of all things, and do count them but dung, that I may win Christ."* I would not trade the anointing for anything on the face of the earth.

Some people don't like our services, because they feel we speak about the anointing too much. I don't know what they're going to do when they get to Heaven. Obviously, they must not be going there, because when they get to Heaven, where can they go to get away from the anointing? If you don't love the presence of God, then something's wrong with you. That's why some people are always moving around in church. They are up and down, in and out, moving from one side of the sanctuary to the other. They are restless, and they don't know why they can't sit still in the presence of God. It's because they've got a devil in them and the devil is agitated in the presence of God.

FLESH, DEVILS, OR THE HOLY SPIRIT

In our meetings, when the presence of God starts moving, there are three things that happen to people, depending on where they are. Either the flesh manifests, or the devil manifests, or the Spirit manifests.

What do I mean by that?

Number One: Some people have a fleshly response—which manifests one of two ways: Either they go overboard and try to act like they are getting touched, but they are yielding to the flesh, not the Spirit. They do it for the attention. Or, they sit there with an angry, resistant attitude. They are opposites of the other, but they are both a carnal response. At least if someone is open, you can correct them through the teaching of the Word. However, if a heart is closed, they will be unable to receive anything.

Number Two: Devils start to come out of people. They can't remain when the presence of God comes down in the place. We don't worry about that, neither do we make a big fuss and draw attention to it. All we do is what Jesus did. We tell the demons to shut up and come out and they have to obey. It's not the demons that manifest that we should be concerned about, it's the ones who hide themselves and keep causing trouble for the person.

Number Three: The Holy Spirit touches people and they submit to His work in their lives. Ultimately, number three is what we want for everybody. Not merely an outward manifestation, but a heart totally yielded to the Lord. We do not stop the manifestations of the Spirit working on a person, but we don't draw attention to them either. Our focus is to lift up Jesus Himself in every meeting, and not anything else.

THE PULL OF HEAVEN

When you lay up your treasures in Heaven, you are putting your heart where your treasure is. The more you treasure Heaven, the less you will treasure earth and earthly things, and the more Heaven starts pulling on you.

Some people don't have Heaven pulling on them, because there's nothing there waiting for them. But when you are laying up treasure in the form of souls, and the seed that you've sown, your worship will change, and stuff will continue to mean less and less to you. Heaven and heavenly things become more real to you than the earth and earthly things. By the time you get to eighty-five or ninety years of age (if Jesus tarries), you will be feeling the pull of Heaven stronger and stronger.

Some years back, I went to see my uncle Les, my dad's older brother, who lived to be ninety-three years of age. He was a Pentecostal preacher who had pioneered a great church and Bible school. During the Depression days in the late 1930s, he had built one of the great churches in South Africa. He founded one of the great Pentecostal theological seminaries on his front veranda. He was a theologian, and a remarkable man of God.

When I was a little boy, I would hang around him for days just to hear what he had to say. We would go to visit him and he would talk for hours while we just sat and listened. The mysteries of God would just flow out of him. We would sit around the breakfast table eating breakfast and listening to him.

The other kids would go out to play, but I wanted to hear what he was saying. We would move to the living room and talk there until lunch, then move back to the table to eat again. That's how it would go for three or four days.

After I moved to America, I went back to South Africa for a meeting and went to see Uncle Les to ask him if he would consider coming to America. I wanted him to teach in our Bible College and planned to capture his lectures on video, because no one had ever recorded more than a few tapes of him speaking. I have several tapes of his sermons, and a lot of his writings and Bible commentaries on different books in the Bible, but I wanted video tapes of the two of us teaching.

When I asked him if he would consider coming, he said: "Rodney, I would love to come, but I'm ninety-three years old, and for the last few months, I have had something unusual happening in my life. I go out for a walk every morning just outside my yard. I love walking amongst the trees. But lately, as I walk along, I have noticed that the grass and the trees disappear, and I find myself walking on streets of gold. The pull of Heaven is getting stronger."

As I looked at him, I realized that he was going to go home soon. I leaned over and kissed him, then knelt by him. He laid his hands on me, prayed for me, and handed me his study Bible. I walked out the door knowing I would never see him again this side of Heaven. He died soon after my visit.

The tug of Heaven is strong on the person who has walked with God for many years, but now find themselves in their later years. When Kenneth Hagin went to be with the Lord, Dr. Oral Roberts (who was eighty-six years old at the time) wrote a letter thanking God for Brother Hagin's long years of ministry. He added: "I will join him soon, for I too now feel Heaven's tug."

BE MOVED BY THE HEAVENLY REALM

You know, when you are young you have your whole life ahead of you. It is easy to get caught up in the natural realm—going to work, taking care of your wife and children—all the things we do in this realm. But so many people never think about the heavenly realm, even though people are crossing over to it every second.

Don't miss that heavenly realm. Realize that people are dying—children, young people, older folk—going into that realm. But there are people who are dying all the time who don't know about a heavenly realm, and they are going to a devil's Hell. That should motivate us to win souls. Without Jesus, they will end up in Hell, but we can show them Heaven, and they will want to go there.

Let me be honest with you: the heavenly realm is what moves me. It's what motivates me. Heaven is a place where there's no depression, no sadness, no sickness or poverty. Heaven is a glorious place. Psalm 16:11 says: *"In thy presence is fulness of joy; at thy right hand there are pleasures for evermore."* You can be born-again, enlightened, taste of the good Word of God, and be made a partaker of the Holy Ghost. You can enter in and taste of the powers of the world to come. It's time for the Body of Christ to grow up and come to that place of maturity.

When the Apostle John was on the Isle of Patmos, he was caught away in the Spirit, and the whole of the book of Revelation came forth. Peter was on top of the housetop praying when he fell into a trance and saw a vision. I tell you, these things must become more commonplace in the Church. People are walking around paying too much attention to the natural. They are too much after the flesh.

There are times when the glory comes on me so strong that I can't speak. That's because it is a joy that's unspeakable, full of glory, and the half has never yet been told. 1 Peter 1:8 says: *"Whom having not seen, ye love; in whom, though now ye see not, yet believing, ye rejoice with joy unspeakable and full of glory."*

The Lord once told me: "It's not your job to convince people that this is Me. It's not your job to force them to come. Just set the table and invite them." So, the Lord has set the table before you that is plenteous and good. The Master says: "Come and dine." You are invited to come and sit at the banquet table, eat of the heavenly bread, drink of the living water and the new wine. You can have your head anointed with oil. When you get up from the table, you will find that your cup is running over, and goodness and mercy will follow you all the days of your life. Come and taste of the powers of the world to come. Again, come! Let us go higher in the realms of God!

15

THE FIRE OF GOD
Don't Leave Home Without It

If you were to ask me what the anointing looks like, I would tell you it looks like several different things. But, if you ask me for just one example that would best represent the anointing, it would come down to one word: FIRE. Luke 3:16–17 says:

> John answered, saying unto them all, I indeed baptize you with water; but one mightier than I cometh, the latchet of whose shoes I am not worthy to unloose: he shall baptize you with the Holy Ghost and with fire. Whose fan is in his hand, and he will throughly purge his floor, and will gather the wheat into his garner; but the chaff he will burn with fire unquenchable.

Now, fire can be a great blessing, but it can also be very destructive. Fire is needed, even in the forest. In the western part of the country—especially California—they don't want to see any forest fires. But, a small forest fire can really be very good, because it gets rid of all the leaves and dead stuff that accumulate on the ground under the trees. If you don't ever have a regular small forest fire, there's a good chance that in ten or fifteen years, there will be so much build up that there is too much fuel for the fire, and instead of just burning up the dead stuff, the fire grows so large that it burns the green as well and destroys all the trees. The whole forest goes up in smoke. If the small fires aren't allowed to burn, when fire does come, it does major damage. If the wind is strong, many thousands of acres are speedily destroyed, together with houses and towns.

A fireplace in your home can be nice on a cold evening, and a fire in your oven is a blessing when you are cooking your food, but a fire under your bed would not be so good. A fire that breaks out in your living room will be dangerous to you and your family.

In short, there are good fires and there are bad fires. Fire can have a good effect or a bad effect. The fire of the Holy Ghost that comes and purges you is good fire. The fire of Hell that will burn you—if you aren't saved—is bad fire.

People have asked me for years what this talk of "Fire, Fire, Fire" is all about. Is the Church going to burn up? No, but all that's carnal will burn up. Some people don't want the fire of God here and now, but they'll have to face the fire of Hell later.

You choose. If you allow the purging fire now, you will have the anointing fire for service. The fire of God burns up everything that is not of Him. Whatever is pure will survive the fire; whatever is not, will not. Even when you get to Heaven, your works will be tried by fire. Paul explains it this way:

> For other foundation can no man lay than that is laid, which is Jesus Christ. Now if any man build upon this foundation gold, silver, precious stones, wood, hay, stubble; Every man's work shall be made manifest: for the day shall declare it, because it shall be revealed by

fire; and the fire shall try every man's work of what sort it is. If any man's work abide which he hath built thereupon, he shall receive a reward. If any man's work shall be burned, he shall suffer loss: but he himself shall be saved yet so as by fire.

1 CORINTHIANS 3:11-15

John the Baptist told his followers about Jesus: *"He shall baptize you with the Holy Ghost and with fire"* (Luke 3:16). This fire is the same fire that purges you now and anoints you for service.

It says in the Word: *"Who maketh his angels spirits; his ministers a flaming fire"* (Psalm 104:4). When you speak, people can feel the temperature of your heart. If you listen to some people speak, you feel icicles and the temperature dropping. But when you are a carrier of the fire of God, His fire burns within you, and everywhere you go, you light fires in others.

I am a Holy Ghost "arsonist," come to destroy the works of the devil. I go all over the world and set fire to the Body of Christ. And I tell you, it doesn't bother me how dry it is where I go. When I go to churches where they've never had the fire, the "leaves and sticks" have built up over the years. We go in there on Sunday morning, the fire of God comes, and the whole place goes up in smoke. Most of the time, there's no dead thing left when He's finished. Because, when the fire of God comes, it's going to burn up the dead stuff and make way for new life.

When we go to South Africa, or other countries, we are going in the flames of fire. We are carrying the fire of God into that nation. We're going to light fires—we're not going in there to be invited back—we are going there to get things done. A leading, prominent minister I met when we first came to America was talking to me as we were playing some golf together. He said: "Listen, let me tell you the secret, the key to ministry in America. When you go out to preach, don't unload everything. Just give them a little bit, and leave them wanting more, so that the people will want you to come back."

I looked at him and thought, "What! Is that what you are doing? You are in the wrong business." I don't go anywhere to give a little; I go there to give everything I've got. I get up and preach as though it will be the last time I ever preach on the planet. I go in there and I hit that thing hard. How can I go there and take what is a big fire on the inside of me and turn it all down to a little flame? If every preacher were touched by the fire and gave everything he has, America would be shaken. But unfortunately, most of them are trying to hang on to just a little pilot light.

YOUR OWN PERSONAL FLAME

It is so important for you to understand what I'm going to share with you now. The disciples walked with Jesus, and they talked with Him. They not only saw the miracles that He did, but they were involved in the miracles with Him. When He left, He told them to go and tarry, because they were going to receive power.

They could have said: "But, Lord, we already have it." They didn't realize they were operating under delegated power, and under the power of His Word. He wanted them to get their own personal flame, because it's very hard to operate under somebody else's flame. God wants you to have your own personal flame. Everyone should have their own personal flame.

I look at some preachers and I know they couldn't have got their fire from the same altar I did. They got their fire from a traditional altar—from the altar of religion and tradition, or from the altar of their denominational headquarters. When you get a fire straight from the throne of God like the prophet Isaiah did, you will cry out, like he did, for God to use you.

> In the year that king Uzziah died I saw also the Lord sitting upon a throne, high and lifted up, and his train filled the temple. Above it stood the seraphims: each one had six wings; with twain he covered his face, and with twain he covered his feet, and with twain he did fly. And one cried unto another, and said, Holy, holy, holy, is the LORD

of hosts: the whole earth is full of his glory. And the posts of the door moved at the voice of him that cried, and the house was filled with smoke. Then said I, Woe is me! for I am undone; because I am a man of unclean lips, and I dwell in the midst of a people of unclean lips: for mine eyes have seen the King, the LORD of hosts. Then flew one of the seraphims unto me, having a live coal in his hand, which he had taken with the tongs from off the altar: And he laid it upon my mouth, and said, Lo, this hath touched thy lips; and thine iniquity is taken away, and thy sin purged. Also I heard the voice of the Lord, saying, Whom shall I send, and who will go for us? Then said I, Here am I; send me.

ISAIAH 6:1-8

I see preachers all the time who have some fire, but they are not giving it out…it is a controlled fire. A preacher with real fire is one who has the Word of God in him. He sets himself on fire, and people come to watch him burn. Of course, there will be those who come with wet blankets to put the fire out, but God will set the whole meeting on fire anyway.

Don't let people sitting in the pews dictate the amount of fire that is in you. Be like William Seymour, the old African-American preacher who prayed: "Lord, dip me in the kerosene of thy Spirit; set my heart ablaze that I may burn for You." Hallelujah!

We were preaching in California when a man came to one of the meetings. Actually, he spent most of the week on the floor, under the power of God. After we left he went into his living room to pray early one morning, and he said he was engulfed in white flames and intense heat as he prayed. Others in the meetings came, but they went home the same way they had come—nothing had changed.

This is not a game where you come to get prayed for, fall down and then just get up and go home. You can't wait for someone else to do it for you—you need to plug in yourself. You need to make the connection. This is about getting a touch from Heaven.

Remember, Jesus told the disciples to go and tarry at Jerusalem till they received. I believe that is one of the biggest problems people have today—they aren't willing to tarry. Many people don't get the fire because they are not prepared to press in. They want everything to be instant, with little or no effort or commitment from them. The early Pentecostals used to have what they called "tarrying meetings." They are not just meetings in which to hang around. They are meetings to press in, to diligently seek Him.

Jesus told the disciples to go wait for the coming of the Holy Ghost and they did, and the Holy Ghost came at Pentecost. We don't tarry today because we are waiting for Him to come. I have news—He has already come.

We prepare our hearts and expectantly press in for God to come to us and touch us, because everyone must have their own personal Pentecost. The disciples, and the others with them, however, did what Jesus had said; they went to Jerusalem and tarried—waited—for the Holy Spirit. And the Holy Spirit showed up in power and fire.

How much easier it would be to receive what He has for us if we just listened to the words of Jesus and did what He has told us to do. Look at Acts 2:1-4 (AMPC):

> And when the day of Pentecost had fully come, they were all assembled together in one place, When suddenly there came a sound from Heaven like the rushing of a violent tempest blast, and it filled the whole house in which they were sitting. And there appeared to them tongues resembling fire, which were separated and distributed and which settled on each one of them And they were all filled (diffused throughout their souls) with the Holy Spirit and began to speak in other (different, foreign) languages (tongues), as the Spirit kept giving them clear and loud expression [in each tongue in appropriate words].
>
> ACTS 2:1-4

HUNGER FOR YOUR OWN FLAME

We should not stop preaching about the fire until everybody has their own flame. Everyone should press in. Get hungry, get hungrier and hungrier, until you get your flame. Jesus is the baptizer in the Holy Ghost and fire. Seek Him. The fire will come and purge you. The fire will purify you. The fire will set you apart. The fire will make you a vessel sanctified for the Master's use.

There have been times when I have been aware, as I'm speaking, that my words are going out of my mouth as if it was a flame-thrower, and the fire of God begins to hit people. The Lord told me: "Don't preach people full—preach them hungry—preach them thirsty—so when they leave the meeting they are not just full, but saying: 'I've got to have more, more of that.' But, if you are not hungry, they will not be hungry. They will have to hear the hunger in your voice. Then they will hear the cry of your heart, a cry for more of the Lord. And it will provoke them to press in for more."

Jesus said that if you hunger and thirst after righteousness you will be filled! (*See* Matthew 5:6.) He said in James 4:8: *"Draw nigh to God, and he will draw nigh to you."*

This fire is available for every child of God. Could it be that the Lord will set you ablaze and send you to a city or to a nation? Then you'll burn for Him and set others on fire as well. Remember, even as children we sang the little song:

> *Give me oil in my lamp, keep me burning,*
>
> *Give me oil in my lamp, I pray.*
>
> *Give me oil in my lamp,*
>
> *Keep me burning, burning, burning,*
>
> *Keep me burning 'til the break of day.*

When I was a boy, we added a lot of other verses for fun. "Give me gas in my Ford, let me putt, putt for the Lord," and "Give me unction in my gumption, let me function, function, function." They were fun for us to sing when we were young, but still good for us to remember as adults. We need His oil and we need to stay full and never stop burning!

THE FIRE OF GOD

Fire is not something that you get with your head. Fire is something you have to get with your heart. No one can get the fire for you. You have to desire it with a great fervency, with everything that is on the inside of you. You have to desire it more than life itself.

I was raised in Pentecost, born-again at the age of five, and filled with the Holy Ghost at the age of eight. I received the baptism of the Holy Spirit, and first spoke in tongues, at home, just lying on my bed. I loved to preach to my teddy bears and my brother. I'd line up all my bears, lay hands on them and they'd all fall out under the power.

I'll be honest with you: the "bears" haven't changed much over the years. Some of them still have the stuffing sticking out of them and they need to be sewn up and repaired! But as I grew older, I knew one thing for sure. If I was going to go to the nations of the world I had to have the fire!

The Fire of God will work in all of the countries and regions of the world. Don't leave home without it. Make sure you go to the altar, get the fire from off the altar and put it in your heart. Once you have fire from the altar of God Almighty, it will never burn out. As long as you obey Him, the fire will *never* ever go out.

I am the third of four brothers. I had a brother fourteen years older than me, Mervyn, and I have one twelve years older, Gil. Then I have another brother two years younger, Bazil. My oldest brother, Mervyn, died in August 1978. He had been washing the oil and grease off of his hands at work in a chemical designed only to clean the machinery. It had gone into his bloodstream and had caused leukemia. The Lord had called him to preach, and he was having miracles in his ministry. In fact, the week after he went home to be with the Lord, a letter came from one of the leading denominations, accepting him as their full-time evangelist. He was only thirty-one years old and left a wife and three children.

Our whole family was devastated. I remember standing at his bedside, looking at his body on the bed, and I made a vow. I told the devil: "You'll pay for this—you'll pay for what you've done. People will laugh at you around the world!"

At the time, I didn't know what I was saying. I knew that I would be in full-time ministry. I knew that I would be doing whatever God wanted me to do—lifting His Name up around the world. I had no idea that the Lord would give us a ministry of joy! I have done my best to keep that vow and make the devil pay, by winning souls and seeing people healed, delivered, and set free by the power of the Name of Jesus.

Later, I vowed again at another deathbed, my daughter, Kelly's. I vowed one-hundred-million souls and a billion dollars for world missions. By the grace of God, we will keep this vow as well.

When the fire of God comes, it is always at an altar. I'm not just talking about a church altar—your altar is wherever you are at the time. An altar is a place of death; something has to die. The more of God and His will that you want in your life—the more you need to yield to Him, the more of your own will and plans and desires you need to die to. Unless a seed falls into the ground and dies, it cannot become what it's meant to be (John 12:24). Unless we lose our (lower) lives, we will never find our (higher) life (John 12:25).

If you are truly hungry, and have an intense desire for God, you will be running toward the altar, not merely after natural things like a new home, a new car, or jewelry. That is just "stuff." If you are truly hungry for God, you will put yourself on the altar—a living sacrifice—and stay there until something happens (Romans 12:1).

People tell me all the time that they want to go to the next level, they are hungry, they want more of God—but they are too lazy to press in. Rather they are content to sit in front of the television for hours watching movies. "Rubbish!" I say. You are not hungry. You may think you are, but you're obviously not hungry enough to make the change. You have to separate yourself, consecrate yourself to God, and lock into one thing only: "I *will* receive the Fire of God in my life."

It reminds me of someone who was brought to a meeting because he needed prayer for a terminal disease. In fact, he was expected to live only a few more days. But he couldn't stay for the service because he was in a hurry. For what? If he was dying, a Holy Ghost meeting would be a good place to die.

It all depends on how desperate you are. He obviously wasn't desperate enough to press in to receive what he needed from the Lord. I thought about asking him what he wanted sung at his funeral.

There was a time I didn't realize that I had to be hungry all the time—not just when I felt empty but *all the time*. As a young man, I saw God blessing some friends that I had led to the Lord and I thought: *"Lord, why not me? I have served you all my life. If you are blessing anyone it should be me."*

The Lord told me: "They are hungry and thirsty for me. You are not." Then He used an analogy about a man walking across a desert.

So, the man was walking across an African desert and ran out of water. He had gone days with no water. His lips were parched and bleeding. His tongue was stuck to the roof of his mouth. But he staggered on, crying: "Water, water, water." He looked up and saw a man coming toward him with a briefcase. The man said he had a million dollars for him. The thirsty man pushed it aside and stumbled on crying: "Water, water, water." Then somebody pulled up next to him in an expensive automobile just for him. Still he crawled on, looking for water.

You see, he was so desperate for water there was nothing in this world that could satisfy him but water. When you get that desperate for the fire of God, when there is nothing else the world has to offer that can compare with Jesus, then God will come and visit you. When He pulls up to your house, He will come in a mighty fire. The Fire of God!

How hungry are you? How thirsty are you? How desperate are you? In the early days of our ministry, Brother Richard Moore and his wife, Ronda, were working in the ministry with us, traveling everywhere we went. When I would call the people to form a prayer line he was always the first one in line. I often thought, *This guy is supposed to be helping me, but instead, he's the first one in the line to be ministered to.* I would look at him and he would always say: "I'm hungry. I'm desperate, but the Lord hasn't touched me." I always told him the same thing: "You have to get hungrier." He would say: "Brother Rodney, I am hungry." I would tell him: "But you aren't hungry enough." I am happy to report, that after several months, he did get hungry enough and he did receive the Fire of God!

So, I ask you again. How hungry are you? If one meeting a week satisfies you, then you are not hungry enough for the fire of God. You can be a nominal Christian, but you will never be a nation-shaker. The history books will never include your name as one of the great men or women of God. When they turn to the chapter about mediocrity, or the Pharisees, will your name be there? The people who oppose the move of God, or who ignore it, are not remembered long; but those who press in to get touched by fire and carry it will be remembered by history.

There are hungry people who followed us from meeting to meeting, across the nation, pressing in for a touch from God, and God met them at the point of their faith and they received the fire and the anointing. When the fire falls, people are saved, revived, and called into ministry.

PRAY FOR THE FIRE

I have faith to believe that everyone reading this book has the potential to shake the nations of the earth. I have faith for that, even if you don't. All God is looking for is for somebody to say: "Lord, I'm hungry. I'm desperate. I need Your touch. I don't care if the change is so great even my family doesn't recognize me anymore. I don't care if my friends don't want to associate with me anymore. It doesn't matter. I want You! I want You!" That is true desperation. The same desperation that blind Bartimaeus had. He was desperate!

Sitting by the side of the road begging, he heard that Jesus was coming his way. He shouted, "Jesus, thou son of David have mercy on me!" You can read his story in Mark 10:46-52 to see what "desperate" will make you do.

People don't know what it is to travail in prayer anymore. If you could be transported to the garden of Gethsemane when Jesus was praying, you would see what travail was. It was not a prayer coming out of a human intellect. It was a desperate cry for God from the heart. You can pray in English, or whatever language you understand, but if you're going to really pray, then grab hold of the Holy Ghost and let the Spirit of God pray from your belly. Grab ahold of Heaven.

You can't pray a weak, doubt-filled prayer and expect results. You might just as well say: "Twinkle, twinkle little star, how I wonder what you are. Up above the world so high, like a diamond in the sky." Results have nothing to do with the eloquence of your prayer, either. It's not about pretty words. It's about faith! The Bible says that we should know what our covenant is and we should come boldly into the throne of grace to ask God for help! Those who hear from God, and get answers to their prayers, are the ones who believe His Word and diligently seek Him.

I'm talking about praying with a passion. I'm talking about praying with a fire. The fire is the passion and the passion is the fire. James 5:16 tells us, "The effectual fervent prayer of a righteous man availeth much." The Amplified Bible, Classic Edition renders it this way: *"The earnest (heartfelt, continued) prayer of a righteous man makes tremendous power available [dynamic in its working]."* The fervent prayer of a righteous man, or woman, will be effectual—if will produce results. It is said of David Brainerd, the missionary to the Delaware Indians in New Jersey in the 1700s, that when he was praying out in the snow, all the snow around him melted. They said of Charles Finney, one of the leaders of the Second Great Awakening, that he prayed so fervently, when he prayed all the neighbors up and down the street complained. That is passion—that is the fire of God.

Do you know what it is to cry out to God? To call out to the Lord to get His attention, so Heaven knows your address and God knows where to come? To know that you can actually move the hand of God so it comes and rests on you? Do you know that God marks you? It's like Heaven's firebrand marking you.

The problem today is that people want to try to change lives without the Fire. That's the problem with these seeker-sensitive, hour-long things they call a church. What are they producing? They are producing nothing more than a McDonald's mentality, where you just pull up to the window, grab a Happy Meal and head on down the road.

If you think that's the solution for the world, we're in dire straits. I've heard the excuse that you can't provoke everybody to live for God. Why not? Do we have to live with what this world has to offer right now? Unless people catch the Fire of God, this world is in big trouble. We have to have a mighty revival of the Holy Ghost! The only way is for every person to catch the fire!

WHAT IS YOUR SPIRITUAL CONDITION?

As the Body of Christ, we need to grow concerned about our spiritual condition. We need to grow concerned about our apathy. We need to grow more concerned about our spiritual walk with God. People think because they come to church, carry a Bible big enough to choke a moose, sit there looking dignified and say Hallelujah, Amen, once in a while, that everything's fine.

No, it isn't! God's not going to answer intellectual prayers. He answers heart prayers. He answers a heart's cry. When you cry out, when you sincerely call out to Him, that's when He hears.

Sometimes people get convicted about their inner condition, but they don't want to make the adjustments. They get mad at everybody else—fight with their spouse, fight with their children, and fight with everybody else. They don't understand why they are fighting all the time. They need to turn that stirring into a cry to God, asking Him to come and do what He wants to do!

You don't know who you are till you're on fire. Perhaps you've been warmed up a little bit, but if you ever get on fire and find out who you are, Heaven help us! You talk about a passion—you would have passion!

If you are a senior pastor, and you don't have a passion for God and for souls, you can't expect your other pastors, or your leaders, or your people, to be passionate for God and souls. When you have a passion in you, it will inspire those around you. Then they will catch the fire and carry it wherever they go. Look around you at others you know and ask yourself if you see passion in them. Everyone should have their own passion, everyone, bar none! Your heart is a fireplace; it is either burning or it is not! No exceptions! You're either on fire or you are not!

See, sometimes we want somebody else to get the fire and the passion for us. "If you pray for me then I can get it," they say. I would like to pray for you, but are you prepared to receive it? Is there something there ready to meet whatever's coming? You have to reach out and meet God halfway. Are you prepared to make the changes required? You can't leave it up to somebody else. They can get their own flame, but what about your flame?

God has a flame especially for you. If you want to spend the rest of your life going from meeting to meeting, from conference to conference just to watch somebody else burn, then you'll always just be a spectator, rather than a participator. We do not have the time for only one or two to carry this flame. It's time for the whole Army of the Lord to get ignited with the fire of the Holy Ghost!

When you get ignited, you will burn with a passion for the lost, and you will burn with a passion to build and expand the Kingdom of God and to contribute towards, and fund, the Gospel. God will anoint you to acquire the end-time wealth of the wicked to fund the end-time harvest. You live it, you eat it, you sleep it, you drink it, you walk it, you talk it, and you pray it. If you're a preacher, then you burn with the fire of God! If you're a teacher, you burn with the fire of God! Whatever you do, you burn with the fire of God! Burn in the morning! Burn in the noon time! Burn in the evening time! Burn on Monday! Burn on Tuesday! Burn on Wednesday! Burn on Thursday! Burn on Friday! Burn on Saturday! Burn on Sunday! Let me tell you what will happen: people will come into contact with you, and even if you didn't open your mouth, they would sense God's presence and be touched and/or convicted by the Holy Spirit. You may not even have to say one word.

MY TESTIMONY

Jesus baptizes in the Holy Ghost and fire. I personally came to a place of desperation in July of 1979 when I cried out to the Lord: "Lord, I know You called me into the ministry, but I cannot go without Your fire, without Your anointing. I'm so hungry, I'm so thirsty, I'm so desperate for Your power—Your fire." I was in a prayer meeting, with about eighteen young people present, when I cried out loud: "God, I need Your fire! Please come touch me now!"

Some people pray for ten minutes and think they have moved the hand of God. Some people pray for an hour and think they really pressed in. No, you haven't come to that breaking point. You have not come to that place called Gethsemane. You have not come to that place where you place everything on the altar. You have not come to that place where you have said: "Father, not my will but Thine be done." You have not come to that place of consecration.

The fire is not for the few, but for the majority. Unfortunately, it seems that it's only the few who press in. The fire is not just for those we read about, who have caught the flame. Your name is supposed to be mentioned in there, as well.

So, I made a decision that night in July of '79. I said: "Oh, Lord, tonight's my night." I meant business, because I was hungry. This hunger had grown from August of '78 to July of '79. I had to have this fire. I started shouting at the top of my voice: "God, I want Your fire! God, I want Your fire!" I shouted for about twenty minutes, but I never felt a thing. My voice was going hoarse. Then, suddenly, it was as though somebody poured gasoline over me, lit a match, and set me on fire, from the top of my head to the soles of my feet. I began to burn with the fire of God. It was like electricity going through me. It felt like pins and needles from head to toe.

Instantly, I was beside myself. If you had seen me, you might have said I was drunk. I was laughing uncontrollably; I was weeping uncontrollably; and I was speaking in other tongues, all at the same time. I thought it might last about an hour. But an hour went by, two hours went by; three, four, five, six hours went by. One day, two days, three days went by. Now I'm not praying anymore for God to send the fire. It is so intense that I can hardly stand it. I'm concerned He's going to kill me. He has touched me, and now He's going to take me home. I started praying: "Lord, I'm too young to die."

I knew then why we're going to have to have glorified bodies in Heaven. Because if we didn't, we couldn't handle the presence of God. Natural bodies cannot handle the full weight of the glory of God. Thankfully, we leave these bodies behind when we go. Oh, how wonderful it will be to walk in His presence!

So, finally I had to ask the Lord to lift the fire a little. "Please don't take it away, just lift it so I can bear it." He lifted it a bit, so I could function, and it stayed like that for about two weeks.

The devil's not worried about you if you don't have any fire. It's those who are full of the fire of God who are the biggest threat to the kingdom of darkness. I do not believe for one moment that I would be ministering today, like I am, if it wasn't for my encounter with the fire of God. It's the fire of God that shapes you, makes you, empowers you, enables you, and that will carry you through till you see Him face to face.

CULTIVATE SPIRITUAL HUNGER

It is important for a child of God to know that spiritual hunger does not come overnight, but it must be cultivated. Spiritual hunger is not just acquired. Spiritual hunger must be developed. A spiritual appetite needs to be encouraged more and more. You just can't jump into ten hours of prayer if you can't even pray five minutes. You have to press in; you have to hunger; you have to thirst; you have to desire; you have to develop the intensity of that hunger, that thirst, and that desire.

When you are desperately hungry for God, the first thing you will do on Sunday morning is get yourself to church. When you aren't hungry, you will make excuses. "I was coming, but…" No, if you are hungry for God, you will be the first one there.

That's how I was raised. Our family was the first to arrive at church and the last to leave. Do you know what that instilled in me? Hunger for God! Now, all I can do is try to make you hungry. I can't get hungry for you, or desperate for you. You can say you are busy—we're all busy—but when we make time for the Creator of Heaven and earth, then He makes time for us. He can do for you, or your business, in an hour what you couldn't do yourself in ten years.

THE FIRE HAS A PURPOSE

If God has touched you with His fire, He has touched you for a purpose. Do you know what your purpose is? Do you want to know? Then get in His Word. Find a church full of the fire of God. Do you think you can go to a church where there is no fire and see your children grow into godly young men and women? I believe so strongly in the fire of God, if I had to move across the country to get into a church where the fire of God is, that's what I would do. For the safety of your family, either move where the fire is or start one. You associate with "dead" people and that's what you'll have. You associate with lukewarm people and that's what you'll have.

You may say: "Brother Rodney, you're just too radical."

No, this is not a game. We need to get serious…the time is short. God's about to do something and there will be a separation between those who are on fire and those who are not. They can laugh, they can mock and say we are just radical because we have all this joy. But I'm telling you: the day will come that they'll know how important it is to serve God with all their heart and how important it is for believers to have the fire of God and the joy of the Holy Spirit. When they stand before the throne of God, they'll see and know the truth.

Press in for the fire of God. This is not a game—your very life depends upon it. Your family's lives depend on it! Your future, both here and in eternity, depends upon it.

16

TO YOU, IN YOU, AND THROUGH YOU

Understanding Your Eternal Purpose

The Bible says that the ministry of Jesus was foreordained before the foundation of the world but was manifest in these last times for you and me (1 Peter 1:20). He was sent from the Father to the earth for a specific purpose. Jesus did not just randomly or accidentally show up here. He came on a mission and that mission was to pay the price for the sins of the world.

Our relationship with God has to do with covenants. We have no rights with God without cutting a covenant with Him. A covenant can only be legally ratified through the shedding and mingling of blood. God cut covenants with men all through the Old Testament. He kept His part, but they did not. He needed a Man Who would cut an eternally unbreakable covenant with Him. Jesus was the God-Man—God in a body of flesh and bone. When He shed His blood, it was the blood of God and man that was poured out—a covenant that could never be broken.

JESUS' MISSION

Jesus did not just show up here on earth one day. Yes, He probably could have just turned up in Nazareth as a thirty-three-year-old man. Boom, there He was! But He didn't. It would have been against the law of creation to just "appear." He would have been an illegal immigrant in the earth. So, He came through the door of natural birth, took on human flesh and spent the next thirty years in preparation for a three-and-a-half-year ministry. Today, people spend three years preparing for thirty years of ministry!

Jesus's ministry did not begin when He was a child. I cannot emphasize this enough, because some people have a fantasy that the child Jesus went around performing miracles. They think His mother had problems with Him, because He wouldn't do His homework. Perhaps she would shout at Him to stop showing off, quit walking on the lake. "Jesus," they imagine her saying, "stop turning the water into wine. We are getting tired of drinking wine. And I know you have to practice but leave the dog alone. He is old; he has died four times, and you keep raising him up!"

Jesus did not do any of that. He operated as a prophet under the Abrahamic covenant. Except for His death and resurrection, He didn't do anything here on earth that we can't do. His ministry did not start until the day He went to the river Jordan where His cousin, John the Baptist, was baptizing his followers. Jesus came down to the water and was baptized by John.

> And Jesus, when he was baptized, went up straightway out of the water: and, lo, the heavens were opened unto him, and he saw the Spirit of God descending like a dove, and lighting upon him: And lo a voice from Heaven, saying, This is my beloved Son, in whom I am well pleased.
>
> MATTHEW 3:16-17

When He was baptized in water, He was also baptized in the Holy Spirit. Then God spoke out of Heaven and said, "This is my beloved son in whom I am well pleased." Revelation 1:15 says His voice is as a sound of many waters. You can imagine how you would feel if God spoke out where everyone could hear it. You would probably fall on your face. Your body would shake—everything in you would tremble.

> And John bare record, saying, I saw the Spirit descending from Heaven like a dove, and it abode upon him. And I knew him not: but he that sent me to baptize with water, the same said unto me, Upon whom thou shalt see the Spirit descending, and remaining on him, the same is he which baptizeth with the Holy Ghost. And I saw, and bare record that this is the Son of God.
>
> JOHN 1:32-34

John's disciples, and the others who were there, were witnesses to the event which would signal the beginning of Jesus's ministry on the earth. If He had worked miracles as a child, it would not have been a surprise to see and hear what happened that day. He was called to His ministry from the womb, but it was from that very moment that Jesus was *anointed* and *empowered* for the work of the ministry. On the third day, after His Baptism, He turned the water into wine at a wedding in Cana. John 2:11 describes the miracle this way: *"This beginning of miracles did Jesus in Cana of Galilee and manifested forth his glory; and his disciples believed on him."* If Jesus had done miracles as a child, this would not have been called "this beginning of miracles."

Look at John 3:34. *"For he whom God hath sent speaketh the words of God: for God giveth not the Spirit by measure unto him."* **God gave Him the Spirit without measure.** "For in him dwelleth **all the fulness of the Godhead** bodily" (Colossians 2:9 Emphasis added). The fullness of the Godhead lived in Jesus when He walked on the earth as a man. He had an unlimited supply of the power of the Holy Spirit. All the power of Heaven was at His disposal. Jesus had a discussion with the disciples, particularly Philip:

> Jesus saith unto him, I am the way, the truth, and the life: no man cometh unto the Father, but by me. If ye had known me, ye should have known my Father also: and from henceforth ye know him, and have seen him. Philip saith unto him, Lord, shew us the Father, and it sufficeth us. Jesus saith unto him, Have I been so long time with you, and yet hast thou not known me, Philip? he that hath seen me hath seen the Father; and how sayest thou then, Shew us the Father? Believest thou not that I am in the Father, and the Father in me? the words that I speak unto you I speak not of myself: but the Father that dwelleth in me, he doeth the works. Believe me that I am in the Father, and the Father in me: or else believe me for the very works' sake. Verily, verily, I say unto you, He that believeth on me, the works that I do shall he do also; and greater works than these shall he do; because I go unto my Father.
>
> JOHN 14:6–12

We know from Acts 10:38 what Jesus's mission was: *"How God anointed Jesus of Nazareth with the Holy Ghost and with power: who went about doing good, and healing all that were oppressed of the devil; for God was with Him."* When we receive the anointing, it is for the same purpose: to do good, heal the sick, set the captives free, cast out devils, etc. In fact, the more anointing you get, the more you are going to look and act like Jesus.

UNDERSTAND YOUR PURPOSE

But it's not just about anointing. It's about yielding. You could be called and anointed and yet never yield to Him, and you'll never do a thing. Jesus said: *"The Son can do nothing of himself, but what he seeth the Father do: for what things soever he doeth, these also doeth the Son likewise"* (John 5:19). In other words, even though He was the Son of God, He still yielded Himself to the Father and did what He saw His Father do.

You can go to a Spirit-filled meeting, be touched by God and leave the meeting full of the anointing. But when you walk out of the doors, if you don't carry the anointing to others outside the four walls, you are wasting what you've been given. It was a waste to anoint you with oil and the precious perfume of the touch of God if you aren't going to use it. You will walk right back to the natural, right back to the realm of the carnal mind. God does not pour His Spirit out on you just to play around—just so you can feel good, or feel Heaven, for a little while—and then you go back out there and live like Hell. He pours His anointing out for a purpose. To accomplish something. Every single one of us has an eternal purpose. God has a mighty plan for each of us.

We saw that Jesus came and was anointed to do good, but 1 John 3:8 gives another purpose. *"For this purpose; the Son of God was manifested, that he might destroy the works of the devil."*

When we were born-again, washed in the Blood of Jesus, we became Christians. The word "Christ" comes from the Greek word "Christos" which means *anointed one*. So, a Christian is a "little anointed one." When you say you are a Christian you are saying that you are a follower of Jesus, the Anointed One.

If Jesus came to destroy the works of the devil, did He do it? Of course, we know He did. Then what is our purpose? To enforce and reinforce that defeat. Just like a police officer is not there to write the laws, because they are already in place, but to enforce those laws. You can put a traffic officer out on any highway in full uniform, let him stand in the middle of the highway and raise his hands, and traffic will come to a screeching halt. But you put him out there in his BVDs with his hands raised, and he will end up getting peeled off the front grill of a Mack truck.

We don't have a uniform, but we have His Blood and His Name. When you stand clothed in His glory you can put your hands up and say: "In the Name of Jesus!" and all the forces of the devil have to back off. You have the authority and you have the power.

You have to understand your purpose. If you think it is only to get a job or go back to school for more education, or get married, that's fine. Get a nice little house and car, but you will find out that was not really your purpose in life. God has an eternal purpose for you. You are an important part of His plan. You are not here by accident. No matter what your parents told you—you were not an accident. You are not a mistake. You are here for God's purpose and you need to find out what that purpose is.

We just read that Jesus came so He might destroy the works of the devil, and you are here to enforce the devil's defeat. That's why the devil hates you. He wants to stop you from seeing or experiencing the anointing. He doesn't want you to hear or understand the truth of the Word of God. He doesn't care if you go to some dead religious institution, but He knows if you go where dedicated believers are, you are likely to get a touch from God and you will be filled with the power of God. He doesn't want you to get a revelation of the price that was paid at Calvary. Above all, he doesn't want you to understand what the Resurrection of Jesus accomplished, or what happened on the Day of Pentecost.

As long as you are no threat to him, he will leave you alone. But when he realizes that you are thinking about being filled with the anointing and receiving the joy of the Lord, watch out! People don't know why they are struggling, but it is the devil trying to keep them distracted and prevent them from having a breakthrough. He knows you have a purpose, and although he may not know what God is calling you to do, he sees God's mark on you. He knows you could be dangerous if you ever come into the knowledge of the truth. You could shake a nation if you ever get on fire! He will try to get a bunch of demons to turn his fire hose on you so you can't burn for the Lord.

You have a choice, and you have to make a decision. Go for God or allow the enemy to pull you in the opposite direction. What will it be?

I was driving down the road in 1989 when God spoke these words to me: **"To You, In You, and Through You."** The Lord always speaks to me in sentences or phrases, but that is all I heard. I began to think about it. What did He mean?

TO YOU

What is that? When Jesus came to me, He revealed Himself to me and I was born-again. When He revealed Himself to you, what happened? You were born-again.

Ezekiel 11:19 tells us: *"I will put a new spirit within you; and I will take the stony heart out of their flesh, and will give them an heart of flesh."* When He comes **"to you,"** He comes to live in you. *"Therefore if any person is [ingrafted] in Christ (the Messiah) he is a new creation (a new creature altogether); the old [previous moral and spiritual condition] has passed away. Behold, the fresh and new has come!"* (2 Corinthians 5:17 AMPC).

God gives you a brand new heart—a new spirit: *"For neither is circumcision [now] of any importance, nor uncircumcision, but [only] a new creation [the result of a new birth and a new nature in Christ Jesus, the Messiah]."* (Galatians 6:15 AMPC). He doesn't just renovate the place. He gives you a brand new heart and a brand new nature and throws out anything not of God. He tells the devil to get out. He has had the place for too long. It's God's house now. *"What? know ye not that your body is the temple of the Holy Ghost which is in you, which ye have of God, and ye are not your own?"* (1 Corinthians 6:19). When He comes **"to you"** it is part of His eternal plan for your life.

Keep in mind that there is no such thing as a born-again drug dealer, a born-again bank robber, or a born-again adulterer. You can make all the excuses you want, but it's a fact. You can't serve God *and* the devil.

Now, I am not talking about temptations. The enemy will try to tempt you, but if you are constantly thinking about these things, then you probably need to get saved and your mind renewed. Because, when you get truly saved those things will leave you.

> This then is the message which we have heard of him, and declare unto you, that God is light, and in him is no darkness at all. If we say that we have fellowship with him, and walk in darkness, we lie, and do not the truth: But if we walk in the light, as he is in the light, we have fellowship one with another, and the blood of Jesus Christ his Son cleanseth us from all sin. If we say that we have no sin, we

deceive ourselves, and the truth is not in us. If we confess our sins, he is faithful and just to forgive us our sins, and to cleanse us from all unrighteousness. If we say that we have not sinned, we make him a liar, and his word is not in us.

1 JOHN 1:5–10

Love not the world, neither the things that are in the world. If any man love the world, the love of the Father is not in him. For all that is in the world, the lust of the flesh, and the lust of the eyes, and the pride of life, is not of the Father, but is of the world.

1 JOHN 2:15–16

There is one more verse that is important for you to remember: *"Whosoever is born of God doth not commit sin; for his seed remaineth in him: and he cannot sin, because he is born of God"* (1 John 3:9). That does not mean you will never again miss the mark or make mistakes. It doesn't mean you will never sin again. It means that you won't practice sin as a way of life. You will not wake up in the morning planning something that you know is blatant sin. You will begin to hate sin more and more, and when you do the slightest thing you know is wrong, you will immediately be convicted in your spirit.

Now let me say this. If you have no conviction when you sin, one of two things has happened. Either you have seared your conscience, or you are not saved. You should be convicted the moment you treat anybody contrary to what Jesus would have done or do anything that is not Christ-like. Your spirit should be sensitive and soft, so that you know when you have done something wrong. This also extends to your business life as well. Personally, if I have to make money by doing harm to someone, I would just rather not make any money.

IN YOU

There is a constant work of the Spirit of God taking place in your life after you are saved. How does this happen? Well, when you begin your Christian walk with Him and start feeding on His Word, there will be an increasing desire for more of Him. As we learned in Chapter 2, your relationship with God will grow as you hunger more and more for Him, which will lead you to a desire for the baptism in the Holy Ghost. You will take a quantum leap at that point, as you allow the Spirit of God to come and live within you.

The best way I can explain what happens is that you get baptized in the River of Life. The word "baptism" means to immerse—to put under.

> Afterward he brought me again unto the door of the house; and, behold, waters issued out from under the threshold of the house eastward: for the forefront of the house stood toward the east, and the waters came down from under from the right side of the house, at the south side of the altar. Then brought he me out of the way of the gate northward, and led me about the way without unto the utter gate by the way that looketh eastward; and, behold, there ran out waters on the right side. And when the man that had the line in his hand went forth eastward, he measured a thousand cubits, and he brought me through the waters; the waters were to the ankles. Again he measured a thousand, and brought me through the waters; the waters were to the knees. Again he measured a thousand, and brought me through; the waters were to the loins. Afterward he measured a thousand; and it was a river that I could not pass over: for the waters were risen, waters to swim in, a river that could not be passed over.
>
> EZEKIAL 47:1-5

When you are baptized in the river, you can choose what level you want to go with God. You can be ankle deep, knee deep, up to your waist, or you can go in over your head. The choice is yours. I want to be at the bottom of the river. I want to dive in and I'm not coming back out. If you want to see me, you're going to have to come under the water. That's really the safest place, anyway.

You have to hunger and thirst...it's an ongoing process. You wake up in the morning saying, "Lord, I'm hungry for You: I'm thirsty for You—fill me again. Fill me to overflowing." If you want the Lord to work in you, the cry of your heart should be "I'm hungry, Lord. Fill me again." Hunger is not just a thought that crosses your mind, it's a heart cry. You can be alone, reading a book, or on a rollercoaster with your kids, but your heart can still be crying out for more of God.

Then, you need to be yielded to Him. You need to allow Him to do His work in you. Not just once, but continually. And when the Holy Spirit speaks to your heart, you need to listen, obey, and make the changes He speaks to you about. Humble yourself and allow Him to clean you out, to burn out everything that's not from Him. He will change you for the better. The fruit of the Spirit will be evident in your life.

So, we established that the **"To You"** is when you are saved—born-again. The **"In You"** is when He fills you with Himself through the empowering of the baptism of the Holy Spirit, and when He also continues to do a work in you.

THROUGH YOU

A lot of people are stuck at "To You" and "In You," and never move on to the "Through You" part. God wants to bring you to the place where He is flowing through you to bless others. What good is it if He comes "to you" and lives "in you," but can't move "through you" because you are all blocked up?

When you go to your water faucet and turn it on full force, but only a trickle comes out, you know something is blocking the flow. What is it that is blocking the life of God in you from flowing out of you? What is holding you back from obeying God and ministering to others?

There could be insecurities, fears, or many other things that keep the life of God in you from flowing out. Your husband or wife, your children, your education or lack of it. It could be you are too young or too old to feel useful for God. Perhaps you feel that you have too much money, too many responsibilities. Or maybe you don't have enough money. I have heard people say that they can't be used of God because they don't have good looks. You may think I'm kidding you, but you would be amazed at the excuses people use for not letting the anointing flow through them.

When you come to the place where you decide nothing is going to stop you from being used of God, you will begin to let the water flow from your belly like a river. John the Baptist explained it to his disciples this way: *"He must increase, but I must decrease"* (John 3:30). That's where our yielding to Him comes in. He manifested Himself...His power and His presence...to us, so when we yield all that we are back to Him, we will be a reflector of His life and exhibit His very nature to the world. Let Him flow out of you to a lost and dying world.

If Jesus came to destroy the works of the devil, and *our* purpose is to enforce the devil's defeat, then we are enforcers of His purpose. Remember Paul's words: *"Neither give place to the devil"* (Ephesians 4:27). Don't let him intimidate you. Stand in the authority Jesus has given you. Let the power flow. Keep on telling the world what our Lord and Savior bought and paid for on the Cross. The people who will allow the Lord to use them are the people who yield to the Lord in spite of their shortcomings and what they consider their failures.

There are times when you may not feel like you can take another step. Stay yielded. In one of my meetings, I had a virus hit my stomach and suffered all afternoon with pains and nausea. I tried to sleep so I could preach that night but was getting worse by the minute. I thought perhaps Adonica should preach, but I knew I should, at least, try to give the word the Lord had given me. Several times I sat on the edge of the platform, praying that the Lord would not let me lose my lunch in front of all those people.

As the nausea subsided somewhat, I began to pray for the people. As I touched the first person, he fell to the floor and was gone for two hours. The power of God hit the place and many people were mightily touched that night, who would have missed a blessing had I gone home and not ministered.

So, what am I saying? You have to yield whether you feel like it or not—physically, mentally, and spiritually. You may feel inadequate and weak; you may be struggling, but when you make the commitment, you must determine to yield to Him, no matter what. Then you will see the hand of God move.

To you, in you, and through you! God's ultimate purpose, of course, is to come *to you* and live *in you*. But He wants you to step into that third phase. Will you step in to a place where He can move *through you?* Come on, child of God. Let the life of God flow out of your hands… let the words of God stream from your mouth. Be that person who is totally yielded to the Holy Ghost. One person can shake a nation, but imagine what all of us combined can do.

The history books are waiting to be written about the man or woman who will totally yield to God. Let the anointing flow through you!

17

THE DOUBLE PORTION ANOINTING

Dying to Self...Paying a Double Price

*Y*ou may be totally unaware, as you are reading this book, that God has a double-portion anointing for each one of us. But, it requires pressing in and seeking the supernatural impartation of that anointing. God has a plan for our lives, but we must desire that plan and His will for our lives and seek it with all our heart. I pray that this understanding cuts deep into the hearts of men and women, young and old, who want more...who are desperately hungry for all that God has for you. If that is you, read on. Only eternity will reveal what He can do with a yielded heart.

The ANOINTING

And it came to pass, when the LORD would take up Elijah into Heaven by a whirlwind, that Elijah went with Elisha from Gilgal. And Elijah said unto Elisha, Tarry here, I pray thee; for the LORD hath sent me to Bethel. And Elisha said unto him, As the LORD liveth, and as thy soul liveth, I will not leave thee. So they went down to Bethel. And the sons of the prophets that were at Bethel came forth to Elisha, and said unto him, Knowest thou that the LORD will take away thy master from thy head to day? And he said, Yea, I know it; hold ye your peace. And Elijah said unto him, Elisha, tarry here, I pray thee; for the LORD hath sent me to Jericho. And he said, As the LORD liveth, and as thy soul liveth, I will not leave thee. So they came to Jericho. And the sons of the prophets that were at Jericho came to Elisha, and said unto him, Knowest thou that the LORD will take away thy master from thy head to day? And he answered, Yea, I know it; hold ye your peace. And Elijah said unto him, Tarry, I pray thee, here; for the LORD hath sent me to Jordan. And he said, As the LORD liveth, and as thy soul liveth, I will not leave thee. And they two went on. And fifty men of the sons of the prophets went, and stood to view afar off: and they two stood by Jordan. And Elijah took his mantle, and wrapped it together, and smote the waters, and they were divided hither and thither, so that they two went over on dry ground. And it came to pass, when they were gone over, that Elijah said unto Elisha, Ask what I shall do for thee, before I be taken away from thee. And Elisha said, I pray thee, let a double portion of thy spirit be upon me.

2 KINGS 2:1–9

TAKING ON THE CALL

This story has always inspired me, because of the boldness of Elisha. God chose him to take Elijah's place, but it was not just handed to him. He had to take steps of faith in order to receive the mantle and the anointing. Elisha was minding his own business, plowing a field, when Elijah came by and cast his mantle upon him. Elisha didn't even have time to say goodbye to his parents or to explain to them what happened or where he was going. He slaughtered his oxen, fed them to the locals, and followed after Elijah, and served him.

The prophet Elijah was mightily used of God. God's hand was upon him in a phenomenal way. Everywhere he went, there were miracles, signs and wonders. He was God's man, raised up at that particular time to be a prophet to the nations. God had called him; God had appointed him, and God had anointed him. But the time was nearing when he would be leaving this earth. It was time for a successor.

God chose Elisha, but Elisha had to be willing to take on the call. I believe that there was such a hunger for God in the heart of Elisha. Obviously, he had been watching Elijah, and thought to himself, "I've got to have what he has. I want the same anointing on my life that is on Elijah." God was raising up Elisha for His work, and Elisha recognized that he had better stick close to Elijah until the time when there would be a "download" of impartation of his anointing. Thank God that we don't need to wait for someone to depart this earth before we can receive an anointing. However, the anointing is *caught*, and not *taught*. You may have a calling on your life, but you still need to stay in the presence of God, stay under the ministry of anointed people of God, and press in until God touches and anoints you.

You see, when you are hungry and thirsty for the things of God, then you are going to press in, reach out to receive all that He has for you. You will press in until you get it. I've watched people come to our meetings since the revival broke out in Upstate New York in April 1989. So many don't get it. They just don't know how to yield or how to receive. They won't press in for the anointing…the fire…the glory of God. They come to a meeting, get a little touch from God and think they have it all. Not so! A little dab won't do it. They need to be immersed!

This is not just about one touch. It is not just about coming forward and falling under the power. It is about a change—a transformation. It's when you look at yourself in the mirror after a month or two—perhaps even a year or two—and you don't recognize yourself. Everything about you has been changed because the hand of God has come upon you. There has been a divine impartation by the Spirit of God, and you'll be carrying that anointing. Elisha was not anointed merely by being with Elijah. He had to respect the anointing on Elijah, desire it and receive all he could. As I have said: **"The anointing is not taught—the anointing is caught."** You have to catch it! You have to "get under the spout where the glory comes out."

GETTING YOUR OWN ANOINTING

Remember this. The last thing you want to do is to carry a "borrowed anointing." If all you have is a borrowed anointing, what are you going to do when it runs out? When you start out, you might be operating on a borrowed anointing, but there comes a time and there comes a place when you want to check into that realm for yourself. Do whatever you have to do to get your own anointing. And if you are as hungry for it as Elisha was, you will seek a double anointing.

What are you going to do when your Elijah is gone? What are you going to do when your Elijah is no longer there? Especially when you've been following him and he goes across the Jordan. You realize there is only one way back and no bridge. If you are going to walk in that same anointing, then those waters are going to have to part.

MANY DISTRACTIONS WILL COME

We look at Elisha as he follows Elijah, and we see that he had many distractions. And, as usual, those distractions came from people—people who were the sons of the prophets. They also had insight—the revelation that Elijah was going to be taken away. They went to Elisha and asked: "Don't you know your master's going to be taken away from you?" He answered them: "I know that. Hold your peace." Basically, he was telling them to shut up. He had a goal—a desire—and he wasn't going to let anyone hinder him. He wasn't about to stand around and chat while Elijah was off on his mission to make his appointment with God. He was sticking to him like glue.

Some people are talkers and some are doers. Follow a doer. Be a doer. There comes a point in time when you may have to tell some people to shut up, because they will try to distract you from pressing in for your anointing. They may mean well, but they don't know what the Lord has told you or how He is dealing with you. Everyone has an opinion, but it's only what God tells you that matters.

Some people let other people affect them too much. I've watched people come around the ministry and then leave because they were offended…someone in the parking lot cut them off, or some other stupid thing. They got upset, because it didn't take much to distract them. They wanted the anointing, but it didn't take much for them to be offended and then they lost out on what they were trying to get. They were robbed of their blessing because they allowed other people to get in their way.

When you focus on Jesus, it is necessary to take your eyes off of *people*. Look only to Jesus; turn your eyes on Him, and press in to Him. Don't allow anyone or anything to come between you and your primary goal, which is to receive all that Heaven has for you. Think for a moment. How many people do you know personally in the Body of Christ who are "sitting by the side of the road" because they are bitter? They let the little things, the stupid things, offend them. Now they are distracted from their purpose and from God's plan for their life.

I have watched certain students in our school, the River Bible Institute, come for a year and be filled with anticipation, working in the ministry and looking toward a life of dedicated service to God. Then the second year, something distracts them, and they are swayed. I've watched good couples and good singles come and go, because they allowed somebody else to distract them from pressing in for the blessing and the mantle God had for them. They lost out on their anointing; they missed their mantle.

When you make the decision to follow the anointing, don't be distracted. Elisha could not be detoured. He wasn't interested in hearing what others had to say. He had interruptions and he had distractions, but his heart was set. "I am going to get a double portion of the anointing that Elijah has, if it's the last thing I do."

On three occasions he could have given up, but he was determined to stick to Elijah like super glue. Look at verse 4 in the text: *"And Elijah said unto him, Elisha, tarry here, I pray thee; for the LORD hath sent me to Jericho. And he said, As the LORD liveth, and as thy soul liveth, I will not leave thee."* He wanted that anointing and was not leaving till he got it!

THE DISTRACTION OF OFFENSES

People come through the prayer lines all the time and say: "Pastor, I want a double portion." I think to myself: *You have no idea what you are asking for! How can you expect a double portion when you get offended at the least little thing? If people offend you, if you are easily distracted, the double portion would do you no good anyway.* The anointing doesn't stay around people who have a bad attitude. We, personally, have regular opportunities to quit the ministry. I could be offended and sidetracked from God's purpose for my life and our ministry and miss what God has for us, but I choose not to.

We often think that only people who don't know the Lord, or are not walking with Him, are the ones we need to watch out for, but often it is the ones closest to us that have the power to offend us the most. If we are not pressing in to God or secure in our secret place (*See* Psalm 91:1), we can be offended by those who mean the most to us: wife, husband, children, parents or anyone in our circle of family and friends. The devil's sole purpose is to distract you from your primary goal, which is pressing in for more of God and being used by Him. Choose not to be offended. Decide not to take offense when the opportunity presents itself.

DESIRE THE ANOINTING ABOVE ALL ELSE

How do we get more of Him? Get hungry for all that He has for you. Whatever you press in for is what you are going to get. You know the story of Mary and Martha, the sisters of Lazarus of Bethany. Martha was encumbered about, doing all kinds of service. You can get so busy working for God that you don't have time, or you forget, to press in. Mary, on the other hand, just wanted to hang out with Jesus. She wanted to listen to Him talk. She was hungry for more of God.

Elisha wouldn't allow distractions to stop him; he kept his eyes on Elijah. When you are totally focused on the direction God is leading you, you will ignore the other voices. Elisha was pressing in to God.

All along the way, he had refused to leave Elijah, and they had finally arrived at the Jordan. *"And fifty men of the sons of the prophets went and stood to view afar off: and they two stood by Jordan. And Elijah took his mantle, and wrapped it together, and smote the waters, and they were divided hither and thither, so that they two went over on dry ground"* (vv.7–8).

Elisha had his eyes on what Elijah did with his mantle, because that mantle represented the anointing Elijah had on his life, and that's what Elisha wanted. He didn't just want the mantle. He wanted a double portion of what God had given Elijah.

> "And it came to pass, when they were gone over, that Elijah said unto Elisha, Ask what I shall do for thee, before I be taken away from thee. And Elisha said, I pray thee, let a double portion of thy spirit be upon me. And he said, Thou hast asked a hard thing: nevertheless, if thou see me when I am taken from thee, it shall be so unto thee; but if not, it shall not be so" (vv.9–10).

Elijah knew that Elisha wanted a double portion of his anointing, but it wasn't all up to him. Elijah told Elisha that if God allowed him to see him go, then He had granted his request.

> And it came to pass, as they still went on, and talked, that, behold, there appeared a chariot of fire, and horses of fire, and parted them both asunder; and Elijah went up by a whirlwind into Heaven. And Elisha saw it, and he cried, My father, my father, the chariot of Israel, and the horsemen thereof. And he saw him no more: and he took hold of his own clothes, and rent them in two pieces. He took up also the mantle of Elijah that fell from him, and went back, and stood by the bank of Jordan; And he took the mantle of Elijah that fell from him,

and smote the waters, and said, Where is the LORD God of Elijah? and when he also had smitten the waters, they parted hither and thither: and Elisha went over.

2 KINGS 2:11-14

What a scene that must have been for the young prophet, Elisha, as he watched Elijah taken up in a whirlwind and disappear into the heavens! And the fifty prophets who had been standing afar off were watching the whole thing unfold. What a way to leave the planet—in a whirlwind! Glory to God! I believe God Himself came and fetched Elijah, because in Job 38:1 and 40:6 it says that God answered Job out of a whirlwind. I think a "Whirlwind" is the automobile that God drives. God came and picked up Elijah and said: "Hop in, Elijah. We're going home."

Then Elisha cried out, "My father, my father," he took off his own clothes and tore them into two pieces. What was he doing? He was still wearing his own garments—his own mantle, which represented his own anointing. They represented where he was and what he could achieve. It spoke of what he could do with his old anointing. He didn't want to take his new mantle—his new anointing—and put it on over the old, so he tore his garments in two, destroying the old mantle.

Elisha was saying, "There is no going back now. I can't go back to what I was and what this part of me represented. I have to have the new mantle." He remembered that Elijah had told him if he saw Elijah go, he could have the double portion. "I have seen him go and I **will** have the double portion." So, he took the old things, destroyed them, and picked up the new. He knew it could be nothing less than a double portion of His Spirit, because that is what he had asked for. Elisha was hungry and wouldn't settle for less than all God had for him.

After Elisha took up Elijah's mantle, he was all alone and all he had was a token of what Elijah had said. He didn't have any proof that he had the double portion. So, there he stood on the banks of the Jordan. He knew if it worked for Elijah, it would work for him, because he now had a double portion of Elijah's anointing. Look at the scripture once more.

THE DOUBLE PORTION ANOINTING

> And he took the mantle of Elijah that fell from him, and smote the waters, and said Where is the LORD God of Elijah? and when he also had smitten the waters, they parted hither and thither: and Elisha went over.
>
> 2 KINGS 2:14

The water parted and Elisha went over! God kept His word to Elisha and gave him a double portion of Elijah's anointing. The sons of the prophets knew that Elijah was anointed, but they had no idea about Elisha. They had not seen the hand of God on him yet.

Perhaps they saw Elisha merely as Elijah's servant. When Elijah was taken up, it was like the end of an era for them. But God had another plan. He chose Elisha and He anointed him. Some people only see the anointing on certain people, and they look to them. But the Lord wants us to keep our eyes on Him. He can anoint anyone, as long as they sell out completely to Him.

It was only when Elisha called on the Lord God of Elijah and the sons of the prophets saw the waters part, that they believed he had the anointing. *"And when the sons of the prophets which were to view at Jericho saw him, they said, The spirit of Elijah doth rest on Elisha. And they came to meet him and bowed themselves to the ground before him"* (v. 15).

Now if you study the ministries of Elijah and Elisha and write down all the miracles that Elijah did and all the miracles that Elisha did, they are exactly double. Elisha had a double anointing; he had double what Elijah had. If you are hungry for a double portion, then you have to pay a double price; you have to press in. You have to press in where you've never pressed in before. You have to hunger like you've never hungered before. You have to thirst like you've never thirsted before. You have to yield yourself completely. You have to press into God. When you think, "I've got to have a double portion anointing," you can't be distracted by the things of this world; you can't let your friends, or your family, or any other worldly affection distract you from the hunger for God. Spiritual hunger is not something that comes overnight. But if you ask God, and pray with passion for it, He will give you a hunger and a thirst that will grab hold of you and be with you every waking moment. Late at night, lying on your bed, you will be crying out for more of Him: "Lord, I'm hungry for You. Lord, I'm thirsty for You."

Even though He satisfies you with good things, you should never stop pursuing Him. Psalm 145:16 says: *"Thou openest thine hand, and satisfiest the desire of every living thing."* This desire for God is something that should never end, until the day that you see Jesus face to face.

GOD HAS A DOUBLE ANOINTING FOR YOU

Down through the centuries there have been men and women who have pressed in. People like John G. Lake, Smith Wigglesworth, Aimee Semple McPherson, Kathryn Kuhlman, and others we could name. They pressed in because they were hungry. They were desperate. They were thirsty for God.

I know that there are those in the religious circles who would try to say that they were the exception rather than the rule, but I want you to know that God wants the exception to become the rule, when men and women press in. Because remember, it's not *your* anointing. It's *His* anointing. It's not your mantle. It's *His*.

If you are hungry and you're thirsty, He will come and touch you. There are anointings waiting to be released in the Body of Christ that the earth is in desperate need of, but it's going to take hungry people. It's going to take thirsty people to press in and say: "God, I've got to have the anointing. Lord, I want a double portion of Your Spirit. Let it come, let it rest upon me. Let Your fire come and burn on the inside of me. Burn away all of the dross. Do whatever You want to do—just change me, Lord. I don't care if my friends and family even recognize me. God, I don't care what it takes, and I don't care how many people leave me. If I have to go it alone, then I'll go it alone. I'm hungry! I'm thirsty for You."

When you come to that place, you'll press in and you'll receive from Heaven something that will never be taken away from you all the days of your life. God wants to do great things and He wants to do them through your life. You just have to open up—yield to Him. You have to say: "Lord, I'm available." You have to make the decision that you are not going to be distracted. It's time to focus in on Him and put your eyes only on Him. He's getting you ready for a double portion of the glory of God.

You cannot buy this anointing—it's free when you grab it with your heart. I'm so glad that Elisha pressed in. Otherwise we would never have heard about his ministry and how he pressed in for his double portion.

As you travel around our parking lot at The River at Tampa Bay Church, you can see the flags of many nations. How many of the people in those nations will hear the Gospel because you were touched by God? One day in eternity, they will say: "I'm so glad that you pressed in, because if you hadn't, you would never have been touched, and if you'd never been touched, you would never have come to tell me the Good News." Praise God; you didn't get distracted.

That's what the anointing is all about. That's what our ministry is all about. It's about His touch on us. It's about God's fire, and God's anointing. The same anointing that's on us will come on you when you press in—and even in greater measure. Then you will go out to towns, cities, and villages and see nations touched by the power of God. That's what God can and will do through your life. You may be saying: "But Pastor, I don't want to go to Africa." You don't have to move there. God can send you to a nation for one month and you may shake that nation. You don't have to live in a nation to shake it, but God can send you in there with the power, and with the anointing. (Of course, if He's calling you someplace, it would be best to obey. The blessing is in the place He is calling you to. You are better off in Africa, in the will of God, than in America, out of His will. Obedience is key.)

Thank God that Elisha pressed in. Thank God, He was able to do great things through Elisha, which still inspire and encourage us today.

What is waiting to be written about you? What is waiting to be written about what God did through your life because you pressed in? It's not just about you being touched, being blessed, and feeling good. It's about you getting touched and changed and that, through your life,

God is going to touch the lives of many other people. Through your life, your family is going to be touched; your neighborhood is going to be touched. There is nothing greater than being in the will of God. Pursue the double-portion anointing. Don't stop until you have it!

18

WALKING IN YOUR CALLING
Called, Anointed, Appointed

The Bible makes it clear that we need to draw near to God and He will draw near to us (James 4:8), but it also says, *"Herein is love, not that we loved God, but that he loved us…"* (1 John 4:10). He is the initiator. He first reaches out to us and we respond to Him. He is the One who calls you to a specific calling and will anoint you to do it. Romans 11:29 says: *"For the gifts and calling of God are without repentance."* He is the One who calls you. With His help, you are able to fulfill that call. Without *His* call and anointing, you can do nothing.

Throughout Scripture, we read stories about people who received special anointings in order to fulfill the call on their life. In the last chapter, we saw that God was the One who chose and called Elisha, but Elisha had to press in himself, in faith, to receive the anointing to fulfill his calling. Elisha was determined to get not only the same anointing Elijah had, but double the power and miracles Elijah had demonstrated. And he got it! The miracles Elisha saw in his ministry were double what Elijah had in his lifetime.

We could talk all day about the others who received anointings because they were hungry for God, but there is one who was unique in the way he received his anointing: the Apostle Paul. He was not hungry for God, but he was zealous for the Law. His hunger was directed at abolishing any mention of the followers of Jesus and, in fact, he was intent on killing every Christian he could. He went hard after destroying the Church. It is my observation that a passive "sit in the pew and sleep" Christian will not have a breakthrough. It will be the one who is really desperate for God, or sometimes even the one who is fighting God the most.

Many people out in the world are hungry for God but have no idea what they are hungry for. They are looking for something that is real, and when all they see is phoniness and counterfeit behavior they may use this as an excuse to not receive God's Word. (This begs the question: What do they see in you? Are you real or are you a counterfeit Christian?) The most frustrated people are those who are fighting with the call of God. You may be dealing with loved ones right now who seem totally opposed to anything you have to say about God, but they may be closer to coming to the Lord than those who are just neutral. Many times, the middle-of-the-road people won't be moved by what you say—they don't care one way or the other.

SAUL OF TARSUS

Let's look at Saul of Tarsus. I want to look at him in a different frame of reference—his mantle. He was present at the stoning of Stephen: *"and the witnesses laid down their clothes at a young man's feet, whose name was Saul."* (Acts 7:58). He may not have ordered Stephen's death but certainly approved of it.

> And Saul was consenting unto his death. And at that time there was a great persecution against the church which was at Jerusalem; and they were all scattered abroad throughout the regions of Judaea and Samaria, except the apostles. And devout men carried Stephen to his burial, and made great lamentation over him. As for Saul, he made havock of the church, entering into every house, and haling men and women committed them to prison.
>
> ACTS 8:1–3

Look now at the circumstances of his meeting with the Lord. Remember, Saul was not seeking the Lord; he was not hungry for a relationship with Him; in fact, his life's aim at the time appeared to be wiping out the "people of the way," as the Christians were called.

> And Saul, yet breathing out threatenings and slaughter against the disciples of the Lord, went unto the high priest, And desired of him letters to Damascus to the synagogues, that if he found any of this way, whether they were men or women, he might bring them bound unto Jerusalem. And as he journeyed, he came near Damascus: and suddenly there shined round about him a light from Heaven: And he fell to the earth, and heard a voice saying unto him, Saul, Saul, why persecutest thou me? And he said, Who art thou, Lord? And the Lord said, I am Jesus whom thou persecutest: it is hard for thee to kick against the pricks. And he trembling and astonished said, Lord, what wilt thou have me to do? And the Lord said unto him, Arise, and go into the city, and it shall be told thee what thou must do. And the men which journeyed with him stood speechless, hearing a voice, but seeing no man. And Saul arose from the earth; and when his eyes were opened, he saw no man: but they led him by the hand, and brought him into Damascus. And he was three days without sight, and neither did eat nor drink. And there was a certain disciple at Damascus,

named Ananias; and to him said the Lord in a vision, Ananias. And he said, Behold, I am here, Lord. And the Lord said unto him, Arise, and go into the street which is called Straight, and enquire in the house of Judas for one called Saul, of Tarsus: for, behold, he prayeth, And hath seen in a vision a man named Ananias coming in, and putting his hand on him, that he might receive his sight. Then Ananias answered, Lord, I have heard by many of this man, how much evil he hath done to thy saints at Jerusalem: And here he hath authority from the chief priests to bind all that call on thy name. But the Lord said unto him, Go thy way: for he is a chosen vessel unto me, to bear my name before the Gentiles, and kings, and the children of Israel: For I will shew him how great things he must suffer for my name's sake. And Ananias went his way, and entered into the house; and putting his hands on him said, Brother Saul, the Lord, even Jesus, that appeared unto thee in the way as thou camest, hath sent me, that thou mightest receive thy sight, and be filled with the Holy Ghost. And immediately there fell from his eyes as it had been scales: and he received sight forthwith, and arose, and was baptized. And when he had received meat, he was strengthened. Then was Saul certain days with the disciples which were at Damascus. And straightway he preached Christ in the synagogues, that he is the Son of God.

ACTS 9:1-20

OBEYING GOD'S CALL

Now, how unlikely was it that Saul, the persecutor of the Church, would be chosen by the Lord in such a way? God can use anyone He chooses, if they will just humble themselves to obey. Saul was on his way to Damascus when a light shone from Heaven. He fell to the ground and heard a voice saying: *"Saul, Saul, why persecutest thou me?"* (v.4.) His next question was, *"Lord, what wilt thou have me to do?"* The Lord sent Ananias to enlighten Saul concerning his calling and his purpose and to get him filled with the Holy Spirit and anointed for service. He bowed his knee to Jesus and now became zealous *for* the Kingdom of God, instead of against it.

When Saul had his encounter with Jesus, Jesus was placing a mantle on him that would be with him for the rest of his life. He was now in good company with men who had been anointed for their own particular assignments. Abraham, Isaac, Jacob, Moses. They are all classic examples of God touching a man, and the man touching God, each receiving an anointing and their own mantle.

WHAT ARE YOU DESPERATE FOR?
Throughout the Bible, we see different people who grabbed hold of God, all with different methods and ways. In Mark 5, we saw the woman with the issue of blood…desperate…needing an anointing of healing, who grabbed onto the hem of His garment.

What are you desperate for as you are reading this? Something will happen when you get desperate, hungry, and thirsty for your anointing. Many times we go along, needing a breakthrough, but just resisting what God is trying to do in us. We often try to ignore what the Holy Spirit is dealing with us about, but then one day we say, "Enough!" And we cross the line, submitting to His will and running to get our anointing.

Just as Elisha picked up Elijah's mantle and went on to do twice as many miracles, the woman with the issue of blood reached out to touch Jesus's mantle. She was not there looking for a healing ministry, but who is to say that after she was healed, she didn't have one? Once you have touched Him, you are never the same, and you carry your anointing wherever you go. What is real to you is what you will be able to give away to others.

YOU CAN'T GIVE WHAT YOU DON'T HAVE
People who have been delivered of things by the Lord, like drugs or alcohol, or any other bondage of the enemy, often go on to be the best testimonies of His grace. They usually have great faith to see others delivered, as they were. Have you seen someone healed of an incurable

disease? Perhaps you have been healed of an illness that the doctors said was terminal. Now do you have faith to believe God can heal others? Once you have seen the power of God at work, you will be able to witness to others in a similar situation. When your marriage has been healed by God's power and grace, you will have concern for those still going through their struggles, and you can share with them what the Lord can do for them.

So, remember, whatever you are touched with will end up being what God touches others with…through you. **He can only be as real through you as He is to you**. As real as His saving power is to you, that's how real it will be to others as it comes through you. The Holy Ghost will be seen by others through you, only as real as He is to you. That's why the Apostle Paul said, *"For I delivered unto you first of all that which I also received…"* (1 Corinthians 15:3a). He was basically telling them that what he received he had gotten from Heaven, and that's what he was delivering to them. Jesus told His disciples: *"Freely ye have received, freely give…"* (Matthew 10:8).

You can't give out to others what you don't have. The woman with the issue of blood touched the hem of Jesus's garment and received her miracle. I believe, with all my heart, that her later years were spent giving out to others what she had received. Under Jewish law, she could not go out in public with an issue of blood, so she had been in her home, alone. Imagine being isolated all that time and then being healed—whole again, able to move about in public.

Yes, she told what happened. I believe she spent her life telling everybody what Jesus had done for her. When God has touched you, He expects you to go and touch others.

Look at Luke 12:48. *"For unto whomsoever much is given, of him shall be much required…"* In the book of Mark, we read of an encounter between Jesus and the demon-possessed man who was living in the tombs.

And when he was come out of the ship, immediately there met him out of the tombs a man with an unclean spirit, Who had his dwelling among the tombs; and no man could bind him, no, not with chains: Because that he had been often bound with fetters and chains, and the chains had been plucked asunder by him, and the fetters broken in pieces: neither could any man tame him. And always, night and day, he was in the mountains, and in the tombs, crying, and cutting himself with stones. But when he saw Jesus afar off, he ran and worshipped him, And cried with a loud voice, and said, What have I to do with thee, Jesus, thou Son of the most high God? I adjure thee by God, that thou torment me not. For he said unto him, Come out of the man, thou unclean spirit. And he asked him, What is thy name? And he answered, saying, My name is Legion: for we are many. And he besought him much that he would not send them away out of the country. Now there was there nigh unto the mountains a great herd of swine feeding. And all the devils besought him, saying, Send us into the swine, that we may enter into them. And forthwith Jesus gave them leave. And the unclean spirits went out, and entered into the swine: and the herd ran violently down a steep place into the sea, (they were about two thousand;) and were choked in the sea. And they that fed the swine fled, and told it in the city, and in the country. And they went out to see what it was that was done. And they come to Jesus, and see him that was possessed with the devil, and had the legion, sitting, and clothed, and in his right mind: and they were afraid. And they that saw it told them how it befell to him that was possessed with the devil, and also concerning the swine. And they began to pray him to depart out of their coasts. And when he was come into the ship, he that had been possessed with the devil prayed him that he might be with him. Howbeit Jesus suffered him not, but saith unto him, Go home to thy friends, and tell them how great things the Lord hath done for thee, and hath had compassion on thee. And he departed, and began to publish in Decapolis how great things Jesus had done for him: and all men did marvel.

MARK 5:2–20

The ANOINTING

It's hard to imagine the agony the man must have been suffering. He was howling and cutting himself, bound by a legion of devils. (It says in the Book of Luke that he had been filled with the devils a long time; he didn't live in a house but lived naked in the tombs.) The Bible says that there were 2,000 pigs who plunged down into the sea, so there could have been as many as 2,000 devils in this man. It must have been a huge relief to him when the devils left him, at Jesus's command, and went into the pigs.

He was totally set free. When the people came to see what had happened, the man was fully clothed and in his right mind and they were afraid. Isn't that just like the religious crowd? They did not care about him when he was demon-possessed, but now that he was free, they were afraid. They showed more concern for the pigs than the man, whom God had created in His image. All they cared about was that this man Jesus had killed all their pigs, and they just wanted Him to leave them alone.

But not so for the man who had been set free. Much had been given him, and he wanted to give back. He begged Jesus to let him go with Him, but Jesus told him "No." Do you think it was because He didn't like the man? Of course, not. He had a testimony to share. Look again at verses 19 and 20:

> Go home to thy friends, and tell them how great things the Lord hath done for thee, and hath had compassion on thee. And he departed, and began to publish in Decapolis how great things Jesus had done for him: and all men did marvel.

Here was a man who had been demon-possessed for years...now set free...going to Decapolis, a region of ten cities, telling everyone what Jesus had done for him. He hadn't even been to Bible School, but he knew he wasn't crazy anymore. He had seen the pigs go into the sea, full of devils.

What do you think his message was? Yes, it was about being set free. His sermon titles probably all had "pigs" in them. "The Day the Pigs

Drowned." "The Bay of Pigs." "Deviled Ham." After a while, as he preached in the ten cities, somebody must have gone to him and said, "Look, don't you have something new to say? We were in your meeting in the last city, and you told the same story."

What else could he tell them? Before Jesus healed him, he was naked, he was in chains, he was bound by the devil, and he doesn't remember anything from that time period. All he remembers is that when the last devil left him, he was standing there in his right mind in front of Jesus. On the other side of Jesus, he saw all the swine running down the hill. That's all he remembers. So, what is he going to preach on? "The Day the Pigs Died." He preached what was real to him. You have to stay with what is real to *you*.

You may think God can't use you because you don't have a testimony like the man you heard speak on television who had been in prison for murder and was touched by God. He was saved, baptized in the Holy Ghost, and now has a big healing ministry. You hear their story and you say: "My God, that's amazing. I wish I had a story like that." But you do. You have a story of how God saved *you*. You have a story of how the Lord has touched *you*. You just have to start telling it. You've got to tell somebody!

I have heard people say: "But God didn't call me to preach. I can't speak that well." What do you mean? Most of us talk all the time. Listen to the people around you talking about where they've been, or what they've done, or what they plan to do. Listen to your own words. You're preaching to "someone" about "something." You can talk about frivolous, inconsequential things, or you can talk about Jesus. What better to talk about than what Jesus did for you? There are people who need to hear your story and touch your anointing. But how will they touch your anointing if they don't even know you have an anointing?

ARE YOU WEARING YOUR MANTLE?

Every time you tell someone what the Lord has done for you, then you are wearing your mantle. Jesus wore His mantle all the time. Remember, we looked at the testimony He gave of His calling, when He stood up in the synagogue and declared His anointing from God. Let's look at it one more time in Luke 4:18–19:

> The Spirit of the Lord is upon me, because he hath anointed me to preach the Gospel to the poor; he hath sent me to heal the brokenhearted, to preach deliverance to the captives, and recovering of sight to the blind, to set at liberty them that are bruised, To preach the acceptable year of the Lord.

We usually stop with that verse, but verse 20 says: *"And he closed the book, and he gave it again to the minister, and sat down.* ***And the eyes of all them that were in the synagogue were fastened on him.***" They saw the anointing on Him and heard the power in His words. When people see the reality, the power of God in your life, then they will go out and witness, and tell other people about you. "I'll tell you what—I saw it in that guy's life. Believe me; something happened. Something took place in His life."

Every time you get up and proclaim it with your mouth, you are declaring your anointing. You are demonstrating your mantle. On a Monday morning, when you get up, say: "I am anointed of God." Tuesday, you tell someone: "I am anointed of the Lord to stand in this place." Wednesday, you testify: "I'm anointed of the Lord to utter the Word of God." Thursday, you pray for someone. "I'm anointed of the Lord to lay hands on the sick." And so it goes throughout the week. What are you doing? Your anointing and your mantle are being voice-activated.

When Elisha took the mantle of Elijah, after he had torn his clothes—his mantle—in two, he said: "Where is the God of Elijah?" And he smote the waters. What was he doing? He was activating his new mantle. In other words, he was saying: "If God can do it for Elijah, He can do it for me."

Evangelist Reinhard Bonnke had a powerful ministry in Africa. You may have heard him say: "Africa shall be saved." He held meetings across Africa, and in Nigeria in particular, where he has had more than 1.6 million people in one service. But it is very interesting how his miracle ministry started out. He was a missionary from Germany to Lesotho, Africa.

Lesotho is a kingdom encircled by South Africa. It's never been part of South Africa or the system of South Africa; it has its own king. Lesotho is surrounded by some of the most beautiful mountains in the whole of the South African area, the Drakensberg range. The mountains go up to 14,500 feet and are known for their beauty. As a child, I visited the area with my family. There were places in the mountains where your voice would echo back to you. I would stand and shout, "Hello," and hear my voice echoing back to me, "Hello!" I loved to stand and drink the water as it came off the cliffs...just pure, fresh mountain water.

At that time, Reinhard would preach on the streets and play his piano accordion to attract a crowd. His ministry was small. He certainly wasn't shaking the nation; he wasn't even shaking the city. He was just there as a missionary, holding small meetings. Then he invited a South African evangelist, Dan Bosman, who had a powerful healing and miracle ministry, to come and to speak for him in Maseru, the capital of Lesotho. The meetings were widely advertised as "miracle meetings." Dan preached the first meeting, which was powerful, with many phenomenal miracles and salvations.

The next morning when Reinhard went to pick him up, Dan was in prayer. He told Reinhard that the Lord spoke to him to leave and to tell Reinhard that he needed to preach the remainder of the advertised meetings and that if he didn't leave, Reinhard would not step into his calling. Reinhard said: "No, you can't go; there are thousands of people here to see you. You're the miracle man." Nevertheless, Dan left as God had instructed him, even though Reinhard didn't want him to leave.

What happened next gave birth to Reinhard Bonnke Ministries, which now has seen over fifty-five million people saved. At first, Reinhard was so distraught that he went to God and prayed: "God, I've got thousands of people coming tonight expecting miracles and I can't do this." The Lord said: "I'm with you. Trust Me." He went out that night, by faith, and preached and prayed for miracles. To his surprise, many blind eyes were opened, deaf ears were healed, and cripples walked. God gave him miracle after miracle after miracle and launched his miracle-working and soul-saving ministry around the world.

People come to me all the time and say: "Pastor Rodney, I want to be a blessing to you. How can I bless you?" The greatest blessing that you can be to me is to go out and shake cities and shake nations for the Lord. Let me tell you—money can't even buy that. If you go out and "smack the devil up the side of his head," break the religious spirit off of people, and set the captives free, that's blessing enough. I want nothing else, nothing other than that. That is where the rubber meets the road. That's what it's all about.

The woman who touched the hem of Jesus's garment placed a demand on His anointing. As you declare, by the Spirit of God, that His Spirit is upon you, there will be people who cross your path who are going to place a demand on the anointing on your life. When people call in to our ministry to ask for prayer, we are there for them. They are placing a demand on our anointing. Many are suicidal, suffering breakdowns in their lives; some are needing healing, and they all need prayer.

UNDERSTAND WHAT YOUR CALLING IS

It's important to understand what your purpose is—what your calling is. Jesus knew His purpose, as He stated in Luke 4. He came to seek and to save the lost—to set the captives free. You and I, as born-again, blood-washed children of the living God, should make our life's goal the same one that Jesus had. We should place an importance on receiving the anointing and striving for a double-portion anointing. But we must know what to do with that anointing when we get it. We have been entrusted with a gift from Heaven and a responsibility to use it for Him.

Don't waste what He has given you. I look forward to standing before Him and hearing Him say: *"Well done, good and faithful servant; thou hast been faithful over a few things, I will make thee ruler over many things: enter thou into the joy of thy lord"* (Matthew 25:23).

When we go into any foreign country, we can have huge meetings with pastors from countries all around where we are speaking. We never know what will happen in those meetings. We may have thousands come to the Lord, be baptized in the Holy Ghost, receive their healing and be touched by God with an anointing. If even one pastor receives his double-portion anointing and picks up his mantle from the Lord, everything we have had to endure to get here has been worth it all. We will only know the results when we get to Heaven, but if a minister goes back to his city and country and, like Elisha, does double the miracles that we have in our meetings, then we will have done what God has called us to do.

You have a responsibility. There may be someone who comes your way this week and they will place a demand on your anointing. Don't take it lightly. As I stated earlier, when God has touched you, He expects you to go and touch others. But, you cannot give out to others what you do not possess yourself. Put on the mantle of the anointing. If He did it for Elijah, He will do it for you. If He did it for Elisha, He will do it for you. Walk in your calling. Walk in your anointing.

My prayer is: "Lord, may I be forever marked by Your anointing. May I be marked by the finger of God for all eternity."

19

DON'T TAKE THE ANOINTING FOR GRANTED

Guard the Anointing

You can come to a place in your life, whether you are a believer sitting in the pew or are in full-time ministry, that you find you are taking the holy things of God for granted. It has become easy for you to go through your daily life knowing Jesus has saved you and the Holy Spirit is living in you, but you are really just going through the motions of living a Spirit-filled Christian life. In Leviticus 10:10 (AMPC) we read that the Lord told Aaron: *"You shall make a distinction and recognize a difference between the holy and the common or unholy, and between the unclean and the clean."* Why did He say that?

In the following verses, we read the story of Aaron's sons: *"And Nadab and Abihu, the sons of Aaron, took either of them his censer, and put fire therein, and put incense thereon, and offered **strange fire** before the LORD, which he commanded them not. And there went out fire from the LORD, and devoured them, and they died before the LORD"* (Leviticus 10:1–2 Emphasis added).

GUARD THE ANOINTING

They offered up "strange fire" to the Lord, with no intent or purpose at all. In other words, strange fire would be when you pretend to be anointed. You are just going through the motions. You may say all the right words and use the right clichés. You may do all the right things, but the anointing is not there. That is "strange fire." Nadab and Abihu died because they didn't **guard the anointing**, but "did their own thing" without God's instructions and without their anointing.

This same pattern was followed by another pair of brothers, also sons of a priest. We begin their story with the prophet, Samuel, who was given to the Lord's service as a child, and who was, as a young boy, ministering to Eli—a priest in the temple of the Lord. *"Now the boy Samuel ministered to the Lord before Eli. The word of the Lord was rare and precious in those days; there was no frequent or widely spread vision"* 1 Samuel 3:1 (AMPC).

Why was the word of the Lord rare and precious in those days? Why was there no frequent or widely spread vision? What was Eli doing? Where were the prophets of God? Who was leading Israel and bringing them the Word of the Lord? God chose Samuel and raised him up to speak His Word and His will to His people.

Samuel had not heard God speak yet, since he was just beginning to learn from Eli how to minister in the temple. Verses 2–10 tell of God's call to the young prophet, and in verse 11, we see the beginning of Samuel's ministry, when God told him of all that He was going to do.

The Lord told Samuel, "Behold, I am about to do a thing in Israel at which both ears of all who hear it shall tingle. On that day I will perform against Eli all that I have spoken concerning his house, from beginning to end. And I [now] announce to him that I will judge and punish his house forever for the iniquity of which he knew, for his sons were bringing a curse upon themselves [blaspheming God], and he did not restrain them. Therefore, I have sworn to the house of Eli that the iniquity of Eli's house shall not be atoned for or purged with sacrifice or offering forever."

1 SAMUEL 3:11-14 (AMPC)

Eli had two sons, Hophni and Phinehas, who were totally out of control, and Eli would not, or could not, correct them. It was almost like he had given up on his sons, which would, in the end, cost him his life and the life of his sons. You can see in 1 Samuel 2:22–36 that they were following the same path that had brought about the deaths of Nadab and Abihu. Look now at 1 Samuel 3:15–18 (AMPC):

> Samuel lay until morning; then he opened the doors of the Lord's house. And [he] was afraid to tell the vision to Eli. But Eli called Samuel and said, Samuel, my son. And he answered, Here I am. Eli said, What is it He told you? Pray do not hide it from me. May God do so to you, and more also, if you hide anything from me of all that He said to you. And Samuel told him everything, hiding nothing. And Eli said, It is the Lord; **let Him do what seems good to Him.** (Emphasis added.)

When Samuel delivered the Word of the Lord to Eli, his only words to Samuel were, **"Let Him do what seems good to Him."** His words were spoken in resignation. But, in a way, they were spoken in arrogance—because there was no repentance at all for the sins of his sons and himself. You could have expected: "Oh, that's terrible! God have mercy on us!" But it was basically just: "Whatever." Why? Because the Lord had already told him that just as it had happened to Aaron's house, it would happen to his house. (*See* First Samuel 2:27–34.) And he did nothing.

But that is just the beginning of Israel's problems. First Samuel

4:1–7 gives an account of how Israel was affected by the sins of their priest and his sons.

> And the word of [the Lord through] Samuel came to all Israel. Now Israel went out to battle against the Philistines and encamped beside Ebenezer; the Philistines encamped at Aphek. The Philistines drew up against Israel, and when the battle spread, Israel was smitten by the Philistines, who slew about 4,000 men on the battlefield. When the troops had come into the camp, the elders of Israel said, Why has the Lord smitten us today before the Philistines? Let us bring the ark of the covenant of the Lord here from Shiloh, that He may come among us and save us from the power of our enemies. So the people sent to Shiloh and brought from there the ark of the covenant of the Lord of hosts, Who dwells above the cherubim. And the two sons of Eli, Hophni and Phinehas, were with the ark of the covenant of God. And when the ark of the covenant of the Lord came into the camp, all Israel shouted with a great shout, so that the earth resounded. And when the Philistines heard the noise of the shout, they said, What does this great shout in the camp of the Hebrews mean? When they understood that the ark of the Lord had come into the camp, the Philistines were afraid, for they said, God has come into the camp. And they said, Woe to us! For such a thing has not happened before.
>
> 1 SAMUEL 4:1–7 AMPC

Israel heard the Word of the Lord concerning Eli and his house but, like Eli, they ignored it. What they should have done was humble themselves before the Lord, check their own hearts and make sure that they were right with God. Instead, they went into battle on their own volition and so lost 4,000 men.

NEVER TAKE THE PRESENCE OF GOD FOR GRANTED
Even though Israel lost the battle, they still didn't stop and repent. The loss should have been a sign to them that there was a problem, but

instead, they went to fetch the Ark of the Covenant. They brazenly brought it out, like some kind of talisman. Instead of honoring God, they disrespected Him. You should never take the presence of God for granted. Some people started out with the presence of God on their lives, but without realizing it, because of pride, they moved further and further away from Him. They still act like God is on their side, but He left them a while back.

What did the Ark represent? It represented the presence of God. When the presence of God comes into the camp, something is going to happen. When the presence of God is released, it will not just be a show. When the presence of God is coming, it will be a manifestation of His power, to deal a blow against the forces of darkness, against the enemy, against everything that Hell has to offer. It was there to bring the camp of the wicked to naught.

But, the presence of God in the Ark of the Covenant was not to be put on display like something in a showcase. The Ark was there to do battle—no enemy can stand before Him. It's there to bring about judgment. According to the Word of God, God's judgment brings justice to the righteous and recompense to the unrighteousness.

God's people need to keep their hearts right with God. It is dangerous to become complacent or "too familiar" with the things of God. Don't allow wrong attitudes to slip in and cause you to lose your reverential fear of God. First Peter 4:17 says: *"For the time is come that judgment must begin at the house of God: and if it first begin at us, what shall the end be of them that obey not the Gospel of God?"*

Continue to keep your heart soft and yielded to the Holy Spirit. Continue to allow God's Word to bring correction to your life. We should always remember that we are here to do God's will. He is not here to do our will. God is not your servant. He is your Master.

The Philistines heard the shout of the Israelites and asked: "What does this great shout in the camp of the Hebrews mean?" When they heard that the Ark of the Lord had come into the camp, they knew that the presence of God had come into the camp, and they were afraid. Israel's enemies were afraid of God, but unfortunately, Israel had lost their fear of God. The Israelites should have been afraid, but they weren't.

Israel, and her priests, had lost respect for the Holy presence of God. What does that mean to you today? That means you can have the presence of God in your life but lose it if you lose respect for Him. You can talk about God, you can throw the Name of Jesus around, but if you are out of line, you'll come to nothing. Look what happened to the children of Israel. They ended up losing the ark, and their anointing:

> And the Philistines fought; Israel was smitten and they fled every man to his own home. There was a very great slaughter; for 30,000 foot soldiers of Israel fell. **And the ark of God** was taken, and the two sons of Eli, Hophni and Phinehas, were slain.
>
> 1 SAMUEL 4:10-11 (EMPHASIS ADDED)

I am so thankful that we are not under the old covenant today. I'm so happy that the presence of God is not housed in a box somewhere in Jerusalem. I'm so full of joy that the Tabernacle of God is with men, and God has come to dwell in us. But nonetheless, you can still have the anointing and then lose it. Especially when you take it for granted.

You may ask: "How do I lose the anointing by taking it for granted?" By not placing a demand on it. When you do not place a demand on the anointing you've taken it for granted.

I'll never forget when we first moved to our property, after the Lord gave us possession of the eighty-three acres. It's a long story that I won't go into, although I have told about it many times as a witness to the Lord's goodness to us. It was supernatural how we got this property—with no deposit and with no money changing hands. We didn't have the finances—we just heard the Word of the Lord and acted on it. They brought the documents upstairs to what is now my office, and I signed on the dotted line.

That day, we owned the property that is now The River at Tampa Bay. People thought we must have paid millions of dollars up front, and yet we didn't give them even a dollar. We just walked in, signed a document, and suddenly the property was ours. That's how the Lord does business when He has told you to do something.

Later, I received a letter from a lady who does not come to The River. She told me that she was very excited about the property that had come into our hands. She had seen the property and had always felt that it should be a church. Later on, we found out that many people had thought this should be a church. Numerous people had been coming onto the property just to pray. We walked around the property, praying as we went, and looked through the building with grateful hearts. God's provision was evident. It is the perfect place for a church, with thirteen-hundred parking spots, surrounded by palm trees. The property had belonged to an auto dealership, so the glass-walled showroom was ideal for a large number of people to gather. There were even offices upstairs for our pastors and staff. It was just what we needed, and God had miraculously opened the door for us to have it.

The lady continued her letter. She had been part of a church where the power of God was moving in a phenomenal way. People were saved and healed; miracles were taking place. Then things began to go wrong. If was as if you could feel the anointing of God flying away like a dove—and then it was gone. People began to leave until there was no one left. Weeds were breaking through the concrete in the parking lot. The property was unkempt and looked disheveled and run down. What was once a hub of activity, full of the power of God, was no more. The presence of God, which was always so manifested you could feel it the moment you walked onto the property, was no longer there.

She closed her letter with a warning: "Please, I beg of you. Don't ever let that happen to your church."

I didn't take offense, because I knew it was a warning from the Spirit of God. You may have a beautiful building, but that means nothing. There are empty churches all over America that have taken the anointing for granted. I know of one in particular in the city of Denver that was running 6,000 people on a Sunday morning back in the eighties. When

DON'T TAKE THE ANOINTING FOR GRANTED

we went there to minister in the nineties, the average attendance was 400. Things went wrong, and people developed a "whatever" attitude. They took the anointing for granted.

We can never, never, ever take the anointing for granted, because the moment we do, it's over—whatever we do, we have to do by the anointing of God. As a church, as a ministry, as individuals, in our personal lives, in our businesses, whatever we do, must be done with the anointing of God on it. We should never get to a place where we feel like we've "made it." We should never feel that we've "arrived" or that we've achieved it all. We must always be dependent on Him, relying on Him at all times, because the moment the hand of God is lifted—it's over.

Let's look at verse 5 in our text again: *"And when the ark of the covenant of the Lord came into the camp, all Israel shouted with a great shout, so that the earth resounded"* (1 Samuel 4:5 AMPC). The people were so excited to see the Ark come into the camp that they shouted until the ground shook. At that moment—the defining moment—they could have gone up and prevailed against the enemy had they been in the right spirit. Everything seemed the same as always. The ark was there; they shouted like they had done before, but there was no victory for them this time. Because they showed God no respect, He had removed His hand from them. *"The Philistines were afraid, for they said, God has come into the camp. And they said, Woe to us! For such a thing has not happened before* (1 Samuel 4:7 AMPC).

The Philistines heard the shout. They were momentarily shaken, but they still got up to fight. Just because you make a lot of noise shouting at the devil, doesn't mean he is going to back off. You also need to be walking in your anointing and your authority. (*See* verses 7–9.) *"And the Philistines fought; Israel was smitten, and they fled every man to his own home. There was a very great slaughter; for 30,000 foot soldiers of Israel fell"* (1 Samuel 4:10 AMPC).

The Israelites learned a great lesson that day. The Ark was in the camp. But God's presence was not there to do battle for them. It is a spiritual battle. You can't fight a spiritual battle with natural resources.

Many churches have pushed the Spirit of God to the side and wonder why it is so difficult to get people saved, delivered, healed, and on fire for God. In some churches, they go through all the motions. They sing and shout and run around the building, but there's no power in the place. It's all just a show. You can't defeat the enemy without the genuine power of the Holy Spirit.

Don't take the anointing for granted.

Across America today, there are thousands of people gathered in congregations on Sundays where the shout is heard—but from Monday through Saturday, there are no corresponding actions to go with the shout. They talk the talk, but they don't walk the walk. The Lord wants to show up in our midst and move on our behalf, but we need to make Him feel welcome, we need to allow Him to do what He wants to do in us and through us. God touches us so we can go out and touch others. We need to get filled up with the presence of God and then go fulfill the Great Commission.

When the presence of God is there, it's time to "**Arise and Do**." Boldly get up in the Name of Jesus and march through the land. See the hand of God in operation: Monday, Tuesday, Wednesday, Thursday, Friday, and Saturday. We are taking territory for the Kingdom. Hallelujah!

But that is not what happened in our text. Verse 11 says: *"**And the ark of God was taken,** and the two sons of Eli, Hophni and Phinehas, were slain"* (Emphasis added). Remember, the presence of God was in the Ark. So, no matter how great the shout had been, no matter how the earth resounded, or how secure the Israelites felt with God in their midst, they still lost the Ark. The enemy came in and stole the anointing. The presence of God was taken from the people. The devil will do whatever he can to steal the anointing.

But, that is not the end of the story:

> Now a man of Benjamin ran from the battle line and came to Shiloh that day, with his clothes torn and earth on his head. When he arrived, Eli was sitting by the road watching, for his heart trembled for the ark

of God. When the man told the news in the city, all the city [people] cried out. When Eli heard the noise of the crying, he said, What is this uproar? And the man came hastily and told Eli. Now Eli was 98 years old; his eyes were dim so that he could not see. The man said to Eli, I have come from the battle; I fled from the battle today. Eli said, How did it go, my son? The messenger replied, Israel fled before the Philistines, and there has been a great slaughter among the people. Also your two sons, Hophni and Phinehas, are dead, and the ark of God is captured. And when he mentioned the ark of God, Eli fell off the seat backward by the side of the gate. His neck was broken and he died, for he was an old man and heavy. He had judged Israel forty years.

1 SAMUEL 4:12-18 (AMPC)

The Ark was gone. The presence of God in their midst was gone. Because Israel did not regard the Word of the Lord, and because they disrespected the anointing, they lost everything.

Now his daughter-in-law, Phinehas' wife, was with child, about to be delivered. And when she heard that the ark of God was captured and that her father-in-law and her husband were dead, she bowed herself and gave birth, for her pains came upon her. And about the time of her death the women attending her said to her, Fear not, for you have borne a son. But she did not answer or notice. And she named the child Ichabod, saying, The glory is departed from Israel!—because the ark of God had been captured and because of her father-in-law and her husband. She said, The glory is gone from Israel, for the ark of God has been taken.

1 SAMUEL 4:19-22 (AMPC)

What a terrible thing to call your child—Ichabod—"the Lord has departed from Israel." They often named their children according to events happening, or situations occurring, at the time. Sometimes, you just happened to be born the wrong child in the wrong place. Ichabod was a living witness to the fact that the Ark had been taken, because they had taken the anointing for granted.

STAY OPEN, HUNGRY AND TEACHABLE

Now you may be asking: "In the modern context of things in the 21st century, how could we be sure not to take the presence of God for granted?"

The answer resides with two ingredients: hunger and thirst. We know that Jesus knew their importance because of His Words in the Sermon on the Mount. *"Blessed are they which do hunger and thirst after righteousness: for they shall be filled"* (Matthew 5:6). The moment you lose your hunger and your thirst for the things of God, you're about to lose everything.

As I said earlier, we should never allow ourselves to get to the place where we feel like we've arrived. We have to approach the things of God like little children—expectant, open, and teachable. We must never become blasé about the presence of God. Never, ever watch an altar call and think: "Oh, that's just another altar call…that's what they do here, you know." No! We should always be as excited when another person comes to Christ as we would be if it were our own brother, or our mother, or father, who got saved that day. If it was one of our family, we would stand there, weeping for joy, wouldn't we?

An altar call is not a signal that it is time to get up out of your seat and leave. Many people think: "Oh well, he is almost through now. I've heard all he has to say, so I can go home." I've seen that in many of the churches we speak in. In a religious church setting, the moment you say: "Every head bowed, every eye closed," people start leaving the building. They use the altar call as an opportunity to leave…to get out so they can go to a restaurant for Sunday brunch. There might be someone on the verge of making a decision for Christ, and they will step over them to get out ahead of anyone else. I don't understand that kind of religious thinking. It's really nothing more than lukewarmness manifested.

I tell people that if they are going to leave, do it while I'm preaching, but don't leave during the altar call. If you want to get me mad, start leaving during the altar call. That shows a total disrespect for God and for the Word of God and a callousness toward lost souls.

Don't come to The River if you're in a hurry. Don't come to any of my meetings thinking: "Well, I'm just going to go to a quick service," because we don't do quick services. I don't do drive-thru meetings. Someone told me: "Pastor, some people can't handle more than an hour."

Yes, they can. They do it all the time. They go watch movies that are getting longer and longer. Some of these epic movies are over two-and-a-half-hours long. Do you think people get up and walk out before it is over? No, because they are interested in what they are watching. People go to sporting events, such as a football game, or a hockey match, that goes on for hours, but then they think church must be hurried up, or shortened down.

If that is what you are looking for, The River is not the place for you. We aren't going to cater to that kind of thing. I preach all over the world to people who are hungry for the Word and have a great respect for it. I am not going to change for people who have no respect for God or His Word.

If you have felt the touch of God, and have moved in His gifts, don't make the mistake that Samson did. He had been given strength beyond any other man, and in Judges, Chapters 14–16, we see that he allowed sin to take him to a place where he took his gift and anointing for granted. When his strength was taken from him, by the cutting of his hair—the source of his strength—he was not even aware it had gone. *"And he awoke out of his sleep, and said, I will go out as at other times before, and shake myself. And he was not that the LORD was departed from him"* (Judges 16:20). Do not lose the precious anointing with which the Lord has blessed you.

Don't take the anointing for granted.

20

WHAT WILL YOU DO WITH THE ANOINTING?

Don't Let the Devil Steal Your Seed

*J*esus often taught in parables, but I want to look now at the "Parable of the Sower," beginning with Mark 4:1–3 (AMPC):

"Again Jesus began to teach beside the lake. And a very great crowd gathered about Him, so that He got into a ship in order to sit in it on the sea, and the whole crowd was at the lakeside on the shore. And He taught them many things in parables (illustrations or comparisons put beside truths to explain them), and in His teaching He said to them: Give attention to this! Behold, a sower went out to sow."

Now notice where the seeds landed and what happened to them, in verses 4–8.

> And as he was sowing, some seed fell along the path, and the birds came and ate it up. Other seed [of the same kind] fell on ground full of rocks, where it had not much soil; and at once it sprang up, because it had no depth of soil; And when the sun came up, it was scorched, and because it had not taken root, it withered away. Other seed [of the same kind] fell among thorn plants, and the thistles grew *and* pressed together and utterly choked and suffocated it, and it yielded no grain. And other seed [of the same kind] fell into good (well-adapted) soil and brought forth grain, growing up and increasing, and yielded up to thirty times as much, and sixty times as much, and even a hundred times as much as had been sown.

Jesus finished the parable with verse 9: *"And he said unto them, He that hath ears to hear, let him hear."* When they were alone, His disciples began to ask Him about the parable. They didn't understand what He was trying to tell them.

THE ENEMY COMES TO STEAL THE WORD

I say these same words to you—He that hath ears to hear, let him hear—because I want to tell you why people take the anointing for granted. Let's start with verses 14–15: *"The sower sows the Word. The ones along the path are those who have the Word sown [in their hearts], but when they hear, Satan comes at once and [by force] takes away the message which is sown in them."*

So, one thing we know is that when you sow the Word of God, the enemy comes to steal the Word. He comes to take it by force. Some people ask: "What do I do when he comes?" Reinforce the Word—preach it harder. When you start preaching on healing, people get sick. The devil is trying to steal the Word before it has a chance to be planted and established. That's not the time to say: "Oh, the Word of God doesn't work." That's the time to double down on preaching and praying for people to be healed. Continue to minister healing. Don't let him steal the Word. Reinforce it.

When you begin to share on God's supernatural provision, and you teach tithing and giving, people start coming under financial attack. They will say that it doesn't work. It does work! Keep teaching it. Whatever the enemy is trying to steal from you, reinforce God's Word into your eyes, ears, and heart. The devil knows the Word, and he knows you can defeat him with it.

The devil knows that the best time to prevent the tree from growing up and producing fruit is to snatch up the seed before it even has a chance to germinate in the soil. If he can't prevent the seed from being planted and sprouting, then he will try to destroy the tree while it's a sapling, while it's still young and tender. He knows it will be almost impossible, twenty years later, to come back to pull it up when the tree has grown up to be a tall oak with deep, strong roots.

SEEDS SOWN ON STONY GROUND

So, the opportune time for the enemy to steal the Word is the moment that it's sown. He comes to steal the Word, and you have to be aware of that and realize what he is doing. Read Mark 4:16–17:

> And in the same way the ones sown upon stony ground are those who, when they hear the Word, at once receive and accept and welcome it with joy; And they have no real root in themselves, and so they endure for a little while; then when trouble or persecution arises on account of the Word, they immediately are offended (become displeased, indignant, resentful) and they stumble and fall away.

So, the seeds sown on stony ground are those who hear the Word and receive it, accept it and welcome it with joy, but they have no real roots in themselves. They are shallow. They hear the Word and it sounds good to them, but they don't allow it to make an impact—to bring about a change—in their life. They cave in at the slightest sign of pressure or opposition. When trouble or persecution arise, they are offended. You ask: "Pastor, are you telling me that trouble and persecution arise because of the Word? If that's the case, I don't want the Word." No! You do want the Word…you just want *more* of the Word, so that when trouble or persecution arise you are not offended. The devil's best deception is to attack you and get you to blame God for it. God and His Word are never the problem. They are the answer!

Just grit your teeth and tell the enemy: "Listen, you fire your best shot, but if you think you're getting me off of this, you're mistaken. I'm going to double down on it. I'm going to go lock myself away in a room for three days. I'm going to solidify this Word in my heart. I refuse to be offended because of God or His Word."

The Bible says because they have no real roots they are offended when persecuted. Trouble and persecution arise because of the Word. You ask why? The devil doesn't want the Word to take root in you, because if it takes root, you're going to be dangerous to his kingdom. So, people with no roots become offended, displeased, indignant, resentful until they stumble and fall away.

You want to know why? It's because of the stony ground. The ground is representative of the heart—the heart that's stony, the heart that has rocks in it. Jeremiah 23:29 says: *"Is not my word like as a fire? saith the LORD; and like a hammer that breaketh the rock in pieces?"* That's why we have to allow the Word to come and break up the fallow ground—so we can have a heart that's soft with ground that's ready—so when the Word is sown, it's not blown away and the birds of the air can't just come and pick up the seed and steal it away.

SEED SOWN AMONG THE THORNS

> And the ones sown among the thorns are others who hear the Word; Then the cares and anxieties of the world and distractions of the age, and the pleasure and delight and false glamour and deceitfulness of riches, and the craving and passionate desire for other things creep in and choke and suffocate the Word, and it becomes fruitless.
>
> MARK 4:18-19 (AMPC)

These people hear the Word and receive it. It is planted and begins to grow. But the devil sends weeds and thorns and thistles to choke the plant and steal its nourishment, so it is prevented from growing further or producing fruit. The devil tries to distract people from the truth of God's Word with cares and anxiety. He tries to amplify problems and get people to focus on them, rather than focusing on the solution. When you feel tempted to worry and fret, remember that it's a trap of the enemy. Jesus said: *"And who of you by worrying and being anxious can add one unit of measure (cubit) to his stature or to the span of his life?"* (Matthew 6:27 AMPC)

Worrying is a fruitless exercise. It has no solution but continues to drag you further and further down. Take your eyes off the problem and fix your eyes on God's Word. Don't tell God how big your problem is. Tell your problem how big your God is!

People everywhere have cares and anxieties. Each one of them feels that their situation is worse than anyone else's. People tell me: "But Pastor, you just don't know my circumstances. You don't know what happened last week." Each time you see them, you are afraid to ask how they are, because they are going to tell you. "Well, Pastor, I'm not doing that well." Then you wait for it. It's coming. Buckle your seatbelt, because you are going to have to listen to their problems for the next hour. Why? Because the cares and the anxiety of this world have weighed them down. They are focused on the problem instead of the solution.

The weeds that choke the Word in some people's lives are the distractions of the age—the pleasure and delight, the false glamour, and the deceitfulness of riches. The craving and passionate desire for other things creep in; they choke off and suffocate the Word until it becomes fruitless. 1 John 2:15-17 says:

> Love not the world, neither the things that are in the world. If any man love the world, the love of the Father is not in him. For all that is in the world, the lust of the flesh, and the lust of the eyes, and the pride of life, is not of the Father, but is of the world. And the world passeth away, and the lust thereof: but he that doeth the will of God abideth forever.

People are distracted by movies and entertainment. The Bible says in 2 Timothy 3:4 that the ungodly people of the last days will be lovers of sensual pleasures and vain amusements more than and rather than lovers of God. People desire to gratify their flesh even as they deny their spirit. They can tell you more about the latest reality stars than the men and women of faith.

People are so distracted in today's world that many don't even bring their Bibles to church like they used to. Even worse, they don't even read their Bibles anymore. I've heard them say: "My Bible is on my phone if I need it." But if the battery dies, your Bible is dead. You need to have a Bible that you can familiarize yourself with. One that you can find, even when there is a blackout and you can't charge your phone, your iPad, or your computer.

How good it is to have a Bible that you can actually hold in your hand, turn the pages, and mark the passages that speak to you! When people lose their reverence for the Word, they are in danger of losing the anointing.

Another robber of fruit in a person's life is greed and covetousness. Covetousness is faith in material possessions, rather than in God. Jesus said, in Luke 12:15: *"Take heed, and beware of covetousness: for a man's life consists not in the abundance of the things which he possesses."* A person's worth is not in what they own, but in the quality of their heart. Paul tells us, in Ephesians 5:3, that covetousness, along with fornication and uncleanness, shouldn't even be *named* among Christians. In 1 Corinthians 6:10, he tells us that covetous people will not inherit the Kingdom of God.

SEED SOWN ON GOOD GROUND
Look now at Mark 4:20 (AMPC):

> And those sown on the good (well-adapted) soil are the ones who hear the Word and receive and accept and welcome it and bear fruit—some thirty times as much as was sown, some sixty times as much, and some [even] a hundred times as much.

Some seed will bear thirty times as much as was sown, some sixty times as much, and some even a hundred times as much. But even two times more is better than not bearing fruit at all. Five times more is definitely better than nothing.

So, what do we want to be? We want to be good soil. How can we be good soil? By receiving the Word of God with joy and gladness. By allowing the Spirit of God to do the work in our hearts, and by never approaching the things of God with complacency. And by being totally open in the areas of our worship. Worship and the Word—these two areas go hand in hand.

When we worship God intentionally and with purpose, when we worship with all our heart, there are some people who may think we are crazy—like Michal thought David was crazy. But we're not doing it to be seen. We're doing it for the King. Our worship is not just saved for Sunday. Our worship is for every day of the week. Our worship is in our home, lying on our beds, singing and rejoicing…even in the shower. Some of my best times worshipping Him is when I am driving down the road in my car. You can worship Him anywhere.

NEVER BECOME INDIFFERENT TO THE THINGS OF GOD

However, when you become complacent, the first areas that start sliding are your worship, time in the Word, and your prayer life. You may not even notice the difference, but you are on a path leading to losing the anointing. Many people physically come to church, but it's evident they aren't really there. Their bodies are there, but their minds are somewhere else. They are not participating in the service. The church is filled with spectators instead of participators. They are waiting for something to happen from the platform instead of keeping their eyes on Jesus and being open to receive. (Sadly, many Christians have been trained by their church to just sit and watch while the pastor does his thing.)

When you come to church hungry for God, it doesn't matter what happens from the platform. If you just came to watch what happens, that's all you will ever get from the service—just what happened on

WHAT WILL YOU DO WITH THE ANOINTING?

the platform. But, if you come hungry and thirsty for God, it doesn't matter where you're sitting. The Word of the Lord will come to you. The power of God will bring just what you need.

There are times when I am in church that the worship begins and I start weeping. The Fire of God touches me, and I know I have received from Heaven. I can leave there with what I came to get. There shouldn't ever be a time that you come to church and don't receive what you need from Heaven.

There have been ministers who attended our Ministers' Conferences who stayed in their "ministry mode" all week and never received from God what He had for them. They didn't come expecting to receive anything from God. They were just spectators. If you leave a service without receiving what you need from Heaven, it's not God's fault. It's *your* fault, because there is a banquet table that is set before you, and the Master has said, "Come and dine." When you're hungry, when you're thirsty, He has a table set especially for you.

You must stay in a place—with your heart attitude—to receive. You have to come with an anticipation and place a demand on the anointing. You have to come hungry to every service, coming with the Word in your heart, bringing your Bible, your notebook, writing down things you don't want to let slip, letting God speak to you. Come with an anticipation. Never ever become blasé or indifferent to the things of God because you have "heard it all." God's mercies and compassion are always fresh and new every morning (Lamentations 3:23). His Word never gets old. He is always moving—always working.

Some people, bless their heart, get up and go to the restroom four or five times during the service. Now, I'm not saying you couldn't have a bad case of diarrhea or bladder problems. But I promise you, you're not going to receive from God in the restroom. I'm not trying to make people afraid to get up and go—I'm trying to make a point, because some people are always restless, roving around, going somewhere else, coming back to their seat, only to start over. It's obvious that their mind is not on receiving from God. It's not on worshipping God or giving back to Him. It's the same with their giving. Never just come to the service and just throw something in the bucket. Come ready to worship Him with the fruit of your labor. Come ready to give of yourself.

I teach our people at The River to come hungry, thirsty, ready to participate, anticipating what God is going to do in the service. The anointing comes for a purpose, to bring about taking territory for the Kingdom of God. In the service, the purpose is to save the lost, set people free, deliver the captives. All of this God does through the gifts of the Spirit, which is why we should never take them for granted. Then, as we said in an earlier chapter, there are ministry gifts that God places in the church: apostles, prophets, evangelists, pastors, and teachers. We should never take those for granted, either. They are diverse and they are unique. With each of those gifts come different anointings.

It's very hard to receive from an anointing that you criticize. You might not like someone who comes along with miracles. You don't have to like the vessel, but the Lord can use whomever He chooses! If you need a miracle, forget about the vessel. Just accept your miracle. It's like a person who's drowning. He's not going to argue about who's throwing out the lifeline. He is not going to say: "Oh no, don't throw the rope yet; I know I'm drowning, but first of all let me just check your credentials. I wouldn't want the wrong person throwing the lifeline."

THE ANOINTING COMES ON YOU FOR A PURPOSE

That anointing is not just for in the service. The anointing is extended when you walk out of the doors, then goes into your home, your marriage, your children, your finances, your business, your ministry, and every area of your life. The Lord is with you so that you can see the Kingdom of Heaven come. Remember this: Everything you need is in the anointing, so let it loose!

There is not one person reading this who faces a problem, circumstance or situation that the anointing of God can't cure. There is no one with a problem so great that's it's beyond the anointing. The anointing is there to meet any need, at any time, and in any given situation or circumstance—regardless of what is involved. Your problem doesn't faze God one little bit.

The anointing destroys the yoke of bondage. The anointing brings the release. Perhaps you are having problems in your family. Your family cannot stay the same way. It is impossible! When the anointing comes, it breaks and destroys every yoke. It is impossible to stay under the anointing and not be changed. It's impossible to have the anointing of God come upon you and then remain the same. It's impossible.

The Bible says that we are being changed from glory to glory. (*See* 2 Corinthians 3:18.) Can you say that you find yourself in another dimension of glory from where you were a year or two ago? You're being changed from glory unto glory. Some have asked why God doesn't just do it all at one time. And my answer is that you couldn't handle it all at once. But I promise you—you can handle what He has for you right now—what He has for you today.

You may be thinking: "But Pastor, what can the anointing do for me?" Let me give you several things the anointing will do for you.

- In the anointing is provision.

- In the anointing is protection.

- In the anointing is His healing power…divine health.

Let us never take the anointing for granted, ever. If you read on in 1 Samuel 5, you will see that after the Philistines stole the Ark and took it into their camp, just having the presence of God there began to wreak havoc in their camp. Sin cannot stand in the presence of God! They placed the Ark by their god, Dagon, and he fell over, broken. He could not stand in God's presence. In Chapter 6, after much confusion and destruction, the Philistines sent the Ark back to the home of Abinadab, where it rested for twenty years.

The anointing is a blessing to those who respect it, but it wreaks havoc in the camp of the wicked. Israel didn't need to lose the Ark. They didn't need to lose the presence of God. But, because they played the fool with the anointing, they lost it. They took it for granted.

It's inevitable that God is going to do His will through every single one of you who respect His presence, and who honor Him. God may raise you up in government, and in order to fulfill and function what He has called you to do, you're going to have to stand in the anointing to do it. He may call you into business and in order to continue and function in what He's called you to do, you're going to have to stay under the anointing.

God may have called you in the area of ministry, and you're going to have to depend on the anointing to be able to do it, because it is the anointing that will make a way for you. The anointing is like the icebreaker ship that goes ahead and breaks the ice, making a path for all the other ships to come through.

I don't know what's in your path. I don't know what the obstacles are, but I promise you that you can function under the same anointing that we do. But, it will be used for a different purpose—for the purposes of God for *your* life. Do not ever put God in a box! Do not limit Him. Follow Him. Obey Him. If a door is open, walk through the open door.

Personally, I am going to walk through every door that God opens. I have people all over the world asking me to come with the Good News of the Gospel. I go where I have the peace to go. I am going to hold meetings wherever people are hungry, until the American people are hungry, until they are desperate for the anointing, the fire of God, and seeing His power manifested. America is not yet desperate enough for the things of God.

Things may need to get worse before they get desperate. Am I worried? No, I've done everything that I can. We've been to Washington, D.C. where we spent millions of dollars to get the Word out. I've done everything; we've been in the House and the Senate, praying with people. I've done everything I can do, and everything God told us to do, and I'll do it again, if He calls us.

I'm not going to carry the burden of it; I'm not going to let it kill me. I'm not going to let it kill my wife or my family, and I'm not going to let it kill the church. I'm not going to lie awake at night worrying about the nation. We'll do whatever God tells us to do. We have a country where many of the Christians vote for people who believe in same-sex marriage and abortion. So, how can you even call yourself a Christian and vote for people who stand for these things? How do you call yourself a Christian? There is a problem with that. Do you understand what I'm saying?

There is a problem there. Those two things are totally against the Word of God. That shows you that people do not fear God. So, what does that mean? America has taken the anointing for granted. The day will come when they will shout and there will be nothing that happens, because they played the fool with the power of God. I am including the preachers who have taken the anointing for granted. They'll shout, but there will be nothing.

When you travel like we do, you see the desperation all over the world. In South Africa alone right now, the killing in the townships is beyond anything that you can imagine. Thousands of people have been killed in the townships of South Africa. (Xenophobia: tribes of the north coming down and taking jobs from the tribes of the south—black on black violence.) The killing of the farmers is like a genocide. (Socialism: kill the farmers—destroy the food supply—make the people dependent on the government.) There is sixty-five percent unemployment. There are whole villages in which the people are dying of HIV/AIDS. People are desperate.

THE ANOINTING WILL BRING ABOUT A TRANSFORMATION

So, if you're a child of the Lord, if you're anointed of God, what are you going to do with it? What are you going to do with the anointing that you've been given? If that anointing can't positively affect your personal life, then you may not have one. Maybe you just have religion instead of the anointing.

The anointing will bring about a transformation. It has to. It's impossible to be under the anointing and have it not bring about a change in a person's life. That anointing you've received of Him, who abides in you, must bring about a transformation and the fruit must be seen. Don't give me all the excuses. The anointing is sufficient. It is

The ANOINTING

not based on "this, that or the other" thing. The anointing is sufficient.

We can all run around. We can shout, "Hallelujah, Amen!" We can give the Lord the biggest shout of praise, but when it comes down to it, if there's no application of it, it will not produce results. God has not given you the anointing just to make a noise and then it not be made manifest.

When you know that it's true, when you believe it, when you receive it, when you walk in it, then the anointing of God is working for you every moment of the day. The very power of God is working to bring about a total transformation in your life. When you make the adjustment, within a split second everything can change. Suddenly, you find yourself a recipient of His abundant grace in a certain area of your life. Grace that will open the door in an area of business, for instance. Millions of dollars will come through your hands, and you aren't doing anything different in the natural. But the anointing is now activated in your life. The anointing is now released and has begun working in your life.

Suddenly, the favor of God is made manifest, and you find yourself in the right place at the right time. No man could ever put that together, but God can put it together. You are living in that place of the "suddenlies."

It has nothing to do with your income, your job or where you work. Even if you lose all your income tomorrow, if you are walking in the favor of God, His favor will cause you to supersede and excel without any income in the natural. Because your income is not your source. God is your source. Hallelujah. Your job is not your source; God is your source. Too many of God's people put their trust in everything else but God.

> Now know I that the LORD saveth his anointed; he will hear him from his holy Heaven with the saving strength of his right hand. **Some trust in chariots, and some in horses: but we will remember the name of the LORD our God.** They are brought down and fallen: but we are risen, and stand upright. Save, LORD: let the king hear us when we call.
>
> PSALM 20:6–9 (EMPHASIS ADDED.)

Proverbs 18:10 says: *"The name of the Lord is a strong tower: the righteous runneth into it, and is safe."* Revelation adds *"and his name is called The Word of God"* (Revelation 19:13). Trust in His Name and trust in His Word.

- It's the Word of the Lord that will sustain you.
- It's the Word of the Lord that will go before you.
- It's the Word of the Lord that will make the crooked path straight.
- It's the Word of the Lord that will be like a hammer, that will break the rock into pieces.
- It's the Word of the Lord that is like a fire that consumes the enemy.
- It's the Word of the Lord that is a discerner of the thoughts and the intents of the heart.
- It's the Word of the Lord that comes and divides between the soul and the spirit.
- It's the Word of the Lord that will come and divide between that which is the Truth and that which is not.
- It's the Word of the Lord that will come and separate the sheep from the goats.
- It's the Word of the Lord that will come and burn the flesh out of the way.
- It's the Word of the Lord that will cause the spirit man to rise in power and the anointing.
- It's the Word of the Lord that will cause you to function in the fullness of what God has ordained for your life.

For the word of God is quick, and powerful, and sharper than any two-edged sword, piercing even to the dividing asunder of soul and spirit, and of the joints and marrow, and is a discerner of the thoughts and intents of the heart.

HEBREWS 4:12

Get ready, get ready, get ready for what God is about to do. Do you believe that He's heard your cry? Do you believe that He's heard your prayer? Do you believe that He can do superabundantly above all that you dare ask or think according to the power working in you? Then get ready! Get ready! Join me now in thanking the Lord for the anointing that breaks the yoke—the anointing that sets men free. Open your heart and tell Him you are ready to receive all that He has for you.

I hear in my heart "New Doors." He is getting ready to open new doors for us. He will open doors no man can shut. There will be new opportunities, dreams in the night, and fresh visions from the Holy Spirit. Get ready, get ready, get ready. I'm talking about people whom God has been preparing, getting them ready. You may be asking, "How do I know I'm one of them?" Because as you are reading, the Spirit of God bore witness in your heart. I want you to know: that which is on the inside of you is by the Spirit of God. It will come to pass. It will come to pass!

Glory to God. I see a clarity of mind coming to you, with no confusion whatsoever. Clarity of mind, clearness of thought. I see all fear totally removed by the Spirit of God. There will be no fear concerning your life, concerning your future, concerning anything to come—only faith in God. Blessed be the Name of the Lord. This next year shall be the year of the fulfillment of the promise of God over your life, over your family, over your ministry, and over your business.

Do you receive the Word of the Lord? Say this with me: **I will not take the anointing for granted—ever**. Lord, I will always look to You with anticipation, whether in the service or out of the service. I will trust in God's anointing and the power in God's ability to do whatever is needed. Lord, I'm like a child when it comes to Your presence. I'm desperate, I'm hungry, I'm thirsty and I receive. And, I will never again take the anointing for granted.

Thank You, Lord.

About the Author

DRS. RODNEY AND ADONICA HOWARD-BROWNE are the founders of Revival Ministries International, the River at Tampa Bay Church, and River University in Tampa, Florida.

In December of 1987, Rodney, along with his wife, Adonica, and their three children, Kirsten, Kelly, and Kenneth, moved from their native land, South Africa, to the United States called by God as missionaries from Africa to America. The Lord had spoken through Rodney in a word of prophecy and declared, "As America has sown missionaries over the last two hundred years, I am going to raise up people from other nations to come to the United States of America. I am sending a mighty revival to America."

In April of 1989, the Lord sent a revival of signs and wonders and miracles that began in a church in Clifton Park, New York, that has continued until today, resulting in thousands of people being touched and changed as they encounter the presence of the living God. God is still moving today—saving, healing, delivering, restoring, and setting free!

Drs. Rodney and Adonica's second daughter, Kelly, was born with an incurable lung disease called cystic fibrosis. This demonic disease slowly destroyed her lungs. Early on Christmas morning 2002, at the age of eighteen, she ran out of lung capacity and breathed out her last breath. They placed her into the arms of her Lord and Savior and then vowed a vow. First, they vowed that the devil would pay for what he had done to their family. Secondly, they vowed to do everything in their power, with the help of the Lord, to win one hundred million souls to Jesus and to put $1 billion into world missions and the harvest of souls.

ABOUT THE AUTHOR

When Drs. Rodney and Adonica became naturalized citizens of the United States of America, in 2008 and 2004 respectively, they took the United States Oath of Allegiance, which declares, "I will support and defend the Constitution and laws of the United States of America against all enemies, foreign and domestic." They took this oath to heart. They love America, are praying for this country, and are trusting God to see another Great Awakening sweep across this land.

Believing for this Great Spiritual Awakening, Drs. Rodney and Adonica conducted Celebrate America DC, a soul winning event. They preached the Gospel of Jesus Christ for fifty nights in Washington, D.C., and surrounding areas from 2014 to 2019. Through the evangelism efforts on the streets, in the halls of Congress, and the nightly altar calls, 58,033 individuals made decisions for Jesus Christ.

During Celebrate America, in July of 2014, at the Daughters of the American Revolution Constitution Hall, Dr. Rodney executed a restraining order against the structure that is holding America in captivity, binding it and rendering it powerless and ineffective, from the Supreme Court, to the White House, to the Executive Branch, Congress, and the Senate, in the Name of Jesus. He commanded the Church in America to wake up and for the people of God to come out of their slumber. He declared that it is time to take the Land.

During the Covid era, Drs. Rodney and Adonica took a stand for the Gospel of Jesus Christ. As a result, Dr. Rodney was wrongfully arrested at his home on March 30, 2020, for holding a church service at The River at Tampa Bay Church on Sunday, March 29.

As a result of his arrest, Florida Governor Ron DeSantis declared attendance at churches, synagogues, and houses of worship to be an essential activity. Dr. Rodney's arrest freed up every church in Florida to meet. All the charges were dropped by the Thirteenth Judicial Circuit State Attorney on May 15, 2020, and the date of his arrest and criminal record were expunged by Circuit Court Judge John N. Conrad on February 22, 2021.

Drs. Rodney and Adonica continue to take a stand for the Word

ABOUT THE AUTHOR

of God and for billions around the world whose right to worship freely was removed and has not been, or perhaps will never be, restored. The Stand nightly services have continued for over 300 nights, as they stand for their brothers and sisters around the world who cannot stand freely.

With a passion for souls and a passion to revive and mobilize the Body of Christ, Drs. Rodney and Adonica have conducted revivals and soul winning efforts throughout eighty-five nations with the 300 City Tour, Good News campaigns, R.M.I. Revivals, the Great Awakening Tours, and The Stand. As a result, over 35,035,765 precious people have come to Christ, and tens of thousands of believers have been revived and mobilized to preach the Gospel of Jesus Christ. For more information, visit revival.com.

Connect

Please, visit revival.com or rodneyhowardbrowne.com for our latest updates and news. Many of our services are live online. Additionally, many of our recorded services are available on Video on Demand.

For a listing of Drs. Rodney and Adonica Howard-Browne's products and itinerary, please, visit revival.com. To download the soul-winning tools for free, please, visit revival.com and click on Soul-winning Tools.

Like us on Facebook:
Facebook.com/rodneyadonicahowardbrowne
Follow us on Twitter: @rhowardbrowne
Follow us on YouTube: Youtube.com/rodneyhowardbrowne
Follow us on Instagram: @rodneyhowardbrowne

Other Books and Resources by Rodney Howard-Browne

BOOKS
The Phantom Virus
Socialism Under the Microscope
Perpetual Harvest
Killing the Planet: How a Financial Cartel Doomed Mankind
The Anointing
The Killing of Uncle of Sam: The Demise of the United States of America
Thoughts on Stewardship
The Coming Revival
This Present Glory
The Touch of God
The Gifts of the Holy Spirit
The Reality of Life After Death
Seeing Jesus as He Really Is
The Curse Is Not Greater than the Blessing
How to Increase and Release the Anointing
School of the Spirit
The Anointing
Manifesting the Holy Ghost
What Gifts Do You Bring the King?
Prayer Journal
Sowing in Famine

OTHER BOOKS AND RESOURCES BY RODNEY HOWARD-BROWNE

AUDIO CDS
Prayer Time
Weapons of Our Warfare
Becoming One Flesh
Faith
Flowing in the Holy Ghost
How to Flow in the Anointing
Igniting the Fire
In Search of the Anointing

Prayer that Moves Mountains
Accelerate
The Camels are Coming
Pray Without Ceasing Vol. 1
Pray Without Ceasing Vol. 2
The Touch of God
Mountain Moving Prayer
Having an Encounter with God
God's Mandate
The Anointing is Transferable
Dealing with Offenses
The Vow and the Decree
Whosoever Can Get Whatsoever
Run to the Water
Demonstrations of the Spirit and of Power
The Double Portion
More Than Laughter
The Hand of the Lord
Running the Heavenly Race
The Holy Spirit, His Purpose & Power
The Power to Create Wealth
Walking in Heaven's Light
All These Blessings
A Surplus of Prosperity

OTHER BOOKS AND RESOURCES BY RODNEY HOWARD-BROWNE

The Joy of the Lord is My Strength
Prayer Secrets
Communion—The Table of the Lord
My Roadmap
My Mission—My Purpose
My Heart
My Family
My Worship
Decreeing Faith
Ingredients of Revival
Fear Not
Matters of the Heart by Dr. Adonica Howard-Browne
My Treasure
My Absolutes
My Father
My Crowns
My Comforter & Helper
Renewing the Mind
Seated in High Places
Triumphant Entry
Merchandising and Trafficking the Anointing
My Prayer Life
My Jesus
Seeing Jesus as He Really Is
Exposing the World's System
Living in the Land of Visions & Dreams
Kingdom Business
Taking Cities in the Land of Giants
Spiritual Hunger
The Two Streams

OTHER BOOKS AND RESOURCES BY RODNEY HOWARD-BROWNE

MP3 CDS
The Killing of Uncle Sam Audio Book
The Touch of God: The Anointing
Knowing the Person of the Holy Spirit
The Love Walk
How to Hear the Voice of God
Matters of the Heart
Exposing the World's System
How to Be Led by the Holy Spirit
The Anointing
The Ways of the Wind

DVDS
Mountain Moving Prayer
How to Personally Lead Someone to Jesus
The Fire of God
Vision for America
Living the Christian Lifestyle
No Limits No Boundaries
The Curse is Not Greater Than the Blessing
God's Glory Manifested through Special Anointings
Good News New York
Jerusalem Ablaze
The Mercy of God by Dr. Adonica Howard-Browne
Are You a Performer or a Minister?
Revival at ORU Volume 1, 2 & 3
The Realms of God
Singapore Ablaze
The Coat My Father Gave Me
Have You Ever Wondered What Jesus Was Like?
There Is a Storm Coming (Recorded live from Good News New York)
Budapest, Hungary Ablaze
The Camels Are Coming

OTHER BOOKS AND RESOURCES BY RODNEY HOWARD-BROWNE

Power Evangelism
Taking Cities in the Land of Giants
Renewing the Mind
Triumphant Entry
Merchandising and Trafficking the Anointing
Doing Business with God
Accelerate

MUSIC
Nothing Is Impossible
By His Stripes
Run with Fire
The Sweet Presence of Jesus
Eternity with Kelly Howard-Browne
Live from the River
You're Such a Good God to Me
Howard-Browne Family Christmas
He Lives
Anointed—The Decade of the '80s
Live Summer Campmeeting '15
Live Summer Campmeeting '16
Haitian Praise
No Limits

The River at Tampa Bay Church

THE RIVER AT TAMPA BAY CHURCH was founded on December 1, 1996. At the close of 1996, the Lord planted within Pastors Rodney and Adonica's heart the vision and desire to start a church in Tampa. With a heart for the lost and to minister to those who had been touched by revival, they implemented that vision and began The River at Tampa Bay, with the motto, "Church with a Difference."

Over 575 people joined them for the first Sunday morning service on December 1, 1996. Over the years, the membership has grown and the facilities have changed, yet these three things have remained constant since the church's inception ... dynamic praise and worship, anointed preaching and teaching of the Word, and powerful demonstrations of the Holy Spirit and power. The Lord spoke to Pastor Rodney's heart to feed the people, touch the people, and love the people. With this in mind and heart, the goal of The River is:

To become a model revival church where people from all over the world can come and be touched by God. Once they have been not only touched, but changed, they are ready to be launched out into the harvest field with the anointing of God.

To have a church that is multi-racial, representing a cross section of society from rich to poor from all nations, bringing people to a place of maturity in their Christian walk.

To see the lost, the backslidden and the unsure come to a full assurance of their salvation.

To be a home base for Revival Ministries International and all of its arms. A base offering strength and support to the vision of RMI to see America shaken with the fires of revival, then to take that fire to the far-flung corners of the globe.

To break the mold of religious tradition and thinking.

To be totally dependent upon the Holy Spirit for His leading and guidance as we lead others deeper into the River of God.

Our motto: Church with a Difference.

For The River at Tampa Bay's service times and directions, please, visit revival.com or call (813) 971-9999. Location: The River at Tampa Bay Church, 3738 River International Dr., Tampa, FL 33610.

River University

RIVER UNIVERSITY is a place where men and women of all ages, backgrounds and experiences can gather together to study and experience the glory of God. River University is not a traditional Bible school. It is a Holy Ghost training center, birthed specifically for those whose strongest desire is to know Christ and to make Him known.

The vision for River University is plain: To train men and women in the spirit of revival for ministry in the 21st century. The school was birthed in 1997 with a desire to train up revivalists for the 21st century. It is a place where the Word of God and the Holy Spirit come together to produce life, birth ministries, and launch them out. River University is a place where ministries are sent to the far-flung corners of the globe to spread revival and to bring in a harvest of souls for the kingdom of God.

While preaching in many nations and regions of the world, Dr. Rodney Howard-Browne has observed that all the people of the earth have one thing in common: a desperate need for the genuine touch of God. From the interior of Alaska through the bush country of Africa, to the outback villages of Australia to the cities of North America, people are tired of religion and ritualistic worship. They are crying out for the reality of His presence. River University is dedicated to training believers how to live, minister, and flow in the anointing.

The Word will challenge those attending to find clarity in their calling, and be changed by the awesome presence of God. This is the hour of God's power, not just for the full-time minister, but for all of

God's people who are hungry for more. Whether you are a housewife or an aspiring evangelist, River University will deepen your relationship and experience in the Lord, and provide you with a new perspective on how to reach others with God's life-changing power.

- Programs Include:
- River Bible Institute
- River School of Worship
- River School of Government
- River Bible Español

You can be saturated in the Word and the Spirit of God at River University. Since 1997, River University has graduated over 4,000 students. It is the place where you will be empowered to reach your high calling and set your world on fire with revival. For more information about River University, please, visit revival.com or call (813) 899-0085 or (813) 971-9999.

God Wants to Use You to Bring in the Harvest of Souls!

THE GREAT COMMISSION, "Go ye into all the world and preach the Gospel to every creature," is for every believer to take personally. Every believer is to be an announcer of the Good News Gospel. When the Gospel is preached, people have an encounter with Jesus. Jesus is the only One Who can change the heart of a man, woman, child, and nation!

On the next page is a tool to assist you in sharing the Gospel with others. It is called the Gospel Soul-Winning Script. Please, just read it! Read it to others and you will see many come to Christ because, as stated in Romans 1:16, the Gospel is the power of God.

Please, visit revival.com, click on Soul-Winning Tools, and review the many tools and videos that are freely available to help you bring in the harvest of souls. It's harvest time!

THE GOSPEL SOUL-WINNING —SCRIPT—

Has anyone ever told you that God loves you and that He has a wonderful plan for your life? I have a real quick, but important question to ask you. If you were to die this very second, do you know for sure, beyond a shadow of a doubt, that you would go to Heaven? [If "Yes"— Great, why would you say "Yes"? (If they respond with anything but "I have Jesus in my heart" or something similar to that, PROCEED WITH SCRIPT) or "No" or "I hope so" PROCEED WITH SCRIPT.]

Let me quickly share with you what the Holy Bible reads. It reads "for all have sinned and come short of the glory of God" and "for the wages of sin is death, but the gift of God is eternal life through Jesus Christ our Lord". The Bible also reads, "For whosoever shall call upon the name of the Lord shall be saved". And you're a "whosoever" right? Of course you are; all of us are.

continued on reverse side—

I'm going to say a quick prayer for you. Lord, bless (FILL IN NAME) and his/her family with long and healthy lives. Jesus, make Yourself real to him/her and do a quick work in his/her heart. If (FILL IN NAME) has not received Jesus Christ as his/her Lord and Savior, I pray he/she will do so now.

(FILL IN NAME), if you would like to receive the gift that God has for you today, say this after me with your heart and lips out loud. Dear Lord Jesus, come into my heart. Forgive me of my sin. Wash me and cleanse me. Set me free. Jesus, thank You that You died for me. I believe that You are risen from the dead and that You're coming back again for me. Fill me with the Holy Spirit. Give me a passion for the lost, a hunger for the things of God and a holy boldness to preach the gospel of Jesus Christ. I'm saved; I'm born again, I'm forgiven and I'm on my way to Heaven because I have Jesus in my heart.

As a minister of the gospel of Jesus Christ, I tell you today that all of your sins are forgiven. Always remember to run to God and not from God because He loves you and has a great plan for your life.

[Invite them to your church and get follow up info: name, address, & phone number.]

Revival Ministries International
P.O. Box 292888 • Tampa, FL 33687
(813) 971-9999 • www.revival.com

THE RIVER AT TAMPA BAY CHURCH
ALTAR CALL

CELEBRATE AMERICA
WASHINGTON, D.C.
57,498 SALVATIONS

WINTER CAMPMEETING AT RMI WORLD HEADQUARTERS

THE GREAT AWAKENING BROADCAST WITH CHRISTIAN TELEVISION NETWORK
OVER 15 MILLION RECORDED DECISIONS FOR CHRIST

GOOD NEWS NEW YORK - 1999

MADISON SQUARE GARDEN

48,459 SALVATIONS

GOOD NEWS NEW YORK - 1999

MADISON SQUARE GARDEN

48,459 SALVATIONS

GOOD NEW SOWETO - 2004
SOWETO, SOUTH AFRICA
177,600 SALVATIONS

GOOD NEWS UMLAZI - 2005
UMLAZI, SOUTH AFRICA
286,750 SALVATIONS

SINGAPORE 1995

THE EARLY YEARS
RODNEY, ADONICA, KIRSTEN, KELLY, & KENNETH

THE EARLY YEARS
RODNEY & ADONICA